The new Audi R8 V10.   Vorsprung durch Technik

Extra Urban 27.7 (10.2) – 29.4 (9.6), Combined 19.2 (14.7) – 20.6 (13.7). CO_2 emissions: 327 – 351 g/km.

THE NEW FORESTER DIESEL.
ENGINEERED FOR TODAY'S ENVIRONMENT.

Whatever you use an SUV for, you need to know that its all-round versatility is matched by drivability, safety technology and first-class green credentials. The new Forester's All-Wheel Drive is permanent (unlike some lesser SUVs), and with a totally symmetrical drive train, it matches stunning off road grip with the best possible on road balance. Its unique Boxer Diesel engine sits lower, giving Forester a low centre of gravity, reducing body roll and improving handling. A class-leading 44.8 mpg economy, 167 g/km CO_2 and road tax of just £175 means the Forester also makes real economic sense. With an unbeatable design and superlative build-quality, the Forester is truly built the way all SUVs should be. And from only £20,875 even the price is engineered for today's environment.

CALL 0844 662 6638 OR VISIT FORESTERDIESEL.CO.UK

OVERFINCH

LUXURY, REDEFINED.

OVERFINCH IS THE ULTIMATE EXPRESSION OF THE RANGE ROVER ICON.
A VEHICLE AS INDIVIDUAL AS ITS OWNER.

OVERFINCH

Contents

R-50-TN-AJ

www.brm-manufacture.com

Bernard Richards Manufacture

Bernard Richards Manufacture

photos : Luc Virginux

Introduction

We never forget how incredibly lucky we are to be working on **evo** magazine. Ever since the first issue, back in the autumn of 1998, we've been allowed access to the greatest performance cars on the greatest roads (and race tracks) on the planet. Looking back over 130-odd issues, it's actually been quite tricky deciding what to leave out of this 'best of' collection. In the end we went for the stories that gave us the biggest thrill at the time, the ones where it all just came together (often at the very last minute) to create something special on the page. We hope you enjoy looking back over these highlights of the first ten years of **evo**, and as always we thank you for your support, without which none of it would be possible. Here's to the next ten. We really will have to get proper jobs one day…

Peter Tomalin, managing editor

MAGAZINE

The Best of evo
From the publishers of evo magazine
www.evo.co.uk

Editorial
5 Tower Court, Irchester Road, Wollaston,
Northants NN29 7PJ, United Kingdom
email eds@evo.co.uk
Telephone 0207 907 6310

Subscriptions
0844 844 0039

Managing editor
Peter Tomalin

Designers
Adam Shorrock, Chee-Chiu Lee, Neil Carey

Contributing writers
John Barker, Jethro Bovingdon, Henry Catchpole,
Colin Goodwin, Richard Meaden, Harry Metcalfe,
Peter Tomalin, David Vivian

Contributing photographers
Michael Bailie, Stuart Collins, Gus Gregory, Charlie
Magee, Andy Morgan, David Shepherd, Kenny P

Advertising
30 Cleveland Street, London WIT 4JD
Email ads.evo@dennis.co.uk
Group advertising director Des Flynn
(020 7907 6742)
Advertising director Sarah Perks
(020 7907 6744)
Deputy advertising manager Tim Deeks
(020 7907 6773)

Dennis Motoring
Editorial director Harry Metcalfe
Group publishing director James Burnay
Managing director Ian Westwood

Dennis Publishing Ltd
COO Brett Reynolds
Group finance director Ian Leggett
CEO James Tye
Chairman Felix Dennis

THE DEVIL'S PLAYGROUND

Six of the world's most fabulous cars – Diablo, Maranello, Modena, Zonda, Viper GTS and 911 Turbo – on some of the world's most breathtakingly beautiful roads. Back in 2000, it really didn't get any better than this

LAMBORGHINI
Diablo 6.0 VT

After ten years, it seemed the Diablo had reached the end of the line. Like the Countach before it, it had accrued as many scoops and spoilers as it could carry, and as much power as it could handle. Many of us expected Lamborghini's new German owners to close the Diablo chapter with the GT, launched earlier this year. Not so.

Instead, Audi has given us the 6.0 VT, and an early taste (**evo** 19) led us to believe it could be the best Diablo ever. The remarkable thing is that this has been achieved without resorting to dramatic changes. It has been a process of refinement, of identifying and correcting weaknesses and building on strengths.

It starts with the looks – not even the Gandini original looks this clean and purposeful. Inside, the adoption of Audi switchgear and glossy carbonfibre trim imbues a real sense of solid quality.

Beneath the low-line engine cover is a 550bhp V12 hooked up to viscous-coupled four-wheel drive. Fundamentally the suspension is just the same – double wishbones all round, with electronic four-stage damping – yet whatever subtle changes have been made, they've transformed the Diablo. The VT feels more precise, driveable and faithful. Far from being the last of the line, it feels like a next-generation Diablo. We won't mind waiting for the replacement. **JB**

SPECIFICATION: Engine 5992cc, V12, 48v, mid-mounted **Power** 550bhp @ 7100rpm **Torque** 457lb ft @ 5500rpm **Transmission** Five-speed manual, four-wheel drive **Weight** 1625kg **Power to weight** 343bhp/ton **Suspension** Double wishbones, coil springs, electronic damping, anti-roll bars front and rear **Tyres** 235/35 ZR18 front, 335/30 ZR18 rear **0-60mph** 3.8secs **Max speed** 200mph+ **Price** £152,500

Diablo, Lamborghini, Maranello, pepperoni, Pagani, Chianti, mozzarella… The words are so rich, so redolent, so heavy with promise, of exquisite flavours, hedonistic pleasures, intoxication. Food, drink and supercars. And the landscapes… painterly, like an old canvas, steeped in the juice of grapes and olives. You could tear a strip down from the sky, roll it up and wring it out later, taste the flavours all over again. This, I have decided, is a group test made in heaven, and we haven't even seen the cars yet.

Four of us – me, **evo** MD Harry Metcalfe, art ed Damian Smith and photographer Gus Gregory – have flown out to Pisa as a sort of advance guard. Harry has a villa two hours to the south, right in the heart of Tuscany between Florence and Rome, and we'll be using that as a base for the next three days. You're not the slightest bit envious, I can tell. Right now it's mid-morning, Monday, it's ten degrees hotter than back home, and we're winging it down the autostrada in Hazza's faithful old Mercedes 300 estate, retained at the airport for times such as this. It's our job to recce the countryside for suitable roads and photo locations. Maybe even the odd ristorante…

We catch glimpses of the hills as the big Merc peels back the autostrada miles, but you don't get the full effect until you turn off and head over the first horizon. As the first full-on 100 per cent Tuscan vista appears before you, it's as though someone has rolled down a huge theatrical backdrop. It looks brushed-on, slightly unreal. The colours, the landforms, the scale – it's all simply breathtaking. And the roads – as twisting and tempting as a plate of tagliatelle, and practically deserted. If God created the East Midlands so there'd be somewhere for double glazing salesmen and unattractive teenagers to live, then he surely created Tuscany for artists, poets, sculptors and road testers.

We're here to enjoy ourselves, thoroughly and unashamedly, in the fastest, most fantastic and most emotionally charged cars available to **evo**-man in the first year of the new millennium. From Ferrari, the glorious 550 Maranello, our long-time favourite supercar, and the scintillating 360 Modena, front versus mid-engined, an interesting little private duel. From Lamborghini the new 6-litre Diablo, the purest and most polished yet. Then there's the sensationally quick all-new Porsche Turbo. These are the cars you'd expect to find in any supercar test worth the name. There are a couple of wild cards too – the brutish 8-litre Viper GTS, and the exquisite Pagani Zonda C12. I tell you, to drive these cars on these roads is a seriously big deal for every one of us. Along the way we hope to discover which is the greatest supercar currently in production. And, in the process, attempt to pin down exactly what we mean by supercar…

You'll have your own take on this. For me, it has little to do with pure speed across the ground. On certain roads and in certain conditions a well-driven Fiesta could run rings around a Diablo. More to the point, an Evo VI would be as quick if not quicker than any of the cars here, 95 per cent of the time. But an Evo VI is not, I put it to you, a supercar.

[Supercar Group Test]

The way I see it, there are a few basic rules of admission to the supercar club, and anything based on a fifteen grand saloon is going to be left outside on the pavement, however many exciting bulges and wings it might flaunt at the doorman. Supercars are low and wide and exotic, with vast, near-horizontal windscreens, tarmac-hugging chisel noses and gaping race-car style airducts. Their purpose is to shock and amaze and intrigue. They need big numbers of cylinders and horsepower – at least eight and three-fifty of each respectively. While it's not compulsory to have less over-the shoulder visibility than the Hunchback of Notre Dame, you won't lose any points for it either. Same goes for having the combined thirst of a stag party including Oliver Reed, Paul Gascoigne and two large, thirsty camels. Being harder to get into than a wetsuit

that's one size too small (and without the aid of talcum powder) is taken as read. These are things we secretly admire in a supercar.

And obscene amounts of rubber too. Today's archetypal supercar is the Lamborghini Diablo. Its rear tyres are 335/30 ZR18s. Try fitting those to your Mitsubishi.

Having 'Made in Italy' stamped on the floorpan is a distinct advantage. The Viper and the 911 Turbo are the interlopers here. We'd wanted to bring an Aston DB7 Vantage along too, but Aston were unable to supply a car. Or perhaps they'd guessed what we were beginning to suspect anyway, that in this sort of company a DB7 would feel just a little soft, a little too much the GT. With the imminent demise of the big Aston V8, there is no obvious British supercar to rival the likes of Ferrari and Lamborghini. Lotus's Esprit is starting to feel well past its use-by date; TVR's Cerbera Speed 12 is the Next Big Thing.

So it falls to the all-American Viper and the so-German-it's-painful Porsche Turbo to see if anything can upset the Italian supercar hierarchy in their own back yard. As we slide down the autostrada, somewhere on a French autoroute **evo** co-editor John Barker and road test assistant John Hayman are cruising at unlikely speeds in the Porsche. Round about teatime, Dickie Meaden and **evo** resident snapper Andy Morgan will follow in the Viper and drive through the

night. Tomorrow morning we all meet on Ferrari's doorstep.

But that's tomorrow. Recce completed, we grab a pizza in Sarteano, the local town. Harry tells us about the jousting competition which has been held here for centuries. Each district nominates its own champion and it's the real thing – big sticks, big horses – though these days they aim for targets rather than each others' heads. In fact it's just an elaborate excuse for a succession of feasts and celebrations. Sounds reasonable to me. Later we chill out on Harry's patio, underneath a million stars, clutching cans of Peroni beer (or for those of us with a smaller thirst, a Didier Peroni). The stage is set.

Curtain up on another stunning scene. Watery early-morning light makes the hillsides look even more otherworldly, and there's mist hanging in the valleys just to complete the effect, so the outlines of the hills look almost airbrushed on. We swill down some strong coffee in the chill air, then pile back into the Merc. Another two-hour autostrada drive, this time north towards Bologna, brings us to Sant'Agata, home of Lamborghini. The old 1960s factory frontage is being ripped down, which seems symbolic of the changes since the VW Group took control. While we're waiting for 'our' 6-litre VT to be given a quick wash and

checkover, Lamborghini's charming PRO, Eleanora Negrin, takes us on a whistlestop tour of the factory floor. For a sad old petrolhead like me, this is a major thrill. There's an upbeat air about the place, plenty of Diablos in various state of assembly – and a jaw-dropping line-up of around 20 Diablo GTR racers, just completed and ready to rumble. Most memorable sight of all, however, is the nuclear orange Diablo GT that pulls up at the factory gates, presumably for a service. The scissor door rises to reveal a most unlikely Lamborghini customer: sixty-ish, pot-bellied, brown as a berry, thinning slicked-back hair, and most incongruously of all, braces holding up black Prada jeans. He chats with the gateman while his wife stays in the car; she's sixty-ish too, dressed for comfort, certainly no pneumatic plutonium blonde. For some reason I find this little tableau utterly wonderful.

We're led outside again just in time to see our Diablo roll up at the gates. The shape, now shorn of spoilers and scoops and stripped back to its original purity, is just mesmerising. Not exactly beautiful, but rolling sculpture. And stunning in solid orange, a similar hue to the one they used to paint Miuras in the early '70s.

I'm happy to let Harry take first stint in the Diablo; he's done all the driving so far, and plunging straight onto urban Italian roads in the rush hour in a left-hand-drive Diablo is not the

best way to get up to speed. I take the Merc and follow, as Harry steers a course towards Maranello, 30 minutes away. You might imagine that round here people would be almost blasé about supercars. Far from it. The orange Diablo cuts a swathe through the ranks of Puntos and panel vans, and everywhere people turn and point and stare. When we pull into a public square in Maranello alongside the 911 and Viper which have apparently arrived safely after their epic drive, a crowd gathers in seconds.

The two Johns, Barker and Hayman, are enjoying a coffee in the sunshine. 'The Porsche,' says JB, ' is phenomenal. You put you foot down at 150mph and you can feel it push you back in the seat again…' Meaden and Morgan, we learn, are stealing a few hours' sleep at a hotel 20 minutes down the road after driving all through the night in the Viper.

Harry clambers out of the Diablo. 'Very impressive… It rides a lot better than the GT. And I can't wait to be in the Val d'Orcia instead of being stuck in traffic… I have a feeling it's going to be the star of the show, but we'll wait and see. It'll be fascinating to see how the Zonda compares…'

Ah, the Pagani Zonda. The unlikely-sounding rival to Ferrari and Lamborghini, built just a few miles away from here on the outskirts of Modena. So far only Dickie Meaden has driven

it, and from what he's told us it's a bit special, but the earliest a car is available is tomorrow morning, so we'll have to wait a bit longer to find out. No matter. This is Maranello, and just down the road are the grey gates to Ferrari. Coffee cups are drained faster than you can say Luca di Montezemolo.

Half an hour later, in the central courtyard of the factory, I'm making myself comfortable behind the wheel of a silver-blue 360 Modena. It seems exotically low and laid-back after the Merc. Harry's doing the same in the deep red 550 alongside, while Ferrari's Tim Watson gives me a quick refresher on the F1 paddle-shift. Right to go up the 'box, left to go down, and both together to get neutral. Pull the little lever on the centre console to select reverse. A doddle.

Photographer Gus has asked us to turn in opposite directions as we leave the gates. I suggest it might look as though one of us is lost, but he tells me not to be so silly, it will make a good photo, so I shut up. Ten minutes later, I am in actual fact quite hopelessly lost and looking

FERRARI
360 Modena

The 360 is a radical step on from the much-loved 355, most obviously in styling but most significantly in construction. It's the first of a new generation of all-aluminium Ferraris, employing a superstructure of extrusions and castings, and the technical approach doesn't stop there. More than any production Ferrari before it, the shape of the 360 has been influenced by aerodynamics. There's plenty of clever marshalling going on beneath the car, but airflow has also dictated the proportions and shape of the upper body. It's a handsome car, if not Pininfarina's finest.

The 360's extraordinary V8 – on display through the back window – is an evolution of the 355's. It boasts 400bhp which it delivers with a demonic howl at a dizzying 8500rpm, while a huge amount of work has gone into enhancing its low and mid-range urge. A year into production, the 'F1' paddle-shift is the preferred transmission by some margin and it certainly keeps the 360 on the boil with ease. Even so, die-hards (like some of us) would rather have the open aluminium gate and a bit of left-foot exercise.

At a brisk pace the 360 feels incredibly sharp and responsive, with better steering than the 355. Push a little harder and it isn't quite so poised. Should make for an interesting meeting with its natural rival, the new 911 Turbo, especially as the GT3 pipped it for the title of 1999 **evo** Car of the Year six months ago. **JB**

SPECIFICATION: **Engine** 3586cc, V8, 40v, mid-mounted **Power** 400bhp @ 8500rpm **Torque** 275lb ft @ 4750rpm **Transmission** Six-speed manual (F1), rear-wheel drive **Weight** 1390kg **Power to weight** 82bhp/ton **Suspension** Double wishbones, coil springs, electronic damping, anti-roll bars front and rear **Tyres** 215/45 ZR18 front, 275/40 ZR18 rear **0-60mph** 4.5secs **Max speed** 180mph **Price** £101,24?

in vain for Harry and the 550. All roads look the same. This is where the F1 transmission is at its worst, shunting and jolting as you stop and start. I light a cigarette in an effort to look cool and not at all like an Englishman getting increasingly rattled. I fail miserably.

Thankfully 360s stand out, even in Maranello, and Harry brings me in. We form up into convoy and roll out of the square. By now we're the main event in town, with a sizeable crowd soaking up the sights and sounds of five supercars straining at the leash. I tuck in behind the 550, with the Viper, 911 and Diablo behind. As I pass a family standing watching, a small boy murmurs: 'Bello, bello.' You don't get that in Wellingborough.

Those Tuscan hill-roads are waiting, and Harry leads us back towards the autostrada. Compared with the lavishly wide rump of the Diablo, the 550 looks almost like a conventional coupe, almost ordinary. It isn't, of course, but it can't hold a candle to the Lamborghini for visual drama.

The cabin of the 360 is everything that supercars didn't used to be – very wide, very accommodating, hardly any offset to the pedals, and with a slicker, more mass-produced feel to the facia and trim. The previous 355 wasn't like this, though it had a bit more character, a bit more honesty about it. I'm also missing the open metal gearshift gate; the last 360 I drove had one, and it was the best of its kind I've ever tried – sweet-shifting and massively satisfying – but apparently more customers are opting for the F1. The 360 has a supple ride and an easygoing nature – until you crack open the throttle and its bark rips holes in the air as it surges forward. Glance up in the mirror and you can see the top of the plenum chambers exposed behind the glass panel. It's a carefully calculated mix of civility and savagery.

After 20 minutes we pull into a hotel to collect the slumbering Meaden and Morgan. Stepping out of the air-conditioned capsule of the 360, the full mid-day heat hits me like opening the proverbial oven door. I find Barker eulogising the Diablo. The last one he drove was the hotrod GT. This, he reckons, is a much more rounded, more complete car. 'Straight away the steering quality feels absolutely spot-on – no slack, the weighting just right. The low-speed damping is good too. It feels like a different car, a really sorted car.'

Harry concurs. 'In this form, 550-man, who might previously have dismissed the Diablo as a crude, over the top device, would think, I've got to have a look at this now. He wouldn't have to find excuses for it. He might go for a different colour though…'

Just before our convoy hits the motorway, we pass a chap in a Boxster waiting to pull out of a junction. He's a very smug looking man, with a very German looking moustache. As each of our supercars cruises past, you can see his moustache gradually wilt. Shame.

I am thoroughly enjoying the 360. It's the perfect beginner's supercar – nothing too intimidating, but breathtakingly quick and stratospherically high-revving. The way the exhaust compresses to an urgent blare will have you whooping with pleasure.

The fun really starts as we hit the three-lane. We take turns to lead, swapping positions constantly to get a good view of all the cars. Occasionally two cars fall back, before their

Chalk and cheese: agile, mid-engined 360 pursued by thunderous front-engined Viper GTS

drivers drop the hammer simultaneously in second or third. I'd like to say this is some sort of scientific test, but really it's just bloody good fun. After each redline surge, we settle back to a cruise – 4500 revs in the 360 equates to an indicated 160kmh, or a nice round 100mph. The Ferrari is comfortable, untaxing, but with a muted growl just to remind you what's behind your back.

In my mirrors the rather anonymous looking 911 is overshadowed by the threatening hulk of the Viper, all bulging curves and tarmac-vacuuming snout (later, Dickie Meaden, who's passengering in the Merc while he recovers from his marathon drive, reports that the Diablo and Viper are the two cars that cause all the necks to swivel and jaws to drop). When the GTS rumbles past, it's backside is so muscular it makes the 550 look almost effete. With its twin stripes, double-bubble roof and kicked-up tail, it really could have driven straight out of Daytona.

The Diablo moves ahead next, and I have to say it does look absolutely mindblowing, the huge rear haunches and, from where I'm sitting, arrowhead of a snout reminding me of one of those massive Apollo moon rockets, with the astronauts' tiny pod at the pointy end. The A1 is heavy with trucks, but every once in a while an artic pulls aside to reveal a long clear stretch of road: so we drop a couple of gears and open throttles wide. The 360's tigerish response means it can stay with the Diablo for the first 50 yards, but then the Lamborghini's massive power begins to tell, and gradually but unstoppably it pulls away.

As the A1 begins to carve into hillsides, a new pleasure presents itself. The tunnel. These were originally built by the ancient Romans for racing their chariots through, while trumpeters at the roadside blared the most incredible cacophony of sound to proclaim their passage. Chasing the Diablo up through the gears, hitting maximum

Above: Porsche's answer to the Italians is new 911 Turbo, with twin turbochargers, 420bhp, four-wheel drive and stability control

revs in fourth just as we plunge into near darkness is one of those moments that will stay with me forever. (Orange Lamborghini, driving into tunnel on Italian mountain road; now where have I seen that before?)

One particular tunnel is half-open on one side and the light cuts through the pillars, straking the rear deck of the Lambo as Barker gives it full throttle. It's like heaven come down to earth. The Diablo sounds so animal, so visceral, it makes even the wailing 360 seem slightly synthetic. I flick down another gear while simultaneously winding my window down. You could get drunk on this.

It's pretty nerve-wracking at times, mind, what with narrow lanes and wandering artics. There's an occasional splurge of brakelights and I can almost sense our insurance underwriters holding their collective breath. I feel like breathing in too, as I squirt the Ferrari through another gap.

The 360, I know, won't be the sharpest tool here. The steering is quicker and keener than the 355's but feels a little numb each side of the straight-ahead, and though the chassis' compromise between suppleness and connectedness is more

'The Diablo sounds so animal, so visceral, it makes even the wailing 360 seem slightly synthetic '

convincing, you feel just a little removed from the action at the road. It's not quite as confidence building as a 911.

About 20kms before our turn-off, Harry decides the time has come to give it some serious humpty. The 550 and Diablo, the two horsepower heavyweights, hammer into the middle distance and, once the pursuing pack realises what's going on, Viper, Turbo and 360 storm after them. At an indicated 250kmh (155mph), the 360 has plenty more to give, but the steering is noticeably lighter, it feels rather less than locked to the road, and I decide to leave it at that.

We pause for breath just the other side of the toll booths. Mr Metcalfe reports seeing 280kmh on the 550's dial – 'It's all very refined and composed up to about 250, then it comes on cam and there's lots of mechanical noise and wind rush and it's a bit of an animal.' Barker claims 300 in the Diablo (that's 186mph, by the way). 'It was just getting into its stride,' he deadpans. Hayman says he saw 175mph in the Viper, but adds that the general din, engine boom and wind noise, and the feeling of looseness in the body

structure, didn't make it an experience to relish. And I promise faithfully not to commit any of these figures to print. Oops.

Into the hills, and again the 360 is instantly gratifying. There's a goodly flow of information coming back from the chassis and steering wheel, though the messages aren't always quite what you'd want to hear – after initially sharp steering response, the front end seems short of real bite, reluctant to really key into the road surface. Makes you think you're pushing hard. Maybe it was designed to make less than godlike drivers back off and push no harder…

And now, wouldn't you know it, the clouds are rolling up and as the first drops of rain start to fall and the 360's nose washes wide a couple of times, I decide to leave the ASR switched in. By the time I climb out of the 360 I reckon it's scored consistently highly, but without ever quite setting me all of a tingle, though the engine, it has to be said, is a bit special. Not sure about the looks. There are shades of classic '60s Dino, especially when you stand at the nose and

look down on the curvature of the screen and the way the front wings lap over onto the small front bonnet. It's not Dino-dainty though. Alongside the Diablo, which looks like one long, lithe, muscular limb, it looks almost podgy.

Barker has formed some firm impressions of the Lamborghini. 'It's very wieldy. I remember driving the first one, on roads that weren't as twisty as this, with no power steering, and it was an absolute nightmare. This tucks into corners, steers nicely, little bit of understeer, but you can get the power on early and it just pulls through.' Do you notice that it's four-wheel drive? 'No, it just feels like it's got lots of grip.' What about the width? Is that a hindrance? 'I didn't really think about it. And it rides so well, too. It's going to surprise a few people who might think it's just a brash old dinosaur.'

I slip into the Diablo's supposed nemesis, the 550, the flagship of the Ferrari range, and a car which has shown that supercars don't have to be intimidating; they don't even have to be mid-engined. Straight away, after the 360, it feels more special, more exotic. It's in the materials, the gorgeous hides, the exquisite bucket seats,

FERRARI
550 Maranello

It took a typically brave decision from Luca di Montezemolo to abandon the mid-engined layout for Ferrari's flagship supercar and revert to a layout last seen in the Daytona some 30 years before.

The result was the 550 Maranello, a car that put a modern spin on the Daytona's proportions, powerplant and continent-consuming appetite but exorcised its dynamic demons. Here was a supercar you could live with, a genuinely practical 199mph projectile that was a million miles from the unwieldy nature and Miami Vice image of the Testarossa.

Now, some three years since its introduction ,the 550 is still a masterpiece. Granted, Montezemolo's front-engined dictum denied Pininfarina's pen the freedom to scribe a jaw-slackeningly dramatic shape, and the 550's sheer driveability robs it of the Diablo's animal appeal.

The 5.5-litre, 485bhp V12 is muted but magnificent, delivering a creamy torrent of power and torque through a meaty but easily manageable six-speed gearbox. Feel the V12's tidal surge squeeze you into the driver's seat's buttery hide and savour the refined but expensively busy-sounding engine note, for this is one of the finest driver's cars on the planet. Exploitable, involving and completely exhilarating, it is without doubt one of Ferrari's greatest achievements. **RM**

SPECIFICATION: **Engine** 5474cc, V12, 48v, front-mounted **Power** 485bhp @ 7000rpm **Torque** 415lb ft @ 5000rpm **Transmission** Six-speed manual, four-wheel drive **Weight** 1716kg **Power to weight** 287bhp/ton **Suspension** Double wishbones, coil springs, electronic damping, anti-roll bars front and rear **Tyres** 255/40 ZR18 front, 295/35 ZR18 rear **0-60mph** 4.2secs **Max speed** 199mph **Price** £149,700

There's something shark-like about the 550. It's not the greatest looking Ferrari – rear view may be its best angle, conjuring up thoughts of classic Daytona. 'Little-brother' 360 (right) is more homogeneous shape

the jewel-like detailing, and the complex, seriously expensive sounding hum from the big V12. On the move it immediately feels like a car of real substance, from the precision of the damping to the heavy-engineering feel of the metal gearshift gate.

It's a short drive to the next photo call. As we spill out of the cars again, John Barker is less than complementary about the 360. Seems it feels good up to a point (i.e. my ability) but thereafter not so hot. 'Nervous, edgy,' he says, 'Feels on tippy-toe where the Diablo feels sucked to the road. If you turned the traction control off it could swap ends pretty quickly. Steering feel's not as good either.' Why has Ferrari built-in so much understeer? 'Possibly to protect drivers from what is not a terribly well balanced chassis. It could certainly be a handful.'

Harry has had his hands full of 911. 'It's very good, and you can step right up to the edge with the stability control in. Only trouble is, in wet and tricky conditions you ask for another 10bhp and it throws in an extra 40bhp for free. I'm amazed at just how much grunt comes in on a part-throttle. It's not as delicate as the 550. Because it's so grippy in the dry you wouldn't really notice it so much. And flab doesn't enter its vocabulary – it restricts body movements to a minimum and it doesn't seem to oversteer at all.'

Early evening and we head to the hilltop town of Pienza to refuel. The road snakes up the hillside with a succession of looping corners and a couple of real tight hairpins. It's my first shot at the Diablo, and predictably it feels awkward, intimidating, bulky.

Just climbing inside is like starting an adventure. You sit so low, the scuttle is so high, and you can see none of the corners of the car for reference. Just when your heartbeat is settling to normal, you look in the door mirrors and all you can see are the voluminous rear wings flaring outwards. The starter motor whirrs like a drill and, when it catches, the V12 tears at the air and sets the whole car trembling. While I feel my way in – and wrestle with a gearbox in which the dogleg change from first to second is one of the nastiest I've driven – Harry in the 911, Dickie in the 360 and Johnny B in the 550 set a searing pace up the hill.

Harry is pushing hard, Dickie harder still but, impressively, staying glued to the 911's tail. Barker can enjoy watching from the comfort of the 550 – or rather he would if he wasn't

working so hard to keep up. 'The 550's got, what, 485bhp, the Turbo 420 and the Modena 400, but I seemed to be lacking punch out of corners,' he reports. 'Even on the straights there was very little in it.' Harry is looking pretty chuffed with himself and the 911. Then John chips in: 'Hey Dickie, did you turn the radio off at any point?' Cue gales of laughter.

On the run back to the villa I'm feeling more at ease with the Diablo. The more you concentrate on the driving, the more it shrink-wraps itself around you, and you feel so in touch with what's going on, and the chassis feels so composed, that you soon start to go as quickly as you dare, lining up the exit and really piling on the power. The power steering is one of the best here, in that it doesn't feel assisted at all, just manageable. There's massive grunt everywhere,

911 HUL plate has graced several generations of Turbos. This one's the fastest yet, probably the fastest all-road all-weather supercar there has ever been. Tuscany makes a suitably epic backdrop

but it's from 4500 that it really explodes, bellowing through its stubby exhausts, zizzing and resonating through the whole cabin, reminding you that this car is, in fact, one huge engine platform. And when it sounds like it's just about to burst through the firewall and eat you, then you change up.

Over dinner we marshal our thoughts. There's a general consensus that Lamborghini, with Audi's help, has created the car the Diablo should have been all along, and that so far it's got its nose in front of the Maranello.

The 360 has had a few mixed notices, but Dickie has shown that it's right on the pace if you've the requisite trouser furniture, though even he admits it's 'a bit unpredictable'. Mention of the Viper elicits chuckles.

The 911 has impressed everyone. Harry reckons it's the quickest car here over give-and-take roads, and compares it with his own previous-generation 993 Turbo. 'Like all the current 996s, it's more polished, with better body control. It's still bloody firm, and it won't squat like mine out of corners. I also love the way mine looks – it's as though the body can barely contain the mechanicals underneath. This one looks like it's been designed by someone who has no passion for cars. I think with a supercar, you have to open your garage door and think: 'Ooooooh my god.' By my reckoning that makes my old Series 3 Jag a supercar, but I think I know what he means.

'The Porsche is awesome in its ability,' continues Harry. 'On a track day you'd run rings around just about everything else – you'd take anyone on.' John Barker chips in: 'It's the smug supercar.'

Wednesday morning, and thankfully the skies are clear. I open the passenger door to the 550 Maranello. The smell of leather is as evocative and as heady as the slightly chill, damp air inside a shuttered villa before the sunlight floods in. I'm happy to ride along with Dickie and wallow in the sights and sounds.

The landscape is entrancing: ancient towns perched on hilltops, roads that zig and zag up valley sides, lined by those signature cypress trees like dabs of dark green paint on the canvas. The light is ever changing too, through ethereal dawn, to brilliant mid-day sun that illuminates hillside and poppy field, to the moment when dusk creeps over the land, and finally the red cherry of a sun – a Maranello cherry, as one of our number put it – dissolves on the horizon.

'The Viper's like driving
a bar of soap. You never know
quite when it's going to slip
out of your hands'

CHRYSLER
Viper GTS

A much better driver's car than the original Viper RT/10, the GTS is America's only genuine supercar. Regarded by many as a blunt instrument despite crushing Porsche in GT racing, the Viper is unarguably spectacular and fearsomely potent.

Famously donated by a truck, the Viper's monstrous 8-litre V10 motor was refined and recast in aluminium by Lamborghini before being bolted snugly beneath its sprawling be-striped bonnet. That engine alone booked the Viper a place in supercar folklore.

With a shape that successfully fuses the creativity of Chrysler's designers with a bruising, track-tough stance honed at Le Mans and Daytona, the Viper trades visual punches with the best Europe can offer.

As you'd expect of an American legend, the Viper relies heavily on unashamed brute force. With the power delivery of an AMTRAK freight train, the six-speed gearbox is largely redundant. You won't find any fancy paddle-shift nonsense here.

Don't expect any other techno creature comforts either. Traction control comes courtesy of your right foot. It's a raw, uncensored experience made doubly unique, surreal almost, by the Herculean reserves of torque that rumble from deep within the V10. It's like the forces of nature have been harnessed and hooked up to the rear wheels. **RM**

SPECIFICATION: Engine 7990cc, V10, 20v, front-mounted **Power** 378bhp @ 5100rpm **Torque** 454lb ft @ 3600rpm **Transmission** Six-speed manual, rear-wheel drive **Weight** 1293kg **Power to weight** 297bhp/ton **Suspension** Double wishbones, coil springs, anti-roll bars front and rear **Tyres** 275/40 ZR18 front, 335/30 ZR18 rear **0-60mph** 4.5secs **Max speed** 177mph **Price** £68,825

There's no denying Viper's presence or its muscularity – it looks like it's just swallowed Arnold Schwarzenegger. Torque easily overcomes grip, which is impressive – rear tyres are as big as the Diablo's

Dickie picks up the pace and the 550 feels magnificent, all of a piece, sliding with such balance and progression that power-on oversteer feels like the most natural thing in the world. There's real quality in depth, shot through every component. What's missing is the Diablo's blood-and-thunder soundtrack, and maybe the extra challenge of driving the mid-engined leviathan.

'After the Lamborghini it's almost like driving a 3-series BMW,' says Dickie. 'And in some ways you can get more out of it, do more with it. In many ways it's just a better car – the gearchange for example is vastly better than the Diablo's.'

The 360, on the other hand, he found just a little bit scary, especially on yesterday evening's drying roads. 'The 911 is probably as fast a car in anyone's hands on any given road as there has ever been. Harry in the 911 could just turn in and go, the 360 was more difficult. I tried with the traction control on, but it doesn't let you get on the power when you need to, or you hit a bump and spin a wheel and that kills it.'

What about front versus mid-engined – does it actually matter where the engine is? 'Unless you're going to drive really hard, it probably doesn't matter. Personally I prefer the balance of a front engine. Everything happens more slowly.'

Is it also because in a mid-engined car like the Diablo you're right in the nose, and there's a mass of body and engine strung out somewhere behind you, whereas in the 550 you're much closer to the rear wheels? 'Yeah, I guess this is a bit like driving a big Caterham – you feel what's going on. The visibility also restricts what you can do with the Diablo.' So he wouldn't get the Diablo as out of shape as the 550? 'Oh no, no...

'The 550 is the best of Diablo and 911, but a supercar has to look spectacular too. I mean, I love the Viper, though it's a pretty agricultural thing, because you see it on the road or you get into it and you feel genuinely excited, because of what it is. In some ways it's just as compromised as the Diablo. It's big and heavy, the gearchange is awkward, and it's difficult to place. Everywhere you want to look there's a big lump of bodywork.'

Truth be told, I'm not exactly itching to drive the Viper. Yes, it looks as mean, moody and magnificent as a bison in motorcycle leathers. And yes, an 8-litre V10 is a very amusing concept indeed. But all the talk of wobbly body panels, agricultural transmissions and imprecise controls has kind of put me off. Funny that.

I decide to go for a passenger ride, with Mr Barker. Harry's going to lead in the 360 Modena and he's going to show us some of his favourite roads around the Val D'Orcia, including part of the old Mille Miglia route. Imagine all your favourite bits of roads strung together in a 15-mile loop then draped over the Tuscan hills and you get some idea.

After two days here, Harry is metamorphosing into his alter ego, the hard-driving Italian count Arri Vederci. He sets quite a pace in the 360, and the agile, mid-engined Ferrari looks so right for these roads, I'm thinking any minute now he's going to start opening out a gap. But he doesn't. The great galumphing black beast sticks to his back bumper like it's locked on by some some of tractor beam. What's even more of a bugger, if only Harry knew it, is that while he's flicking up and down the paddle-shift box like the pinball wizard, JB has stuck the Viper's gearstick in third – and he's leaving it there. Even when we pull out of a T-junction at barely 10mph.

Now, I know John's a bit handy, but I'm thinking there's rather more to the Viper than meets the eye. Its pace, not just in a straight line but across really testing roads, is a revelation.

[Supercar Group Test]

Seems you get just as much enjoyment, though, from the passenger seat.

'It's like driving a bar of soap,' says John above the roar of the V10. 'You never know quite when it's going to slip out of your grasp. The pedals are all mushy and there's no real feedback. You tell more about the front running wide from what you can see through the screen than what you can feel at the wheel. At the back you have to be gentle; it can feel like it's on ice. On corners where the 360 is understeering, this is slithering around.

'The engine's fantastic, and sounds better than ever with this exhaust. But there's no precise feel to the throttle – it's difficult to measure out exactly what you want. In many ways it's the opposite to the Maranello in feel, even though the basic layout and power are so similar.'

My go. Love the view out through the pillbox screen over that massively curvaceous bonnet, and the noise. It's a big, breathy sound, smoother than the average V8, almost warbly – not unlike two quattro straight-fives on a common crank. And redlined at a mere 6000, which in this company makes it a real lugger. The gearknob is almost baseball-size - it's a bit like pulling the lever on a one-arm bandit. You just hope you get two big plums when the reels stop.

There's not much finesse. A fruit machine has a slightly better action than the Viper's lumbering gearshift. The pedals are offset – towards the wheelarch! – and the throttle feels like it's attached to a bent knitting needle. But in fact it's quite a benevolent beast to punt along and the V10 makes it feel indomitable. Rides well too, and the brakes are certainly up to it.

Sophisticated? Nah. There's no traction control, not even ABS. And as you hit about 125mph the bonnet starts to judder. Combined with the acreage of hard scratchy plastic inside,

that makes it feel a bit flaky. But it's a big character, and it's supercar-quick all right. As you've probably realised, there's little delicacy or sensitivity about it. Which makes it a bit cartoonish, a bit two-dimensional. Still, it would have bloody Pikachu for breakfast.

It's mid-morning now, and we're getting to know the roads pretty well. John Hayman and I are enjoying the Diablo on a particularly fine 15km stretch between Sarteano and Radicofani. Every time you glance up from the road, there's the most absurdly romantic scenery all around you – and it looks best through the plummeting sideglass of the Diablo. Suddenly the 360 bursts into view, closely pursued by an arrow-headed silver sliver of a supercar.

Neither of us has ever seen one on the road before, but we know instantly what it is. The Pagani Zonda has arrived.

The Zonda looks like a Group C racer crossed

with a Faberge egg: narrow cockpit, pinched waist, extravagantly flared hips and the OTT tail with its cluster of exhausts, and all that elaborate detailing. Makes the Diablo look restrained. It has been driven down from Modena by chief development driver Loris Bicocchi – immensely experienced and a thoroughly good sort. This particular car, he explains, is well used. In fact it has covered 130,000km. He is embarrassed that the pristine demonstrator isn't available. He needn't worry…

While the others pore over the Pagani, I slip into the Porsche. The launch of the Turbo was what prompted us to bring this group of cars together, but down here, in the Diablo's playground, it's almost being ignored and it's not hard to see why.

Turbos have traditionally been among the lairiest 911s, with their swollen rear haunches and outrageous whaletail spoilers. With the 996, it seems Porsche has decreed the Turbo should be the discreet supercar, leaving the way clear for

the GT3 and forthcoming GT2 to be the show-offs. Fair enough, but in this company the 911, especially in midnight blue, looks almost reserved. Of course it only takes a few seconds behind the wheel to realise that beneath the bushel the light burns as vividly as ever.

In fact its sober suit means its monumental thrust is all the more shocking. And there's no turbo lag, just thickly spread torque. It's got oceans of grip, and it puts a grin on your face with its sheer stonk – on the straights, into the corners, and out of them. The steering isn't the most feelful, but the chassis' tightness and precision build your confidence, as do the 911's inherent compactness and visibility.

There's a seriously meaty feel to the Turbo. The ride is firm – on my test route the Diablo had at least as good damping and body control (which shows just how far the Lamborghini has come). There's a wonderful sensation of the back hunkering down as I'm shot out of a long right-hander and into a sun-dappled tree-lined straight.

Above: two front-engined cars, three mid-engined, and a 911. Diablo and Porsche have four-wheel drive, the rest are rear-drive (and Viper and Zonda make do without traction control)

The consistency of the feel and weighting of the controls puts the Viper to shame. Consider that the Turbo costs £86,000, which makes it the second cheapest car here, yet offers all that hardware – twin turbos, four-wheel drive, stability control, ABS – and more all-road all-weather speed than any car on the planet, and as Dickie says, 'It's got everything you want, really.'

So why am I feeling so cool about it? Because a GT3 is more soulful, engages the senses, presents more of a challenge. Because the Turbo makes going quickly just a little bit joyless. The original scary supercar, the 911 Turbo, has become the most efficient, the most sanitised. It sounds stupid, but if you had to put your gran behind the wheel of any of the cars here, this is the one.

'The great galumphing black beast sticks to his back bumper like it's locked on by some sort of tractor beam'

PORSCHE
911 Turbo

We've grown used to Porsche producing the ultimate all-weather supercar. A precedent that started with the 959 has now been ruthlessly honed into a 911 Turbo with almost worrying potency. Twin turbos, four-wheel drive, stability control and 420bhp all contained within less square feet of sheet metal than any other 190mph supercar. A weapon, pure and simple.

Forget the flamboyance that the Italians love so much. Functionality is Porsche's hallmark, and it's stamped all over the Turbo. Hungry, ugly vents shaped and positioned by computers not stylists dominate the Turbo's stern face, while at the rear the trademark spoiler has gained a second fin, pushed into the air-stream by a pair of hydraulic rams. It's a design flourish-free zone, but there's no doubting the quality of the engineering.

In terms of sheer point-to-point pace the 911 has no peer. You can deploy every ounce of power cleanly to the tarmac come rain or shine. The brakes are sensational, steering feedback intimate and with such tight, lean dimensions you can attack where Diablos fear to tread.

In fact only the Turbo's possible lack of raw sex appeal could possibly stand between it and supercar domination. For a car as accomplished as the 911, dynamics are normally enough, but up against Ferraris and Lambos, the outcome is often as dependent on lust as it is on logic. **RM**

arrive at our muster point just in time to see John Barker emerge from the Zonda with the expression of a man who's just tasted a completely new flavour and found it very much to his liking. 'Mmm*MMmm*,' is his first utterance. 'It's actually very friendly, and very, *very* quick. The engine's fantastic – like the Diablo's V12 but smoother, creamier. Doesn't rev as high, hasn't quite got that spine-tingling top-end, but it's a quality supercar sound.

'According to Loris, the suspension on this car is tired, there's a revised set-up coming, and there's a new six-speed gearbox on the way too. The ride isn't as absorbent as the Diablo's, and the gearbox is the least happy aspect of the car. But straight out of the box it's very, very good. It feels light too. It's got, what, less than 400bhp, and the Diablo's got nearer 600. They feel pretty close. I think you're going to like it.'

As you slide inside, you just have to spend a couple of minutes absorbing all the fabulous details. It's like sitting in a 962 fitted out by Jules Verne and Louis Vuitton. Turn the key and six litres of Mercedes V12 erupts somewhere behind you and settles to a throbby idle. Hefty shove

into first, clutch bites progressively. And within seconds you feel totally immersed in the driving.

It's partly because there's such a rush of sensations to take in, through the suspension and the steering, and the rich sounds of the V12. But also because you're seated low, right down there with the chassis. With the wraparound screen and the front wings rising over the wheels, you feel you're almost there between the hubs, right where the action is. And it comes thick and fast. If you thought that compared with the 550 and Diablo, a mere 389bhp might make the C12 feel a tad underpowered, forget it. The mid-range is immense and third gear stretches all the way from dawdling to dazzling. But unlike the Diablo it picks up speed instantly. There's so little inertia. And then you remember that it weighs almost 400 kilos less. In fact with 316bhp per ton, it's ahead of the Viper and the Porsche and both Ferraris, and just a stretch away from the mighty Lamborghini.

There are details to be improved – the instruments are too tiny and reflective, the rear-view mirrors are ineffectual – but these things are easily fixed. The gearchange is heavy and

stiff, but there's a new six-speed 'box on the way. Where the Diablo smothers the road and tracks arrow-straight, the Zonda feels dartier, more reactive, slightly looser. But this, remember, is not the definitive suspension set-up.

Still, it fairly bites into corners. The steering wheel is quite the best I've ever held, a mix of leather and suede and aluminium that seems to have been moulded by my own hands. And the steering itself is perfectly weighted, perfectly geared. Like the Diablo, the Zonda responds best to a neat, measured driving style, but when I give it a bootful too much throttle in second gear, and the tail suddenly swishes, an instinctive half-turn of opposite lock recovers it smartly enough.

It's the sheer sensuality that gets you, though. That and the engine's delivery, the sheer pace of the thing. It doesn't have the Diablo's top-end savagery (what does?) but it makes up for it with a punchier mid-range. There's a cultured, metallic edge to the engine note. And when it's flying, the Pagani just munches up the scenery. With the canopy all around you, the roadside dissolves to a blur of green, the angular, blade-like snout slicing through the air, the rocketship

Old enemies: Ferrari and Lamborghini have been supercar rivals ever since the late '60s. Now there's a new pretender to the throne, in the unlikely shape of the Pagani Zonda (above)

Zonda and Diablo are both traffic-stopping supercars in the best traditions. Lamborghini now knows how Ferrari felt in the '60s – there's a new kid on the block, and Pagani knows some good moves

'Just when the test was forming into shape, the Pagani has driven a silver wedge through all our preconceptions'

exhausts pulsing. Oh, and when I finally clamber out I note its rear tyre sizes – 345/35 ZR18s. Big respect.

Just when it seemed the test was forming into some sort of shape, the Pagani has come along and driven a silver wedge right through all our preconceptions. Everyone emerges from the Zonda grinning, and telling everyone who'll listen just how fantastic it is. Even Hayman, who has spent most of the day conducting a private love affair with the Lamborghini. 'I though it was going to be as monstery as the Diablo, but it's sooo driveable.'

I watch it approach again down the straight, shimmering in the heat-haze rising from the 360's engine cover. This time the grin belongs to Harry. 'This is going to scare Lamborghini,' he says. 'You instantly feel the lack of weight, especially on the twisty stuff. The tyres are biting – they're not fighting weight and grip, they can just do more work for you. The engine is super-strong, velvety, with a real punch. I have a feeling that in many ways this is a better drive than the Diablo…'

And then he puts his finger right on it: 'The Zonda brings the lightness of the Elise to the supercar class. Just as the Elise came along and shook up all our ideas about sports cars, I think this could do the same. Bugger.'

Nicely put, Lord M.

The final morning, and we leave the villa for the last time. I'm back in the Viper. It's a great car to have on your side: so much *presence*. Fact is, if you hadn't driven any of the other cars, you'd be thrilled with its performance, in awe of its ground-covering pace, in love with its throaty V10. And wherever you parked it, you'd always return to

find you had a crowd of new mates.

But to me it feels more of a musclebound GT than a supercar. Harry describes it as 'a big woolly mammoth', and JB says it's a shame about the flakiness: 'The Americans just don't seem bothered with trim quality, and the pedals vibrate madly at three-figure speeds, suggesting there's not much basic chassis stiffness.'

Dickie is happier to overlook its faults. 'I've always had a bit of a soft spot for the Viper, and far from knocking the rose-tinted specs from my nose, this test has just made me like it all the more. Unlikely as it sounds, it also makes a brilliant long-distance car. Despite being sat in the same seat for 13 hours, it didn't feel bad at all. It simply ate Europe at 2000rpm – which is just over 100mph in Viperspeak.

'I think it's a genuine exotic. It has real character and full-on supercar performance. It feels a bit of a monster when you drive it hard – bucking and leaping around over bumps – but it's still surprisingly effective once you accept its limitations and exploit its strengths. It's kind of reassuring to know that cubic inches can still do the job.'

Hardest to separate are the 911 Turbo and 360 Modena. The Porsche's the more rounded car, with less peaks and troughs in its dynamic performance; the quickest too in most conditions. But the Ferrari has the more extrovert character, one of the most thrilling exhaust notes we've heard, and is the more exciting drive – though not always for the right reasons. In the end the Porsche's completeness and more polished chassis give it the edge.

'I'm not sure about the 360's handling,' says Dickie. 'The steering's lovely, and it turns in like a race-car, but it understeers too early and then when you lift off, things get all nasty and mid-

PAGANI
Zonda C12

The Zonda is the product of a tiny company and the dream of one man, Argentinian-born Horacio Pagani. Yet its construction, build quality and dynamic polish would be a credit to Ferrari, Lamborghini or McLaren. The C12 is one of only a few fully type-approved production cars built in carbonfibre. It seems an incredible undertaking for such a small company until you realise that Pagani left Lamborghini's development department to create a (successful) firm specialising in the stuff.

The C12 hasn't been rushed, and it shows – attention to detail and finish are exceptional, even in areas normally hidden. You need this sort of quality to persuade Mercedes to supply its 6-litre V12, though a word in the right ear from friend and fellow Argentinian the late Juan Manuel Fangio helped.

To some tastes the Zonda is a little over-styled, especially in the details, but from behind the wheel it is a most beautiful thing. First for the speed rush you get from seeing the road disappear between the front arches, and second for its agility. It weighs only 1250kg, which is 400kg less than a Diablo and just 100kg more than a McLaren F1, which helps make it incredibly responsive. As we said when we got our first shot behind the wheel (**evo** 11), the supercar Establishment should be very worried indeed. **JB**

SPECIFICATION: **Engine** 5987cc, V12, 48v, mid-mounted **Power** 389bhp @ 5200rpm **Torque** 420lb ft @ 3800rpm **Transmission** Six-speed manual, rear-wheel drive **Weight** 1250kg **Power to weight** 316bhp on **Suspension** Double wishbones, coil springs, anti-roll bars front and rear **Tyres** 255/40 ZR18 front, 345/35 ZR18 rear **0-60mph** 4.5secs **Max speed** 185mph+ **Price** £200,000

'The 360 gives you a proper supercar buzz. Gratuitous gear-changes are a must'

engined. It's a challenge all right.

'It looks amazingly aggressive and very, very modern. The engine noise and response give you a proper supercar buzz… gratuitous gear-changes are a must in this car. If I owned one I'd have my driveway underground just so I could wind the windows down and nail it.

'But I hate the F1 gearbox. It takes too much away from the involvement and sensations of driving. Feels too much like an arcade game to have really enduring appeal.'

We're divided over the paddle shift. I'm with Dickie on this one, but John and Harry can see advantages on these roads. As John says: 'On the fabulous run up to Pienza in the late evening sunshine I couldn't figure out how Dickie driving the 360 was giving Harry in the Turbo so much grief. Driving the 360 next day, in anger, I knew what made the difference – the F1 gearbox. Right up to the apex you have choices, and both hands on the wheel. Which gives you time to concentrate on line and braking, and to take a very late downshift when you're almost at the apex and keep the flat-plane crank V8 screaming. For me, that was the best thing about

the 360. Well, that and the noise. It feels a little two-dimensional. I don't go a bundle on the looks, or the interior either. I'd have a 355… with the 360 engine.'

Harry says the 360 feels almost toy-like – and then apologises for placing the 911 ahead. I know what he means. On my list I have the 360 narrowly in front, simply because it looks and sounds more like a supercar, but I can't deny that the 911 is devastatingly effective.

'It's ruthlessly rapid on any road,' says Dickie. 'It has a really addictive blend of eye-watering acceleration, near-foolproof chassis and user-friendliness. But in this company it fails to fire your imagination once you've walked away.'

'It has so much power, whatever the numbers on the speedo,' says JB. 'We saw 165 on the autobahn down from Basel with more to come. On these roads the nose feels typically 911-light – you still have to get it hooked in before introducing the throttle to the carpet – and I miss the instantaneous, vocal delivery of the GT3. There's not enough rawness, enough edge, I guess. It's a cliche, but it's almost too efficient.'

As we head for our playground for the last time, Diablo, Zonda and Maranello streak away into the middle distance, as Harry, John and Dickie have their final fling. It's fittingly symbolic. The landscape and the roads here are so spectacular, so special, that they favour bold supercar statements, emotional heavyweights. Maybe that's why the Diablo and Pagani move ahead – ahead even of our long-time favourite, the 550 Maranello.

'The 550's a great car to wring out,' says JB. 'So slideable. Then you think, hang on, this is a 199mph, near-500bhp, rear-drive car with a 5.5-litre V12 up front. Yet it shrinks around you, responds keenly and precisely to every input. You never question that it costs more than twice as much as the Viper, which has a similar layout.'

Dickie describes the 550 as the best blend of supercar power and practical packaging. 'It's very well sorted for rapid driving – a much nicer car to rag than the 360. Maybe it's not vocal enough, but it oozes polish and refinement. But while it's exceptional in isolation it's a bit too sensible in this company. It just seems a bit ordinary somehow. Did I just say that? Oh dear…'

Top row: the supercar Establishment. From left: Diablo's 6-litre V12, 360 Modena's 3.6-litre V8 and 550 Maranello's 5.5-litre V12. Second row: the challengers. Viper's 8-litre V10, Porsche's 3.6-litre twin-turbo flat-six, and Zonda's 6-litre Mercedes V12

Ordinary is one word that will never be applied to the Diablo. It stirs people up, gets them excited about cars, sometimes almost despite themselves. The reaction to the Diablo in Italy suggests an almost religious experience. In England you'd probably be called a tosser and people would try to stop you pulling out of junctions. Here they cheer and smile and give you the thumbs up, not the finger.

We're all agreed this is the best Diablo ever. As much as anything else, it suggests Lamborghini is safe with Audi. The Germans have handled the old devil with sympathy, brought out what it does best, not spoilt a thing. As Barker says, 'Someone has really sprinkled some magic over the Diablo. It looks and sounds like an old-school supercar, but it drives so much better. Usually they come unstuck, feel dangerous even. With this you can creep up to the edge, read the signs and decide what to do.'

Harry reckons that for the first time a Diablo gives you the confidence to push really hard, even on unfamiliar roads, more so than in the ostensibly more conventional Viper.

JB's most memorable moment was on the autostrada. 'I don't know whether Harry's right foot unconsciously eased from the throttle of the 550 as we passed 280kmh but it was at about that point that we began to close. I saw 300kmh on the dial before H backed off hard.

'At about 260, just after I'd shifted into fifth, it got a bit squirrelly. I'm not sure if it was the wake from the 550 or the lack of rear wing, but as we slowed down for the turn-off I noticed that my palms were slightly moist. It's been a long time since that happened. What a machine! The ride is so good, the faithfulness and poise astounding, though just as in the 911, you can't disguise where the weight is when you're really pushing on – through long motorway curves that old tail-heavy balance creeps in and sends a warning – but at any sane speed the Diablo simply feels lithe and driveable.'

'If there's a more awesome looking car on the planet I haven't been lucky enough to see it yet,' says Dickie. 'It's easier to drive than you might imagine, though it's still about as crazily compromised by its shape as any car could be. Through left-hand bends you stare worriedly at the windscreen pillar, and turning into right-handers you seem to look into the passenger footwell for guidance. The soundtrack is positively evil, but the interstellar gearing is frustrating. It takes too long to hit its stride.'

Part of the task we set ourselves was to try to nail what exactly is a supercar. According to John, it's got to have more cylinders and bhp than a road car reasonably needs. And stuff practicality; a supercar should be visually dramatic, exotically engineered and a challenge to drive (so long as it rewards too). It doesn't have to be mid-engined but it does have to prickle the nape with thrill rather than fear.

It's a good definition, but there's an even better one, and it's even pithier. Diablo 6.0 VT. And if it hadn't been for a late arrival in our midst, we'd now be declaring it a clear winner…

As you'll have realised by now, there's another car here which, in certain critical areas, is moving the game on. At the outset we wondered if either the Viper or the 911 Turbo could upset the supercar establishment in their own back yard. We should have been looking closer to home. The Pagani is quite astonishingly good for a first car from a new manufacturer.

For me, it's simply the most intoxicating road car I've ever driven, though I have serious reservations about the looks. The lines are awkward and unharmonious from some angles – and those exhausts are at best in dubious taste – but there is no doubt that it creates a stir in the best supercar tradition.

The only other major reservation is the bought-in Mercedes engine. Nothing wrong with the unit itself – it's fabulous. But most of the truly great supercars have had their own bespoke power units. It's largely a form of snobbery, of course. As with the rather glitzy, flashy looks, it certainly doesn't seem to bother Pagani's customers: 12 cars have already been delivered; the order book is looking very healthy thank you.

What turns us on is the way it drives. 'It just

Growing old gracefully. Gone are all the extraneous wings and bulges and scoops: latest 6-litre VT Diablo is just as God and Gandini intended

blows you away,' says Dickie. 'Watching each and every one of us emerge from the Zonda with mile-wide grins is proof enough that it's the most memorable car in the test to drive.'

Any conversation about the Zonda keeps coming back to lightness. As John says, 'Imagine taking the Diablo's new-found agility and response and unburdening it to the tune of 400kg. In other words, throw a quarter of its mass away. That's the Zonda. No simple weight reduction programme could possibly hope to achieve this. Carbonfibre is the key.'

OK, so Gordon Murray and McLaren got there first with the F1, but the Zonda weighs only 100kg more and costs a third of the price. Some of that extra weight, maybe 25kg, has gone on powered brakes and steering – items that Murray wouldn't countenance – and the result is a car that feels astoundingly light for a broad-beamed, fat-tyred supercar. As Harry said, it's the Elise of supercars.

'In a straight line the F1 is ferociously, relentlessly and mind-numbingly accelerative,' says John. 'It makes the Zonda feel slow. However, come the first corner, the unassisted McLaren is as unwieldy and weighty as the old

Diablo, which I found hugely disappointing.

'The Zonda is brilliant in these areas and I believe it points to a future that no-one thought the genuine, traditional, mid-engined supercar had. The dinosaur could make an evolutionary step that will secure its future.'

With the latest suspension and new gearbox it should feel even better, but we'll have to reserve final judgement. And in three weeks time, Pagani launches the 'S' version with a 550bhp 7-litre AMG version of the V12…

Harry: 'Supercars are all about emotions. If I had to choose an owner to be best mates with, it would have to be either the guy with the Diablo or the Zonda. The Zonda's the best supercar chassis in the world, but in the Diablo there's that magic moment when you're almost kissing the rev limiter, and there's this incredible intensity of noise and speed. It's still the biggest event.'

After three long days – three of the best days of our lives – it all comes down to this. And though it's been on the canvas a couple of times, by the narrowest of points decisions it's the Lamborghini. But the Diablo's days could well be numbered. Twenty one, and counting. ■

V295 HGS

www.PULLICINO.com

AUTODROM MUNSTER

Pictures: Gus Gregory   Archive pictures: Nigel Snowdon/Klementaski Collection

F A N T A S Y
I S L A N D

The Targa Florio road race on the isle of Sicily was one of the greatest
tests of car and driver ever devised. In 2001, Richard Meaden tackled
its 700 corners in a 911 GT3 and relived a famous Porsche victory

Above: magnificent
996 GT3 feels
immediately at home
in Sicily. Below: in
1973 the 911 RS gave
Porsche the last of its
Targa Florio triumphs

've always thought it something of a
travesty that Porsche should name one
of the unhappiest-looking, least
focussed 911 models after the oldest,
most intensely challenging road race
in history. I'm sure it made perfect
sense to Stuttgart's marketing suits.
After all, the 911 Carrera had taken its
name from another great road race,
the Carrera Panamericana, so it must
have seemed perfectly logical to take
Sicily's epic race, the Targa Florio, and use the
name to give the new removable-roofed 911 a bit
of credibility. Sad but true.

What makes the decision all the more
unpalatable is that Porsche appreciated the true
significance of the Targa Florio more acutely than
most. With ten victories on the island, six of
which were scored in the last nine years of the
Targa as a full-blown championship race, Sicily
was as happy a hunting ground for the Stuttgart

marque as Le Mans. What's more, those wins
were made all the sweeter by giving the
combined might of Ferrari and Alfa Romeo a
very public drubbing on home soil.

Porsche's last victory came in 1973. Something
of a shock for the fiercely partisan Italians, this
surprise win by an out-gunned 911 RS is the
inspiration for our pilgrimage to sun-baked Sicily.
Our chosen transport? Why, that glorious road-
racer's great grandson, the 911 GT3 of course.

I don't mind admitting it's been a logistical
nightmare to get here. Sicily's not the easiest
place to get to on a budget, so Gus Gregory and I
have flown out with Ryanair to Lamezia, a
godforsaken place on the southern Italian
mainland. At a faintly ridiculous £9 return we
can hardly complain though. We're left with an
hour or so's drive by hire car (three hours in
anything else) to Villa San Giovanni, where we're
due to catch a ferry to Sicily. I'm not keen on
boats, but **evo** road test assistant John Hayman

and **evo** reader Paul Thorpe are driving the 2000 miles from Blighty in Paul's GT3, so a 30-minute boat ride is a pretty cushy number.

Once safely on Sicily, Gus and I head along the coast from Messina towards the capital, Palermo. It's a long haul, especially when the autostrada peters out and we have to take the narrow coast road. It must have been quite a traffic jam along here when the race was on, with brightly coloured team transporters from around the world snaking their way towards Campofelice and the Targa course itself.

The shrill tone of Gus's mobile 'phone snaps us back to the present day. It's Hayman and Thorpe, just about to board the ferry. They've made excellent time, but just as we're about to warn them of the steep ramps on and off the ferry, an expensive graunching sound crackles from the earpiece, followed by a nervous-sounding Thorpe explaining that the 911 is beached on the hard steel deck. Oh bugger.

'A quarter of a century after the last race, it remains one of the most evocative stretches of tarmac on earth'

nable to offer anything other than sympathy, Gus and I point our willing Fiesta rental towards Campofelice. I've brought along a compilation of old Targa Florio race reports for inspiration – published by Brooklands Books, it's a fascinating insight into what the Targa was like, not to mention a great source of clues with which to trace the circuit and photo locations for Gus to get his teeth into.

Butterflies start to flutter in the pit of my stomach as the Madonie mountains come into view. We're getting close. Some 45 miles long, the Targa Florio's Piccolo Madonie circuit is, as its name suggests, a smaller version of the original Targa course, which snaked for a monstrous 90 miles through the mountains. The more compact Piccolo course uses the same public road that

threads its way inland from the coastal town of Campofelice, down to Cerda, then further inland to Caltavuturo before heading back out to the coast via Collesano.

Piccolo or not, it's an awesome place to drive any car, let alone a full-blooded race car. Apart from one long straight where the racers would slot top gear and hold it there for minutes at a time, the remainder of the circuit is an endless stream of tricky twists and tortuous turns. Long and complex enough to make the Nürburgring look like a kindergarten but just short enough for the very best drivers to learn and attack it like a conventional race track, the Targa Florio was the ultimate challenge for those brave enough to accept it. Even today, around a quarter of a century after the last race, it remains one of the most evocative stretches of tarmac on earth.

By 1973, the Targa Florio's fearsome open-road format was viewed as increasingly unsuited to the World Championship for Makes (an early version of the World Sportscar Championship). The new breed of sports prototypes had simply out-grown the roads. Moves had already been made to tame the cars from their fierce peak of 1971, when big-banger V12 prototypes like Ferrari's 512S weighed just 570kg and kicked out 620bhp. But while the toned-down Ferraris and Alfas of '73 may have weighed 80kg more and had 120bhp less to work with, it was still clear that faint hearts had no place here.

Anachronism or not, the lure of winning the last ever true Targa Florio was too much for Ferrari and Alfa to ignore. The two had been fighting a civil war on the world's race circuits for years, but it was the crumbling roads of the Madonie

mountains that provided the most appropriate and dramatic backdrop. So, when the fastest sportscars and drivers in the world descended on Sicily in early May, the scene was set for one last epic battle.

Somewhat overlooked amidst all this Italian bravado, Porsche arrived with a trio of Martini-liveried 2.9-litre 911 RSs. The pumped, squat, whale-tailed 911s were far less dramatic than the Ferrari and Alfa prototypes, but because of some homologation wrangles over the enlarged rear spoilers, modified suspension and new engine crankcases, they had to run in the same class.

Although there was undoubtedly consternation in the Porsche camp at the time, the 911's compact dimensions and robust build were well-suited to the confined and gruelling Targa course. Even so, chances are you'd have been able to get

good odds in any Sicilian bookmaker's on one of these very obviously road-based Porsches getting anywhere near the home-grown drivers and machinery.

If people power could make a difference to the outcome, Ferrari would have had the race sewn-up, as sharing one of the two factory 312Ps was a man by the name of Nino Vaccarella. A native Sicilian and a former Targa winner, he carried the hopes of all Sicilians on his shoulders every time he drove. Few knew the course quite as intimately as he, nor did any other driver have their name daubed on quite so many stone walls or patches of the road surface as the beloved Vaccarella.

Though Targa veterans in their own right, the lead Porsche duo of Gijs van Lennep and Herbert Müller might have felt somewhat

Above: what must the Targa Florio have been like? Imagine Le Mans race cars running through your local town, with thousands of cheering people lining the streets. Below: the old pits at Cerda. Opposite page: retracing the tyre-tracks of the RSR. Far left: entering Collesano

overwhelmed by the combined might of Ferrari, Vaccarella and the 700,000 roaring Sicilians that lined the circuit. And who could have blamed them? But the pressure was on Ferrari and Alfa to perform, and with such a weight of expectation and the Targa's infamous attrition rate waiting to claim them, there must have been an air of relaxed optimism in the Porsche camp.

As Van Lennep said before the start of the race, 'We are just going to go out and go like hell and see what places we can pick up. That kind of driving is fun.'

'I suspect this is the first time a GT3 has driven these roads, yet it copes with them so well it feels like a homecoming'

Apart from the advancing autostrada that runs like a bleached concrete ribbon along the top of the island towards the capital, Palermo, it's hard to believe that much has changed on Sicily in the last 27 years. The land is largely unspoilt, the pace of life glacial once you get up into the hills, and, if you look carefully, you can still see Vaccarella's name in fading, flaking white paint on the weathered stone buildings. Sometimes it's so quiet you can hear the blood pumping around your head.

Rewind to May 13, 1973, and the whole island must have been in utter chaos. The race was scheduled to be an eleven-lapper – or 491.04 miles to be precise – and the roads would have been closed to the public a good few hours beforehand. With the first car due to start at 9am, and the rest following at 20-second intervals, spectators had to make for the mountains the night before the race, 'parking' their battered Fiat 500s in ditches and securing the best vantage points for the morning. With bonfires flickering, stomachs full of local wine and home-cured meats and heads full of anticipation, it must have been quite a night as all of Sicily partied

under the stars. Waiting.

With the intrepid Hayman and Thorpe now safely on the island, and our hotel rooms waiting in Palermo, we reluctantly head back to civilisation. After a delicious pizza and a few Peronis, we can look forward to a more comfortable night's sleep than those hardy spectators. Our bliss is short-lived, though, for as is customary on a Gus Gregory photoshoot, it's still dark when we meet downstairs the following morning. Our plan is mercifully simple for such a hellish hour, and involves nothing more complex than heading for the town of Cerda, and the old start line and pit complex.

To our complete surprise, many of the original buildings are still standing proud, lending the place a ghostly atmosphere reminiscent of the old Reims GP circuit. After a fevered cleaning session on the travel-stained Porsche, the sun is just beginning to climb from behind the mountains as Gregory's Hasselblad sucks in the first shot of the morning. Today is going to be a good day.

From Cerda we follow the direction of the race traffic, along the stringy, knotted roads that skirt the hillsides en route to the craggy, sun-bleached mountain town of Caltavuturo. It's a breathtaking drive, with seemingly every corner revealing an even more wonderful vista. I can't remember ever driving a road as satisfying as this. It's quiet, tranquil almost, and yet far from wanting to slow and admire the scenery, you feel compelled to push on as hard as you dare as a mark of respect for what has gone before on this great road.

Already the route is a merciless stream of head-spinning twists and turns, gut-wrenching fresh-air drops and spine-pummelling lumps and bumps. These, it soon transpires, are Targa constants – the ever-present dangers, if you like.

You can never quite get your head around where the road goes next, making it almost impossible to decide how big a risk you can take. To be able to take a line and stick with it would take real familiarity, like Vaccarella's. Then and only then could these tangled corners be unravelled into one smooth 44-mile string of utter commitment. Without it I struggle to make sense of more than four or five miles at a time, and have to content myself with nailing a few open corners and feathering the rest.

I suspect this is the first time a 911 GT3 has driven these roads, and yet it copes with them so well it feels like a homecoming. Despite the chin spoiler sitting no higher than an upturned fag packet from the road, the unyielding body control ensures it never swipes the grainy, sun-baked surface, leaving my pre-emptive grimaces comically redundant. As with any 911 there's plenty of grip, but even in lowered, stiffened quasi-racer spec it remains beautifully adjustable. Steering feel is plentiful, and the faster you go the more explicitly informative it becomes. You need it too, for driving fast here means looking as far ahead as you can, living on your wits for the rest. For Van Lennep and Müller, pushing right to the limit in that hairy old RS, the early laps must have been utterly exhausting, a maximum-attack run through some sections of the course, literally dancing on the edge of oblivion.

Qualifying had been very close for the 57th Targa Florio, with Ferrari and Alfa slugging it out for the fastest lap. Records tumbled as each team pushed that little bit harder – too hard

Below: the Ferrari 312P of Arturo Merzario and local hero Nino Vaccarella. This wasn't to be Vaccarella's or Ferrari's day…

The evo crew in Sicily, left to right: Meaden, Hayman, GT3 owner Paul Thorpe, and photographer Gregory

Wish you were here?

I've only myself to blame. After all, I did offer my GT3 to evo for any forthcoming features, and when they mentioned the words 'Targa Florio' it took me at least four tenths of a second to say yes. But this is the moment of truth, when I find out if I'm going to regret it.

Picture the scene. Road test assistant John Hayman and myself are standing on a Sicilian hillside, looking out for local traffic. Photographer Gus Gregory has just laid in the road on the apex of the corner (Gus's mum, please stop reading at this point).

Now we hear the distinctive mechanical growl of the 911 approaching over the horizon. The car darts and squirms through the twists, co-editor Meaden making constant small adjustments. Now he's approaching 'our' corner, close to the limit, and there is Gus, prone on the tarmac, just inches off the perfect line.

The car is now in a deftly controlled power-slide and Dickie nails it off the apex and passes within inches of Gus's left shoulder. Thousands of small rubber pellets are deposited over Gus and the Sicilian landscape, as power, briefly, defeats traction. Throughout all this I hear the camera continue to whir. As the GT3 disappears over the horizon, I turn to Gus and ask how on earth he got the message to Dickie that he was going to be lying in the road. His nonchalant reply: 'I didn't get any message to him – he's just used to my antics.' Then we do it another dozen times but a bit faster and a bit closer!

Later I have a chance to sit beside Dickie as he drives the section one last time and head off for the next one. Dickie is a true master of car control and, when he's really in his stride, it's almost as if time runs slower as each section of a corner melds to the next, accompanied by measured corrections to the helm. We approach each corner with pinprick accuracy, his 'heel and toeing' almost imperceptible to the passenger. Turn-in is crisp, deliberate though not overly fast, but apex-and-out is a delicious crescendo of noise and g-force as the car seems to release a pent-up energy force… Fan-bloody-tastic.

As a reader of car magazines for some 20 years, I've often enjoyed articles like this that link present and past. I will now read them in a different light, knowing how much effort and artistry goes into each piece.

Paul Thorpe

'When the Targa Florio circuit asks you a question, you'd better be ready to answer...'

sometimes, as Alfa driver Clay Regazzoni proved by rolling his car into a ball. The final times were astonishing, with the quickest lap of 33min 38.5 secs being set by Vaccarella's Ferrari team-mate Arturo Merzario, who fired his 312P around the Targa's tortuous 44 miles in a mind-boggling 33min 38.5secs. As for the Porsche of Van Lennep, it was quickest of the road-based prototypes but some 3 minutes behind all the Ferraris and Alfas, on 36:52.1. Clearly out-gunned, the time was still a heroic effort, given the 911's massive power deficit.

It's all put into perspective on a fantastic charge along one of the twistiest, bumpiest section of the course. Gus and I have spotted a good corner for some action shots – a fast, third-gear right-hander with a nasty bump on the exit which will

hopefully help hoist a wheel in the air. Cornering shots are excellent fun because it requires roaring back and forth a dozen or so times along the same stretch of road. Normally the process has no more significance than that, but today such repetition allows me to look at the road through Van Lennep's sharp eyes.

Pushing harder and harder with every run past Gregory's well-aimed Nikon, I can at last attempt to unleash the GT3. The difference between driving at eight-tenths and ten-tenths is like night and day, both in terms of the level of concentration needed, and the sheer punishment it inflicts on the car. The pummelling is unbelievable as we launch off the numerous crests and thump into the compressions, skimming from bump to bump like a smooth, flat pebble

tossed across a glassy lake.

Every landing knocks the breath from my lungs, clatters my chin off my breast bone. The 911 doesn't come off any more lightly, with every millimetre of suspension travel used, every treadblock scuffed and squeezed in an effort to keep us on the road. Corrections come thick and fast, sharp stabs of lock, constant variations of throttle. It's not so much a challenge as a relentless interrogation of your driving ability. Clearly, when the Targa Florio circuit asks you a question, you'd better be ready to answer.

Aside from the endless combinations of dips and crests that are the essence of the Targa, wandering herds of goats and sheep add to its unique dangers. As if meandering livestock didn't cause enough problems, hefty milestones and jagged kerbs wait

Below: the 911 was – and still is – perfectly suited to Sicilian roads. It's compact, nimble and, perhaps above all, strong

in the scrubby roadside verges, jutting just enough to wrench wheels and smash suspension from under the careless, impatient or downright unlucky driver.

It's these variables, the unforeseen hazards, that made the Targa such a savage, unpredictable event. Many a race result was decided by the cruel intervention of a concealed item of road furniture. I decide it's as well to remind myself of that fact every ten minutes or so.

It's bizarre, but there's a distinct 'line' around these roads. With so little traffic and the locals' propensity for driving down the middle of the road, there's more dust and debris than you might expect on the fringes of the road. Stray from the clean line and the grip falls away quite suddenly, giving you the feeling of being sucked towards the barriers, walls and ditches that wait to swallow the unwary. The bumps pose attention grabbing problems too, the awkward, serrated frequency of the poorest surfaces upsetting the GT3's otherwise foolproof ABS and lengthening the braking area by a few heart-pumping feet.

Combine all this with the personal pressures of a race and, if you were driving one of the prototype cars, the frequent need to pass a slower car, and you'll have some idea of how tough it must have been to get through the Targa in one piece. Understandably it was quite common for the faster cars to nudge slower traffic increasingly hard until the driver got the message or lost control, such was the general reluctance for either party to venture willingly into the scrubby verge.

'It's the variables, the unforeseen
hazards, that made the Targa such
a savage, unpredictable event'

As the '73 race got under way it was clear
that the Ferrari/Alfa battle would be
intense. The Vaccarella/Merzario
Ferrari started first, to huge applause
from the crowd, followed by the Alfa of
Adamich/Stommelen, the Ickx/Redman Ferrari
and then the 911 RS of Müller and Van Lennep.
Almost immediately the crowd's favourite car
suffered a puncture, and in his eagerness to get
back to the pits, Merzario drove too fast on the
deflated tyre and inflicted serious damage to the
transmission. Although he would continue for
two more laps, the gearbox would eventually cry
enough before Vaccarella even got in the car.

Shortly before Merzario ground to a halt, Jackie
Ickx, racing in his first Targa, in the second
Ferrari, lost concentration and thumped a large
piece of stone. Wheels smashed, the car off the
road, Ferrari's hopes of one last Targa victory
were gone.

Now with more than five minutes' lead over the
Porsche of Müller and Van Lennep, Alfa were
looking good. There was no need to push to the
limit, but slower cars needed to be passed, and it
was while overtaking a Lancia Fulvia that the
Alfa was shoved into a marker stone and wrecked.

No such trouble for the 911, which continued
to run like clockwork, Van Lennep and Müller's
36-minute laps from hell easing to an altogether
less fraught 41 minutes as the opposition faded
away and the finish drew within sight. The
competition wasn't as hot as it could have been,
but as the Ferrari and Alfa teams would testify,
beating the opposition was the easy bit. Beating
the Targa Florio was another matter entirely.

THRILL
CLIMBER

The 340R might have been made for hillclimbing. In 2000, Harry Metcalfe took it to the ultimate hillclimb...

've had the 340's throttle welded to the aluminium bulkhead for miles now. Above 120mph you really start to *feel* the speed, you're so intimate with this car, the road surface whipping past the translucent side panels. Gus Gregory and John Hayman in the pursuing Golf TDi camera car are a receding red dot in the mirror as I make a glory bid for the outer limits of the speedo dial. I'm not sure why, but show any Brit car enthusiast an empty autobahn and he'll do the same. We're incapable of letting a stretch of unrestricted tarmac go to waste; we just have to max whatever car we're in at the time, even if it happens to be a rented Nissan Micra. The Germans have a similar inability to walk past a sunbed without throwing a towel on it, even if it's raining. Call it a quirk of the national character.

A footling 218kph (137mph) is all it will finally muster. Occasionally I think the needle is going to make a final lunge for the 220kph decal on the speedo but it hits the proverbial brick wall and that's that. This car seems to have the drag characteristics of the Tate Modern, the huge rear spoiler working overtime – combined with the undertray, it generates substantial downforce at higher speeds. So you can hit 215kph in

fourth, but then it's as if an airbrake has been flicked on – you make a move for fifth gear and you've lost 10kph before it engages. We seem to be stopping for fuel more regularly than I'd hoped, too. In fact cruising through France at around 95-100mph doesn't see more than 20mpg, and when we're really pressing on, a tankful is slugged back at the rate of 16.3mpg. Apparently the 190bhp conversion makes the notoriously rich-running K-series engine run even richer still, so you're the poorer as a result.

Finding out just where the speedo needle stops climbing is not the reason we're here though. I'm on a mission to prove a pet theory – that the Lotus 340R could just be the hottest road-going hillclimb car ever made. To test the theory we're on our way to the ultimate hillclimb… no, make that *mountain* climb, the infamous Klausen Pass in Switzerland. This amazing place used to be a regular feature on motorsport calendars in the 1920s and '30s, but after Switzerland decided to ban all forms of motorsport after the war, it was consigned to history. Obviously the climb's still there and somehow the authorities were persuaded to let the event be resurrected in 1993 and again in 1998 with 450 competitors all trying to beat the hill record which was set on an epic day in August 1934. So far no-one has…

The Klausen Pass has two incredibly tortuous, twisting sections, joined by a long, straight section through a valley floor. It's one of the world's truly great roads. Far left: blasting through one of the old tunnels, no longer used by road traffic

'Sixty six years on, Caracciola's record
still stands. If any road car can touch
it, the 340R must stand a chance'

I n 1934 the Schumacher of the day was Rudi Caracciola. Recovering from a heavy crash at the Monaco GP the previous season in which his hip had been shattered (his right leg was now two inches shorter than the left), Caracciola was determined to confound all the doubters who thought his great career was over. He entered the Klausen Pass mountainclimb in a works Mercedes W25, its 8-cylinder 4.3-litre engine pushing out 445hp. The event turned into a head-to-head with his great rival Hans Stuck in the amazing rear-engined 452hp V16 Auto Union designed by Ferdinand Porsche. This was the era of the original, legendary Silver Arrows.

The Klausen hillclimb is a tortuous and demanding 13.4 miles, making it the longest in the world. It climbs 4000ft to 6404ft, its myriad twists and turns embracing 35 hairpins, several tunnels, and a straighter section half-way up a valley where these pre-war monsters would reach 160mph. Caracciola already held the record at 15min 50secs which he set in 1932, but on that day in 1934 he posted an extraordinary time of 15min 22secs, smashing the record by

28secs. Stuck had it all to do and was flying on his final run in the Auto Union when the huge car suddenly tried to spin off the mountain near the top. Stuck gathered it together but lost to Caracciola by 3secs. No-one else was anywhere near their times, third-place driver Whitney Straight being almost a minute behind in his Maserati. The crowd had witnessed an extraordinary display of man and machine at the limit on the ultimate mountainclimb. Sixty six years on, Caracciola's record still stands.

If any roadgoing production car can touch it, I reckon the 340R must stand a chance. Lotuses have always made good hillclimb cars, being so light and agile that they often embarrass more powerful machinery. Indeed the Lotus Seven and its variants have been so successful over the years that the regulators recently decided to ban them from the production class and put them in a class of their own. That still left the Elan, the '60s rear-drive original, and I campaigned one in hillclimbs for several years with no little success, though that had more to do with Colin Chapman's brilliance as a car designer than any driving talent of mine…

When the Elise arrived it was so successful it was moved into the Modified Production Class. Which brings us to the 340R, which by my reckoning ought to be the quickest of them all. You only have to look at the options list to see that it means business: 190bhp upgrade, titanium sports silencer, a trick camshaft pulley to advance the inlet cam… You can turn the Stack instruments into data-loggers, recording lap times, hill times, 0-60 and quarter-mile times. You can even overlay your own times on a track against a pro Lotus driver in a 340R. The ultimate option, though, has to be the six-speed sequential helical gearbox – only serious racers need apply with a list price of £9995 plus fitting. This is a hardcore options list: no air-con or drinks holders here. Not a car you'd usually choose to drive half-way across Europe…

T he weather isn't helping, for as soon as we turn off the motorway and head for the Pass, it starts to rain again. On the autobahn the speed keeps the rain away from the driver; you can watch the water gather in vortices at the base of the

Metcalfe and 340R
follow in the tracks of
Caracciola and the
mighty Mercedes W25

windscreen surround, by the side mirrors, before doing a little dance and flicking away – some of it catching your sleeve, some running down the side panels and onto the floor (so that's what the holes in the floor are for). But at low speeds you're forced to shield your eyes from the raindrops. Which isn't fun.

Worse is to come. When we get to the western end of the Pass we find there's a barrier across the road. After driving most of the day, all I want to do is get to our hotel, but that's at the other end of the Pass, which means we'll have to take a 80-mile detour. Things couldn't look bleaker.

Eventually we arrive in Linthal, at the base of the Klausen Pass. It's late, and we've driven the 750 miles from home in one hit, but I can't resist driving to the start of the climb itself. And there it is, right there in front of us, beginning with a cobbled, banked hairpin. I'm tempted to have a recce up the hill, but not only is it still raining but fog has descended too.

Instead we check into the Hotel Raben. And over a few welcome beers our spirits are soon lifted. Chatting to the locals, we learn that the Pass is closed for much of the year because it gets

blocked by snow – but it's going to be open this weekend for the first time this year.

Trouble is, Switzerland is not the best place for a noisy 340R to make a bid on a hill record on a public road; there's a danger we'll make the wrong sort of impression on the locals, especially the ones in the smart uniforms with guns round their waists. But there's more good news. We get a tip-off that the barrier, which is three-quarter-way up the climb, will be lifted at 4pm the next day, giving us a chance to drive the course before word gets out that the Pass is open again and it fills with traffic. Looks like I might get a shot at the record after all. Outside, the 340R sits in the deserted car park with its Prada-style nylon showercap hopefully keeping the weather out of the cockpit. Inside the hotel, photographer Gus proves what we've always suspected about him by ordering horse for dinner (very tasty, apparently).

Next morning the fog has gone and snowy peaks are briefly visible as the clouds start to break. The scale of the place is amazing; things are definitely looking up. Until, that is, it's time to check the 340R – and find that the Prada

showercap is completely useless at keeping the rain out of cockpit. The seats are soaked, the Alcantara seat-trims looking like electric blue chamois cloths that have been soaked in a bucket overnight. Fortunately the owner of the hotel takes pity and provides bin-bags to sit on, then escorts us to the only car wash for miles and insists on treating the Lotus to an early-morning hot-shower-cum-powerwash. The 340R collects dirt like no other car I know and 750 miles of accumulated grime disappears before our eyes. Checking the oil is a bit of a fag – the engine cover is attached by no fewer than nine Allen bolts – but all seems well and virtually no oil has been used.

The plan is to get the photography out of the way before the barrier is raised, so we set off to see the pass for the first time, the Golf leading. The 340R's crazy Yokohama tyres take time to acclimatise to. At first there seems less grip than you might expect, given their radical hand-cut appearance, but they soon warm up and then start providing amazing levels of grip, even on this morning's damp surface, their bite into corners making a mockery of the Golf's more

Below: the course of the Klausen Pass hillclimb, all 13.4 miles of it. Swiss authorities banned motorsport years ago, but Metcalfe and 340R slipped through

Start

Finish

conventional tyres. On the run down yesterday I was less impressed with their wet weather performance. Driving at night I had two scary moments when unseen standing water sent first the front and then the rear of the car into lightning aquaplaning slides with no warning: if you intend using the car in all conditions, I would go for a less schizophrenic tyre which would be easier to live with, saving the A038 for track work.

The higher you climb the more the scenery leaves you in awe. This is an incredibly beautiful, unspoilt corner of Switzerland: with yellow flowers peppering the mountain pastures, it looks so flawless it's as though someone has given the valley a spring-clean just before we arrived. Some of the snowy peaks surrounding the pass are nearly 11,000ft high, and the light is perfect. Gus has brought his special 'landscape' camera with him. It looks like it's going to get a lot of use today.

Part way up, we come across an old tunnel which would have been in use in 1934 (another, much larger tunnel has been cut through the rock alongside it to carry today's traffic). The old tunnel looks as if it was chiselled out of the rock by hand. It's very narrow, barely 4m wide, curved and paved in cobbles. Every 30m or so there's a window to the outside world, shedding pools of light into the darkness. Then you're briefly out in the sunshine before another, straighter tunnel continues the climb upward. The fact that they used to race through here at three-figure speeds with no lights on the cars almost defies belief. I imagine Carraciola and Stuck in their Silver Arrows, drifting through the unforgiving corners on the slippery stones before blasting back into daylight at the far end of the tunnel some 300m away.

After a leisurely lunch I prepare for my run up the hill. Most of the pictures are in the can, but we're yet to see the final part of the climb beyond the barrier. Gus and our good buddy John Hayman go on ahead to confirm that it's now open (It is!) so the time has arrived to strap myself in and start the run. I'm just a little nervous, not quite sure how hard to push, but after travelling all this way I'm desperately excited to discover what the next 13.4 miles have in store.

340R was simply dazzling on the deserted mountainclimb; it could have been made for this. It makes even an Elise feel slightly flabby

'The higher you climb, the more the scenery leaves you in awe. Some peaks are nearly 11,000ft high'

I click my stopwatch as I cross the start line and the exhaust barks as I begin the assault. Climbing up through the trees, damp patches still remain on the surface from last night's rain, and I can see a swirl of leaves behind me in the mirrors from the draft as the Lotus blasts through the debris left since the winter. The level of grip the 340R develops is beyond excellent – surreal is more like it – and you have to force yourself to push past normal roadcar limits and up to almost single-seater levels of grip, until you begin to sense the nose starting to push wide.

So far second gear is perfect, the engine on song from 5000rpm upwards. Straight-lining a series of bends, I catch a glimpse of some flowers tied to the railing, presumably where some poor soul has plunged over the edge. I make a mental note not to get too carried away.

Just as I leave the trees behind I'm into the tunnel and the air is filled with the glorious sound of a screaming K-series reaching its 8000rpm limit. The change-up light blinks, into third, and out into the sunlight before plunging back into another tunnel with a sharp left-right combination. The tarmac is polished and offers little grip but this car is so controllable I'd like to go back and do it again and again. But now there's a more unusual challenge ahead, one I've never met before on a hillclimb: roadworks with temporary lights. I'm praying they're on green as I round the corner; otherwise this is all going to be rather pointless. Fantastic – a green light beckons me on, but a truck is backing into my path. Fortunately he sees me, chugs forward and waves me past.

The way the 340R hoovers up dust and dirt from the roadworks with its 'venturi' undertray is amazing. I can hear the tinkle of tiny stones on the alloy floor and behind it looks as if I've hit a 'smokescreen' button on the dash. The gradient is now less severe and the flat middle-section of the climb opens up before me, only it's not that flat – the road is rippled with the sort of uneven tarmac you find in the Fens. I know that to get anywhere near a decent time I've got to keep it nailed through here. Matching the 160mph of the old Grand Prix cars is out of the question, but I'm still flat in fourth.

There are magic moments here when the 340R enters a twilight zone and the suspension starts to work overtime. This is where the genius of Lotus's gifted chassis designers shines through. In my mirrors I can see the cycle-wings over the rear tyres become almost a blur, yet the body remains flat and the car never bottoms-out.

Next hazard: the tiny hamlet of Urner Boden, with its 50kph limit. I trundle through, taking a welcome breather. I'm about nine minutes into the climb, but the respite is short-lived: it's back on the pace before the start of the next twisty section. I've climbed nearly 2500ft and I'm starting to feel the power ebb away as the engine is gradually starved of oxygen. A deer jumps out from the trees, as snow starts to appear at the edge of the road. This really is surreal. The recently opened barrier flashes past as the road starts to narrow. I'm making more use of first

'Some of the hairpins are seriously tight, my arms are starting to ache, but there's at least four minutes to go...'

Above: dry-road grip is just phenomenal, as the 340R chases the old record. Below: Rudi Caracciola in the W25 Mercedes – 450bhp and skinny tyres meant the tail was rarely straight

gear up here. Some of the hairpins are seriously tight – the only way a V16 Auto Union would get round would be with a bootful of throttle – and my arms are starting to ache, but there's at least four minutes to go. The smell of hot brakes wafts into the cockpit.

A car appears, coming in the opposite direction, then another. I can't push so hard now – there's bound to be more. There's more snow too, and rivers of water across the road. Gus and John appear stage-left in a lay-by, setting up a shot for later. How much further to the finish can it be? I fluff a gearchange, slotting third instead of first, typically in earshot of the others – the vague shift is one of the 340R's few shortcomings.

The road is just a ribbon of tarmac between deep snowbanks now. One last push for the top, into third – and suddenly there's a snowball the size of a football in the middle of the road. Oh sh**. There's no time to avoid it and it explodes over the car, showering me in fine grains of ice. But no harm done. At last, elation bubbles over as the finish appears. There's a café, with bikers already gathering outside, preparing for their moment of glory. I stop the clock and glance down, having no idea what sort of time to expect. The digital readout shows 15mins 36secs, 14secs outside Rudi's record. But what a ride, what a road, and what a car. I reckon the 340R could well dip under the hill record, given a closed road and a bit of practice.

But I don't want it to. Caracciola's record should remain forever. His drive 66 years ago, powering that mighty Mercedes up this magical ribbon, the ultimate mountainclimb, is beyond heroic. From where I'm sitting, the man's a god. ■

Precision, Engineered

Developed for maximum response at speed, Proxes T1-R gives you the ultimate experience in precision handling. Tested to the extreme, engineered to perfection.

TOYO TIRES | www.toyo.co.uk

LOCH, STOCK AND TWO SMOKING BARRELS

In 2001 the new Aston Martin Vanquish was the most significant British supercar for years. We spent three days and 1200 miles with it on the UK's most breathtaking roads

Y834 MWL

W hen the 550 Maranello first broke cover, Ferrari and its flamboyant figurehead, Luca Montezemolo, were credited with reinventing the classic Gran Turismo supercar. It was an accolade that, one suspects, must have had the chaps at Aston Martin ever so slightly peeved. Why? While the Prancing Horse steered clear of building a front-engined supercar for a quarter of a century or more, a succession of ever faster, ever more dramatic bow-powered behemoths had rumbled out of Newport Pagnell. To have Ferrari bowl in and claim this territory as its own must have hurt.

While you won't find anyone in this office bad-mouthing cars like the knee-trembling twin-supercharged V8 Vantage, it was in truth an anachronism, the spectacular symptom of a car company that lacked the funding, direction and ambition to take on the likes of Ferrari at the cutting edge. Relying on hand-built exclusivity, sheer bulk and barely controllable power at a time when rival supercar makers were producing advanced cars with far superior dynamics and performance together with efficient packaging and superb refinement, the V8 Vantage was a GT from the Jurassic period. The Maranello was the meteor that wiped it out.

In a way this very public drubbing saved Aston from extinction. Parent company Ford wanted a

high-profile, high-performance technical 'shop window', and with the help of men like Bob Dover, fresh from overseeing Jaguar's vital and very successful XK8 project, the seeds for cars like the Vanquish were sown into fertile ground. The first fruits didn't take long to appear. Though still compromised by its ageing XJS underpinnings, the DB7 Vantage was a confident step in the right direction. A new V12 engine provided the soul many missed in the original straight-six DB7, while a supple chassis and realistic pricing made the new £90,000 Vantage appear conspicuous value in the wake of its £200,000, two-ton stablemate. But this was only the beginning.

It's just under a year since we got our first close

With a new British supercar at our disposal for three days and a mission to find Britain's best driving roads, there was only one way to head. Scottish highlands provided a fitting backdrop to Aston's all-time high

'With three rapid tugs on the right-hand paddle, the gearbox punches from sixth to third'

look at the Vanquish. Frustratingly a drive was out of the question, but you didn't need to drive it to appreciate its potential. With a radical chassis that combined bonded aluminium and composites, a six-speed paddle-shift transmission and a more powerful, more vocal version of the DB7's V12, all wrapped in super-plastic-formed aluminium panels, the Vanquish was a car on a mission. We knew better than most, for our own Mr Metcalfe was the first scribbler in the world to bag a passenger ride, thanks to his unrivalled combination of guile, audacity and innate jamminess. And what was the Metcalfe verdict?

'We're only brushing its limits, but it encourages you to go there, unlike some of its predecessors. If this car embodies the new Aston philosophy, count me in as a fan. It's going to be a ball…'

Well, Harry, it gives me great pleasure to be the one to find out for sure whether you were right. But first we've got to collect it from the famous Newport Pagnell works. We arrive along with three other magazines invited to try the car over an extended period before the main press launch. With four identical Vanquishes primed and ready, it's an impressive if slightly edgy gathering. Pleasantries are exchanged but, rather

like a game of poker, none of us hacks wants to let slip where we're going or what we're doing with the car. Comparison tests and performance figuring have been strictly forbidden by Aston's very own ayatollah, PR boss Tim Watson, which is why there's no 550 Maranello alongside it in the test. There's also a mileage limit, but I have a sneaky feeling we're going to push our luck with this. If you don't see any more features written by me next month, it's safe to assume I've been bundled into the back of a van by one of Watson's PR fundamentalist reprisal squads.

It all seems worth the risk when I'm handed a

Y834 MWL

key. The Vanquish really does have the most immense presence. Chiselled, muscular and pebble-smooth, it just sits there, defying you not to gawp like a schoolboy. There's a thread of DB7 in there somewhere, but the shape has more edge, a powerful, pointy aggression that hints at a much rawer character than the lounge lizard-like DB7 Vantage. There are some elements of Ian Callum's design that don't seem to gel at a standstill – the scalloped sill, for instance – but as the first magazine rumbles away, it's immediately apparent that the form gains the required cohesion on the move. One thing's for sure: you don't need a Maranello next to it to decide which looks the most compelling. I'll give you a clue; it's not the Ferrari.

Before we can leave, Ian Minards, Vanquish project leader, gives us a brief guided tour of the controls. For starters there's no gear lever. Instead two fixed paddles sit invitingly behind the steering wheel, Ferrari 360 Modena style. To get a gear, you depress the brake pedal, curl a

Vanquish is fitted with an electronic traction control system, which reins in the horsepower and even applies the brakes to prevent it stepping too far out of line. A quick detour to Knockhill revealed what can happen when you switch if off...

finger around the right-hand paddle and squeeze it towards you. Neutral is selected by pulling back on both paddles simultaneously, reverse by pushing a button on the dash. It's a system that benefits from logical development. Gone is Ferrari's daft toggle between the seats for selecting reverse, for the truth is you don't need a surrogate gearstick to feel comfortable with the paddle-shift system. It also promises faster, cleaner cog-swaps than the 360, despite being produced by Magnetti Marelli, supplier to… yep, you guessed it, Ferrari.

And if all that isn't enough fun for your digits to cope with, there's the big, crimson, dash-mounted starter button that burns bright when the 6.0-litre V12 is primed and ready for action. Time to give it a prod.

When you do, it triggers a chain of noises that can't fail to make you grin like an idiot. First the starter motor spins like a power drill, cranking a dozen cylinders into motion. Then there's an explosion of deep, guttural decibels as the combustion cycle kicks in, before finally the revs slide back to tickover and the noise-level settles to a busy, seismic beat simmering from the prominent tail-pipes. Can't wait to discover what it sounds like at 7000rpm in third. To this end we say our polite farewells and make straight for the M1, pointing the Vanquish north and settling into a frustrating but immensely refined 85mph cruise. 7000rpm will just have to wait.

Our destination is Scotland, Fort William to be precise: a round trip that exceeds our mileage limit by some considerable margin. To be perfectly honest, though, I don't really care, for once tucked snugly behind the Vanquish's fat leather wheel it's impossible not to want to drive until you run out of road. It's a wonderfully comfortable car, with a good driving position, firm seat-cushioning and effortless cruising ability. Wind noise is almost non-existent, even at three-figure speeds, and the engine, so vocal at start-up, remains hushed at part throttle. If there's a car more suited to chomping through

> **'As expected, with so much power and torque on tap, the rear tyres are easily overwhelmed on cold, wet tarmac'**

continents, I've yet to drive it.

After hours of cruising amongst motorway traffic, like a shark stalking through the open ocean in search of food, we slink into the fringes of Glasgow, skirting the congestion on our way to Loch Lomond and the epic highlands beyond. It's our first close contact with onlookers and, judging by their reactions, Aston has got the Vanquish just right. There's no hint of the vulgar hysterics a Diablo provokes, nor are there the thinly veiled sneers that can accompany urban Ferrari driving. Clearly the Vanquish possesses the same coolly aristocratic air of its ancestors, for the glances are longingly lustful but tinged with admiration and respect.

If it all sounds a bit aloof, don't worry, for when you crack open the throttle the Vanquish's strident, surroundsound bellow lights up their faces and treats their ears to a noise they'll never forget. For the innocent bystander, supercar experiences come no more vivid than this.

It's in urban conditions you first appreciate the paddle-shift transmission. Pre-Vanquish, driving a big Aston in town required the calf muscles of a Tour de France cyclist to pump the leaden clutch pedal up and down. Now you don't even need to flex your fingers, thanks to the fully auto ASM mode, which slurs through the gears for you. It also leaves you time to look around the interior. The only question mark hangs over the durability of the clutch, for when you need to perform a hill-start or reverse up a niggly slope, the clutch gets expensively pungent. It's not a problem unique to the Vanquish, as every paddle-shift Ferrari we've tried suffers from the same problem. If you pride yourself on your sympathetic clutch control, it's something that makes you cringe every time.

With not a splinter of walnut veneer to be seen, it's not your usual Aston interior. Sure there's plenty of leather and chrome-rimmed dials, but the bold, laid-back slab of silver centre console is a bit of a shock. If you're uncharitable you'd say it's more Ford Cougar than Aston Vanquish, although it does an effective job of drawing your eye away from the transmission tunnel, which looks a bit odd without a conventional gear lever. One thing that really does grate is the clock, which looks like it fell out of Jac Nasser's cracker at the Ford Christmas dinner. The instruments don't look convincingly classy either, especially as they sit in a car that costs £160,000. In a post-Audi TT world, there's just no excuse for poor interior detailing in a car this expensive.

Perhaps the answer is that Aston blew the budget to smithereens on the hardware, for a couple of feet ahead of that awful clock sits one of the finest engines in production. Though based on the mellow V12 found in the DB7,

All the basics of the cockpit are right: comfortable, supportive seats, excellent driving position, and slick-acting paddles for the gearshift. Not so impressive is the silver slab in the centre of the dash and the tacky clock. You expect more somehow

'With not a splinter of walnut veneer to be seen, it's not your usual Aston interior'

Cosworth's brief was to hone it into a sharper, angrier, more rev-hungry engine, and to this end installed new inlet manifolds, camshafts, valve-gear, crankshaft and exhaust system. Power is up by 10 per cent – 40bhp to be precise. Not a huge leap then, but the way in which it delivers is far more dramatic, encouraging you to wring out each gear to the red line rather than short-shift using the torque. Clear of Glasgow, the roads improve, and although the possibility of being spotted by McPlod remains high, opportunities to snatch quick bursts of acceleration are too good to miss. With three rapid tugs on the right-hand paddle, the gearbox punches from sixth to third seamlessly, the downshift accompanied by a hearty blip of the throttle. With my right foot

pushing the alloy throttle pedal firmly into the Wilton, the Vanquish clears its throat and punches hard towards the horizon, V12 yowling like a 1960s Le Mans racer, speedo needle surging relentlessly around the dial.

Like any true supercar, the Vanquish's gearing is leggier than Elle McPherson: second gear all but stretches to 90mph, third winds out to an exquisite 130 or so. Consequently the claimed top whack of 190mph seems positively conservative but, not wishing to make a star appearance in *Police, Camera, Action*, we restrict our full-bore fun to the lower gears. It's a stride that, given the room to stretch, can destroy lesser cars in one almighty surge. No wonder our poor long-term SEAT Leon camera car is constantly

playing catch-up. When inevitably it starts to rain, huge plumes of spray erupt from the Vanquish's stubby tail, sucked skyward by clever, high-speed stability-enhancing underfloor aerodynamics. For John Hayman, battling along in our wake, it must be like chasing an offshore powerboat.

We're charging across the eerie Ranoch Moor now, fast closing in on Glen Coe. I've driven these roads before, in a supercharged V8 Vantage, and although the Vanquish lacks the Vantage's mountainous muscle, it's light years ahead dynamically. Unleashing the old car was a simple exercise in survival as 550bhp declared war on two tons of mass. Cornering was a violent rodeo ride, the suspension struggling to

Above: Vanquish's 6-litre V12 is based on DB7 Vantage engine. The modifications – including a lightened valvetrain, strengthened crankshaft and revised inlet and exhaust systems – lift power by 40bhp to 460bhp and give it a much freer-revving character

cope with the weight, power and lateral forces pulling in three directions at once. And if you were unfortunate enough to get the thing sideways, the Government declared a state of emergency.

The Vanquish devours the straight bits with relish, but unlike any previous Aston it also has a ravenous appetite for corners. At 1835kg, it's not what you'd call a lightweight (just for the record a Maranello weighs 1716kg) despite the advanced construction materials and techniques, but the

structure feels so darned stiff the suspension has a purity of response that almost defies belief. It's so supple and fluid, so controlled and precisely damped, you're barely aware of all that weight at work through the bends. It feels like it has endless wheel-travel but no roll or inertia when committed to a turn. It even rides well, despite painfully low-profile tyres.

Back in issue 19, we pitched a 550 Maranello against an Impreza P1 to see how the ultimate real-world weapon faired against the ultimate driver's supercar. While the Ferrari had power to spare and admirable poise in most conditions, its weight really started to work against it under braking and over savage, bump-stop-bruising compressions. Despite the fact that it weighs more, I'm convinced the Vanquish would cope better. Not only is the chassis more composed right up to the limit, but the feedback is weightier through the wheel, which gives you terrific confidence. And, as we discovered in the 360 F1, those paddle-shift changes allow you to attack much deeper and later into corners without fear of upsetting the balance under braking. Talking of brakes, Brembo has made a fine job of the Aston's anchors, endowing it with

'Chiselled, muscular and pebble-smooth, the Aston just sits there, defying you not to gawp like a schoolboy'

immense stopping power and delicate, linear feel. It's a joy to be able to work the brakes hard repeatedly and not feel like you're burning the life out of them.

With Scotland providing its customary warm, summer welcome (10deg C, biting wind and driving rain) the traction control had more cause to spring into action than normal. It's a testament to the levels of grip and traction that, while driving quickly but not genuinely hard, the system never flickered into life once. Curious to see just how the system reacts, a deserted roundabout provides the opportunity for an optimistic but not outrageous application of power in second gear. Predictably the tail quickly kicks into a slide, but were it not for a sizeable stab of opposite lock I'm sure we would have been broadside. Somewhat surprised, we scuttle off with no harm done, but subconsciously my faith in the traction control's electronic safety-net is shaken. Later in the day we repeat the process on a slightly larger roundabout and the system reacts swiftly and cleanly while still allowing a small amount of oversteer. Whether our first experience was the result of an electrical glitch in a pre-production car I'm not sure, but Aston has

promised to investigate.

Before returning to Newport Pagnell we want to get some safe but spectacular cornering shots, so rather than risk any heroics on the road we drop in at Knockhill. Using our favourite corner – the uphill, gently cresting Clark bend – it's now the time to switch the traction control off. As expected with so much power and torque on tap, the rear tyres are easily overwhelmed on cold, wet tarmac. The initial breakaway is rapid but, so long as you're quick with the steering, once the Vanquish is sliding it can be controlled very smoothly on the throttle. The balance is really sweet, allowing you to adjust the attitude of the car purely on the throttle.

While this doesn't have much relevance to everyday driving, the fact that the Vanquish has such polished, benign dynamics, even when pushed to extremes, is mighty impressive. Not to mention proof that after years of working with one hand tied behind its back, given the resources Aston's engineering team can produce a front-engined supercar that redefines the breed. As Murray Walker might say, Aston Martin has never really been away, but with the Vanquish it's well and truly back. With a vengeance. ■

Specification

VANQUISH

Engine	V12, 5935CC
Max power	460bhp @ 6500rpm
Max torque	400lb ft @ 5000rpm
Transmission	Six-speed manual with paddle-shift and auto-shift option. Rear drive with LSD. Electronic traction control system
Suspension	Double wishbones, coil springs, gas dampers, anti-roll bar
Brakes	Ventilated discs front and rear, 355mm front, 330mm rear. ABS
Wheels	9 x 19in front, 10 x 19in rear, alloy
Tyres	255/40 ZR19 front, 285/40 ZR19 rear
Weight (kerb)	1835kg
Power-to-weight	255bhp/ton
0-60mph	4.5secs (claimed)
Max speed	190mph (claimed)
Basic price (2001)	£160,000

EVO RATING ★★★★★

RED ROUTE

The Mille Miglia was the greatest road race and a key part of Ferrari's heritage. In the summer of 2000 Richard Meaden drove part of the classic route in the fabulous 360 Spider

Edward Eves

Above: Brescia, May 1957, just before the start of the final, fateful Mille Miglia and the crowd in the Piazza Vittoria press in on the cars during scrutineering. Peter Collins, the young English ace, was entered in his new Ferrari 335 Sport. His co-driver in the race would be photographer Louis Klementaski, who captured many of the classic images you see on these pages

There's never been anything quite like the Mille Miglia. One thousand miles of flat-out racing through towns and open country, it was motorsport on a massive scale. Open to a vast array of machinery, from 750cc bubble-cars to hugely powerful V8 and V12 road-racers based on the Grand Prix cars of the day, the Mille Miglia brought drama, danger and heart-pounding spectacle to the doorsteps of five million Italians.

Starting from Brescia in the far north of Italy, the route twisted its way to the Adriatic coastline. From here it hammered down through Rimini and Ancona, then across the Appenine mountains to Rome, up along the backbone of Italy through Tuscany, over the Futa and Raticosa passes, before descending into Bologna, Modena and eventually back to Brescia. It was a race that consumed an entire country.

Last run as a competitive event in 1957, the Mille Miglia is still a source of fascination for many enthusiasts. Not only was it the scene of some of the most Herculean drives in motor racing history, but as the vast majority of the route is still used as public road today, it is entirely possible to follow in the tyre-tracks of Moss, Fangio & Co.

It's this promise that brings us to the Piazza Vittoria in the heart of Brescia, home of the Mille Miglia and the starting point for our story. We're privileged to be driving Ferrari's new 360 Spider; the ideal car for such a challenging drive as it shares technology and takes inspiration from today's F1 cars, just as the quickest Mille Miglia racers did in 1957. I say privileged because we are the first magazine in the world to be allowed to cover some serious miles in the 360 Spider after its launch in Monte Carlo. As we intend to drive as much of the Mille Miglia route as we can in the time available, serious miles they most definitely will be.

'400 searing horsepower, six-speed Formula 1-style paddle-shift, 0-60mph in under 5secs, top speed of 185mph, and an engine note that makes your ears bleed'

MILLE MIGLIA
Km. 1564

Left: the route of the Mille Miglia (Thousand Miles). Actually it's 972 miles long, but what's 28 miles between friends? Above: the Piazza Vittoria on a quiet Sunday morning. Right: Collins and Klementaski roar out of Brescia and into the dawn. Closeness of crowds made the event special – and ultimately deadly

Some of you might be of the opinion that a soft-top Ferrari is a soft option, the purer driver's car being the coupe. That has often been the case in the past, but the 360 was designed with a barchetta version in mind from the start, giving it the best possible chance of matching the dynamics of its berlinetta brother.

The result is, without any shadow of doubt, the world's most savage soft-top: all-aluminium construction, 400 searing horsepower, six-speed Formula 1-style paddle-shift transmission, acceleration from 0-60mph in under 5secs, 100mph in a shade over 10secs, top speed of 185mph and an engine note that makes your ears bleed. If this isn't in keeping with the spirit of the Mille Miglia, then I don't know what is.

On race day in 1957 the piazza would have been a seething mass of exuberant Brescian spectators, race officials, bustling mechanics and impatient drivers, but now, at 7am on a peaceful mid-summer Sunday morning, the town has sensibly elected to stay in bed.

It's a fittingly dramatic starting point for such an enormously gruelling race, with the imposing Post Office building towering above us, making us

feel very small and insignificant as we fire off a few static shots of the Spider.

Hood down it's a wonderful sight, a combination of sharp, pointy 21st century edginess and classic Ferrari curvaceousness. It's the twin humps behind the head restraints that do it for me, harking back to its racing forebears that still haunt this historic civic square.

Fittingly, Ferrari were race favourites in '57, although previous winners Stirling Moss and trusty co-driver (and journalist) Denis Jenkinson were much fancied in their fearsome 400bhp Maserati 4.5. The fastest cars started last, the final handful leaving Brescia at around 5.30am, their exact start time being their race number.

Car number 534 was Ferrari's best hope of victory, driven by British ace Peter Collins, accompanied by Louis Klemantaski, the finest motoring photographer of his day, who would act as Collins's co-driver and document the race from the passenger seat of the 4.1-litre V12 Ferrari. It's mostly his amazing work that you can see in this feature, alongside that of **evo** photographer Gus Gregory, a man after Klemantaski's heart if ever there was one.

Static shots completed, we leave the town square and complete the short blast along

Left: the Ferrari of
Wolfgang von Trips is
pushed towards the
starting ramp. The
number signified the
start time (5.32am).
Below: Piero Taruffi
accelerates away
from the Rome
Control. Above: a
typically eye-popping
stretch of road.
Opposite above: the
Collins/ Klementaski
335S moves in on
two slower cars

Peter Coltrin

cobbled backstreets to the start ramp at Via
Rubuffone. The 360 Spider ambles across the
uneven surface, its Pirelli tyres slapping a
knobbly, staccato beat on the road, while its
electronic dampers coolly isolate the washboard
bumps. Pedestrians and cyclists whistle and wave
as we pass, their passion for fast, fabulous cars
still wide awake even at this ungodly hour. The
sun is low but warm, the atmosphere already
sticky – a precursor to another scorching Italian
summer's day.

From Brescia the route heads first for Verona.
Running pretty much straight and flanked by
elegant, proudly shuttered town houses and tall
horse chestnut trees, the road out of Brescia is
nothing short of a suburban drag strip. Almost
immediately you're struck by the fierce challenge
that lies ahead. Given the freedom (and courage)

that Collins and Klemantaski had in 1957, we too could quite easily be topping 160mph or more within the first few miles, but instead the 360 is chomping at the bit as we burble through the Brescian traffic.

When gaps do appear, its razor-keen throttle response and flip-shift gearbox whip us to indecent velocities. But to avoid a night or two's stay at the pleasure of the local carabinieri, we reluctantly settle for enjoying the excellent low-speed ride quality, incredible tractability and short but fabulous stabs of engine noise bouncing off the buildings and trees.

After a quick cappuccino stop in Verona, it's clear that even a brand new, bright red Ferrari is going to struggle to cut through the dawdling ranks of Fiats and Alfas. We decide to cut our losses and dive onto the autostrada to make up

some time on our journey to Ravenna and the arrow-straight roads along the Adriatic coastline.

The 360 Spider is already a sublime companion. We've had the roof down from the start, and with the air-conditioning taking the sting out of the sun and the clever aerodynamics eradicating any buffeting, even when cruising at well over 100mph, it seems likely that we'll only raise the roof for overnight halts.

From Ravenna the road is eerily straight, and it is nothing short of awe-inspiring to think that even if we could travel back some 43 years, to May 1957, our state-of-the-art 400bhp, all-aluminium, all-singing, all-dancing 360 Spider would struggle to keep pace with Ferrari's Mille Miglia racers. Imagine the Mulsanne straight running from Calais to Paris and you'll have some idea of what the coastal run is like.

I t's hard to imagine the noise, heat and fierce concentration that would have filled the Collins/Klemantaski Ferrari as they hammered flat-out towards Ancona in excess of 170mph, peering into the shimmering heat-haze in an attempt to pick out fast approaching and potentially lethal S-bends. For a more graphic illustration of how fast they were travelling, take a look at a map of Italy and imagine driving from Brescia to Rome via Verona, Ferrara, Ravenna, Rimini and Ancona in just five hours, including pit stops and the tight mountain run inland. That's an average speed of 107mph, in case you were wondering. I almost feel embarrassed to be driving on the same piece of road.

It's the first week of the Italian holidays, and judging by the number of mopeds and cars on the

'For the first time, the 360
feels like it's working hard, the
engine note hard and insistent'

[360 Spider on the Mille Miglia]

road, all of Italy has decided to have a day at the seaside. By now it's clear that there's no way we'll be able to do the whole route and complete all the photography we need, so rather than slog all the way down the coast and then across the mountains to Rome, we high tail it to Lord Metcalfe's Tuscan retreat. It's a wise decision, as tomorrow we'll be tackling the toughest section of the Mille Miglia, over the hills of Radicofani towards Siena, Florence and the switchback-laden Futa and Raticosa passes.

Fascinating though it was to experience the wide open coast roads, they didn't tell us much about the Spider, but the breathtakingly quick SS2 that slices through the wonderful Tuscan scenery of the Val D'Orcia is a far sterner test. The climb to Radicofani is the most memorable,

the road cresting and falling like a bitumen rollercoaster. For the first time, the 360 feels like it's working hard, the engine note remaining hard and insistent, the cornering and braking loads more severe. Increased engine and wind noise apart, there's no other indication that you're in a convertible. The steering and turn-in are as sharp and instantaneous as in the Berlinetta, and the suspension is just as taut and tolerant of mid-corner bumps. It feels together, cohesive, tight as a drum. Without pushing beyond eight-tenths we're still chomping through this fabulous stretch of road, but the proximity of trees, not to mention walled bridges positioned on tight bends, means it is an unforgiving playground for journalists, and a potentially lethal test for the race drivers of 1957.

With close to the same power as our 360, but

with narrow tyres and no seat belts, let alone traction control or ABS, it is no wonder drivers described competing in the Mille Miglia as like walking a high wire without a safety net. Nevertheless it was a challenge the very best drivers relished, and a perfect backdrop on which to display their dazzling talent.

By this stage Collins and Klemantaski were romping away from the opposition. Not only were they ahead of all their Ferrari team-mates, but such was their pace that Moss and Jenkinson's 1955 record time was seriously under threat. One of the fastest drivers in the world at the time, Collins was looking forward to the tortuous mountain stages of Futa and Raticosa, just north of Florence. Despite having been driving solidly for more than seven hours, he was confident of stretching his lead even further. If only he knew what really lay ahead, for as Klemantaski described in his report for

Right: classic Klemantaski study of Collins' gloved hands on the 335S's wood-rimmed wheel. With its 4-litre V12 producing around 400bhp, it was capable of over 180mph. Above left: 360 Spider retraces the Ferraris' tracks across the Futa Pass. Top right: Alfonso de Portago and co-driver Edmund Nelson leave their last stop. A tragic end to the race awaits

Motor magazine, it would be a far sterner test than they imagined.

'Every corner of note had a crowd on it, all waving us on excitedly, for they knew we were winning. This was second gear work all the time, with a drop down to first gear for the hairpins. The steering ratio was such that on the hairpins, using the wheel and the throttle, Peter could get around without having to take another bite at the wheel. As we reached the top, the sky to the north of us, towards Bologna, was black and soon a physically welcome but morally distressing rain began to come down.

'Goggles misted up, faces were stung by the raindrops, and then, worst of all, we began having difficulty in getting around right-hand corners. Almost simultaneously a slight crunching noise was occasionally heard, coming from the region of the back axle, on left-hand bends, and I tried to think of a connection between the two. The rain

stopped, leaving the roads terribly slippery, then it turned to sleet…'

Quite where Collins got his stamina from is beyond me, as we pitch into the first of countless hairpins. It is an incredible run, the seemingly endless SS65 twisting and turning first over the Futa and then almost immediately after, the Raticosa pass. From wide open sweeps and fresh-air corners, the character of the road can change in an instant, as trees close in at either side, casting deceptive shadows across the tarmac.

The prospect of man-handling Collins' fearsome car along this stretch on streaming tarmac sends a shiver down my spine, but now, just as you'd hope, the 360 is absolutely in its element. The feelsome power steering and darty front end carve into the tightest turns with utter confidence. You begin to push yourself harder and harder, relying more and more on the Spider's reserves of grip and poise.

Having the latest generation F1 shift is a massive help too, as it allows you to grab a lower gear as soon as you see the corner tightening. Seemingly no matter how late you flip down a gear the Spider remains planted to the road, and the shifts are absolutely flawless, with perfectly judged heel-and-toe style blips every time. The upshifts are now smoother too, proving conclusively that the second generation F1 system is much more satisfying than it used to be. I've always been a bit of a Luddite when it comes to self-shifting transmissions, but now even I have to concede that it frees you to concentrate more on the road ahead.

And you need to if you're to stay one step ahead of the SS65, for this road seems to take great pleasure in reeling you in with its hypnotic, rhythmic sequences of second- and third-gear

'Most corners are second-gear,
the fastest straights topping out in
the shrieking upper reaches of third'

[360 Spider on the Mille Miglia]

corners, only to pitch a savagely tightening switchback into your path.

Any mistake, no matter how small, punches your pounding heart into the back of your parched throat. To be a passenger here, as Klemantaski was in the leading car, must have been like being caught in the eye of a storm, pitched and tossed from corner to corner, his life held in Collins's whirling string-back-gloved hands.

If the brain-out missile-run down the coast from Rimini to Ancona was an almost sadistic test of the driver's courage, and the true domain of those with the tallest final drive and the biggest

balls, then the relentless tarmac bobsled run from Florence to Bologna was for the artists. Only those drivers with sensitivity, exquisite car control and an almost telepathic ability to read the road ahead could balance their over-powered machines on a knife-edge for hours at a time.

The great masters of the Mille Miglia could cope with the monstrous demands of both sections, but for me this is by far the most exciting, largely because it is immeasurably less daunting. Most of the corners are second gear, with the fastest straights topping out in the shrieking upper reaches of third. There's less

time to think here – you simply become immersed in your own world, concentrating on each and every bend, revelling in the acceleration, noise and fierce braking forces. For the drivers of 1957, making a mistake over the Futa or Raticosa was one of the few occasions where it would simply mean an exit from the motor race rather than the human race.

It would still have hurt though. Wicked concrete fences line the valley side of the road, while equally unyielding rock, trees or stone walls run close to the left-hand side of the car. In the Mille Miglia heyday much of this would have also been lined with people, drunk on the spectacle, not to mention the odd swig of chianti and hunk of salami. Today we share the SS65 with a constant

Above: one of the great motor racing photographs. The Collins/Klemantaski Ferrari is leading the race at a record pace and charges through the mountains on the approach to Rome

stream of exceptionally noisy, hard-ridden Ducatis. Mixing it amongst them is fun, and gives us some idea of what it must have been like for Collins and the other Scuderia Ferrari drivers dicing amongst themselves and dispatching slower traffic.

The corners come at such a pace it is almost impossible to watch your mirrors *and* the road ahead, but the 360 Spider has so much in reserve that it is laughably easy to empty our

mirrors of distractions. None of the bikes can live with the combination of 400 prancing horses and the adhesive qualities of four Pirelli PZero tyres. It takes no more than three corners to leave them in our venturi-tunnelled wake. On tight, intensely tricky roads like this, the 360 rules supreme.

We've recently criticised the 360 Modena for washing into understeer prematurely, and then snapping into oversteer when you inevitably

back-off. On the Futa and Radicosa hill-roads, the corners either seem to be tight unsighted second-gear bends or fast sequences that you can straightline with confidence hard in third or fourth. At high speeds, understeer isn't a problem, and you can feel the underbody aerodynamics start to draw the Ferrari closer to the tarmac. In the thick of the tight stuff, the fact that the front-end gives in before the rear conditions you to focus all your concentration on your braking points and turn-in speed. There simply isn't the scope for gathering up an excess 5 or 10mph's worth of scrabbly understeer, so you don't push into the last 10 per cent or so of the Spider's ultimate ability. With Armco, stone walls, trees or – worse still – a fresh-air drop waiting to embrace us, it just isn't worth it.

Besides, there's another 360 Modena weakness that remains. The brakes, though fade-free and feelsome, have a spookily unpredictable habit of what feels like prematurely triggering the ABS when really pressing on. Stranger still, the problem seems worse when the suspension is in Sport mode. What's really hard to explain is that the brakes can be fantastic for five or six corners, and then for no apparent reason the pedal hardens, pulses at a higher frequency than you'd get by triggering the ABS, and halves the effectiveness of the brakes for a heart-stopping moment. Unlike the tendency to wash into understeer, this particular trait is impossible to drive around, unless you brake very early all the time, and it's hard to predict because it can happen when the brakes are very hot or stone cold. Weird.

Collins and Klemantaski had more to worry

Left: the Ferrari team cars being prepared in the courtyard at Maranello, which is where, 43 years later, our man Meaden reluctantly hands back the keys to the 360 (far right). Top right: Collins/Klemantaski about to take the lead. Mechanical woes would end their race just 100 miles from the finish

about. After surviving the sleet-covered mountain roads, their ailing Ferrari deteriorated rapidly, the battered transmission finally failing just 100 miles from an historic victory.

As the knotted tarmac starts to untangle its way towards Modena, we decide to peel off the Mille Miglia route and head to some of our favourite roads in the hills above Maranello for one last blast before taking the car back and reluctantly handing over the keys.

We knew it already, but this last thrash just goes to underline the 360's magnificence and its addictive spirit. Far from being the poor relation, the Spider feels more immediate and involving than the Berlinetta, if only because with the roof down you genuinely fear for your hearing every time the revs pass 6000. To put it another way, the 360 Spider is the sort of car for which you'd set your alarm for 4am and then drive to Scotland and back just for the hell of it.

Collins' and Klemantaski's misfortune opened the door for fellow Ferrari driver Piero Taruffi to win the Mille Miglia after failing to finish more than a dozen times. In fact Ferrari would fill the next two places as well, but celebrations were short-lived when news filtered through of a massive accident involving another Ferrari driver, the King of Spain's nephew, the Marquis de Portago. Witnesses reported his Ferrari careering off the road at well over 160mph having suffered a puncture or possibly a wheel or transmission failure. Completely out of control, the car was launched into the air by a granite mile marker and snapped a telegraph pole in half before spearing into the crowd with hideous consequences. The Marquis and his co-driver were killed instantly, along with nine spectators. Inevitably the Mille Miglia died with them. They were less than 30 miles from the finish.

The speed and power of the cars (the factory teams were talking of cars hitting 200mph in 1958), and the huge uncontrolled crowds lining the streets finally became too lethal a combination, leaving the Italian Authorities with no option but

to abandon any future events.

There's no doubt the Mille Miglia was a brutal race, an anachronism, but it was also an intrinsic part of Italian culture, and formed a major thread that runs through Ferrari's genetic code. The 360 Spider might be a million miles safer and more refined than the racers of 1957, but you only need drive it on the Mille Miglia route to discover that the same raw passion that powered them to victory in 1957 still burns inside every one of Maranello's red cars. Peter Collins would have approved. ∎

Copies of Louis Klemantaski's classic photographs, including his 1957 Mille Miglia pictures, may be ordered from the Klemantaski Collection.

For more information contact:
The Klemantaski Collection, PMB 219 - 65 High Ridge Road, Stamford, CT 06905-3814 USA. Tel & Fax: 001 (203) 461-9804. Website www.klemcoll.com

the LAKE

Speed ace Donald Campbell drove a string of Jaguar sports cars. When he was killed on Coniston attempting to raise the water speed record to over 300mph, he had driven there in his E-type. In 2000, Peter Tomalin retraced the story in an XKR Silverstone

T his is the strangest feeling I have ever known. In my hands I hold an item of headgear made from canvas, leather and bakelite. It is the inner helmet that Donald Campbell was wearing on his final attempt to raise the water speed record. You may have seen the black and white film of Bluebird K7 arcing in the air – gracefully, almost in slow motion – before crashing violently back into the water, bouncing along the surface and finally disappearing in a vast cloud of spray. The boat sank quickly – of Campbell himself no trace was ever found.

In such a violent impact, items of clothing on the body's extremities – shoes, socks, gloves, helmets – are often thrown off. It happens in air

crashes too. That's how a young man called Anthony Robinson came to find Campbell's crash helmet and soft inner helmet floating on the surface of Coniston Water minutes after the impact. As a member of the support crew, he'd watched the terrible drama unfold from a boat moored just one hundred yards away.

Thirty-three years later, he places the inner helmet in my hands. All that speed, all that heroism, all that mortality bound-up in its fabric.

DONALD CAMPBELL would have liked the XKR Silverstone. The supercharged 370bhp XKR is the most sporting production Jaguar since the E-type, and the 'Silverstone' is the limited edition model – just 100 built, all of them sold. It has unique Platinum silver paint, red-stitched leather, and all the tastiest 'R Performance' options from Jaguar's catalogue – 20in BBS alloys, giant

Brembo brakes, tautened CATS suspension. It's our favourite Jag, a car of exceptional speed, desirability and rarity.

In fact we had to wait a while for our drive, so great was the demand for Jaguar's demonstrator – a couple of weeks earlier it could be seen smoking its tyres all the way up Lord March's driveway at Goodwood with one J Herbert at the wheel. But it was worth the wait. The XKR is a wonderfully lithe-looking beast. It has the Jaguar DNA shot through it, but it's a natural evolution of the breed, unlike the contrived S-type. The 20in wheels seem to pump out its wheelarches, adding to its muscularity, while the huge cross-drilled discs promise real *edge*. The detail stuff – the vents in the bonnet, the wire-mesh grille, the XKR Silverstone badges – strike just the right notes of subtle aggression. It looks what it is: an extremely potent device.

Inside the muscled torpedo of a bodyshell, the cabin is lined with black leather and strips of grey-stained bird's-eye maple veneer. Jaguar cockpits have always been snug, intimate, the seating low-slung, the interior folding around you.

You can't buy a Silverstone now, of course, but you can buy an XKR with all the R Performance options – wheels, brakes, etc – for £66,005. That's a lot for a Jaguar, but console yourself with the thought that a Ferrari 360 costs almost thirty-five grand more, isn't that much quicker, and is nothing like as usable. Treating the back seats as a second luggage locker, as most owners presumably do, the XKR swallows Michael Bailie's camera gear and several squashy bags without blinking, and we set out from Cambridgeshire on a typical English summer morn, droplets of rain dancing gaily across the screen, sullen skies reflecting in the paintwork. The XKR then proceeds to breeze the four-hour drive to the Lakes with such absolute ease that we arrive feeling we've barely started.

Considering the Pirelli PZeros' paucity of sidewall, the ride is astonishingly good – tauter, obviously, than a regular XK8's but with none of the judder or jarring that other manufacturers would have you believe is the inevitable trade-off for low-profile rubber's added bite. The 4-litre V8 is commensurately smooth – most of the time the heavy soundproofing allows only a subdued hum with a peripheral woofle to permeate the cabin, rising to a turbine-like wail with a top dressing of metallicky supercharger whine when you mash the throttle deep into the carpet and hold it there. It's not jolt-in-the-back fast, but the acceleration is inexorable – rising and swelling, scarcely seeming to diminish until highly illegal, spirit-of-Campbell-invoking speeds are attained. The words hello and officer come to mind.

Above: Campbell memorabilia, including Bluebird team overalls, medal from the International Federation, and the inner helmet with its built-in headphones. Below: Bluebird K7 at speed on Coniston, and Donald with his father, Sir Malcolm

At least the M6 slips by painlessly enough. A wake-up blast, heading west along the A590, brings us to the southern tip of Coniston Water. It's still early afternoon, so we've plenty of time to explore the roads around the lake and find some suitably atmospheric locations for the pics. If it's sombre we want, the weather's playing its part – the skies are the same colour as the slate they dig out of the mountains around here. The water looks choppy, grey, forbidding.

It was Donald's father, the autocratic, multi-record-breaking Sir Malcolm Campbell, who first came to Coniston just before the outbreak of the

second world war with an earlier boat, Bluebird K4, which raised the record to 141mph. He returned after the war, but he was a sick man. When he died in 1948, Donald, then aged 27, took the biggest decision of his life – to take on his father's mantle. Incredibly, he had never driven anything more powerful than the family car. It was as though he felt obliged to carry on the Campbell tradition, to keep the speed records for Britain. He was driven, too, by a need to prove himself, having been consistently under-valued by his father.

There would be many visits to Coniston in the '50s and '60s, and they were heady days for the village. Whenever a record attempt was in the offing, the population was swollen with news crews, reporters and interested spectators. The locals took Donald to their hearts, and he came to view Coniston as his second home.

He still has a presence here. The local brewery brews Bluebird Bitter; the village museum has a section devoted to the Campbells. And then there's the Bluebird Cafe at the waterside; filled with paintings and photos of K7 screaming along the lake. We ask if we can take some photos on the shingle beach in front of the cafe, but the owner insists we pay him £150 for the privilege, so we shrug our shoulders and slip back into the XKR.

Fortunately the management of the Water Park outdoor adventure centre, back at the southern end of the lake, takes a more charitable view and allow us to scrunch down onto the foreshore with all five miles of Coniston Water stretching into the distant murk. We are not alone for long. A group of inner-city youngsters are staying at the centre and soon shamble down to gawp at the Jaguar and the two nervous-looking journalists. The XKR works its magic; within seconds they are cupping their hands at the windows, whistling through their teeth, and demanding to know how much, how fast, is it yours, and can I have a go?

We make our excuses. It's only early evening, but the light is so dismal we decide to call it a day and head for the Coniston Lodge. Back in 1967 this was the Robinson family's bungalow – they offered it to Campbell as somewhere he could stay, away from the media glare. Today it's a hotel run by Anthony and his wife. The XKR wafts us along the western side of the lake, and we leave the youngsters to build their driftwood bonfires.

Anthony Robinson was just a lad when Donald Campbell first came to Coniston to break records. The Campbells always stayed with the Robinsons, who ran a succession of pubs and guest houses in the village. 'My first memory would have been in 1949, when I was five,' he says. 'There was still rationing, and I remember we had to stop using sugar in our tea and on our cornflakes because the Campbells were coming – they always wanted lots of hot sweet drinks to keep them going. It always caused excitement in the village, and being a kid and being that close to them was incredibly exciting.'

Where Campbell senior had been a rather aloof, martinet figure, Donald had more of the common touch – happy to muck in, mix with the locals. He was good company, a charmer. But he was also a complex man, riven with insecurities and doubts. Which, in a way, made his achievements all the more heroic.

His first attempts at the water speed record were in his father's old boat, K4, ending in dramatic fashion in 1951 when it hit a submerged log at 170mph. He was lucky to escape with his life, but the boat was wrecked – today the steering wheel hangs on the wall of the sitting room of the Coniston Lodge.

With the water speed record now in American hands, Donald commissioned a completely new boat, K7 (the K signified that it was registered with Lloyd's in the Unlimited class, 7 meant it was the seventh boat to be registered in the class). K7 was a far more modern design, a three-point hydroplane (meaning it raised itself out of the water and skimmed the surface) powered by a Bristol-Siddeley Orpheus turbojet engine developing up to 5000lb of thrust. The craft was 30ft long, 10ft 6in wide, and consumed 600 gallons an hour at top speed, when a full tank lasted less than six minutes.

K7 first skimmed along Coniston Water in 1956 and returned in successive years until by 1959 the record stood at 260.35mph. Campbell, though, like his father, also had one eye on the land speed record, and the following year he crashed massively on the Bonneville salt flats at 360mph, fracturing his skull. His health never fully recovered.

Still, four years later in Australia he achieved the unique double record of 403mph on land and 276mph on water. It should have been enough to lay all the ghosts to rest. But, perhaps because it happened on the other side of the world, it didn't seem to register with the British public.

Left: Coniston on the XKR's sat-nav system. Silverstone has all the best options, including 20in alloys, biggest wheels ever fitted to a production Jaguar. Above: Campbell (centre, white shirt) in the bar of the Black Bull, which was run by the Robinson family

'Campbell would have liked the XKR, the most sporting production Jaguar since the E-type'

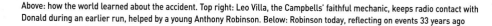

Above: how the world learned about the accident. Top right: Leo Villa, the Campbells' faithful mechanic, keeps radio contact with Donald during an earlier run, helped by a young Anthony Robinson. Below: Robinson today, reflecting on events 33 years ago

Or as Anthony Robinson puts it: 'His father was a hero to every schoolboy in England. Donald was living in a different age. When Malcolm set the land speed record at over 200mph in the '20s, there were few aircraft that travelled that fast. By the 1960s there were aeroplanes travelling at well over 1000mph and rockets going into space.'

Still driven, still feeling he had something to prove, Donald returned to Coniston in October 1966, despite the reservations of chief mechanic Leo Villa, who had been with both Campbells through all their record attempts. K7 was already more than ten years old and they were, of course, pushing into the unknown. The target – 300mph.

The Robinsons, naturally, welcomed the Bluebird team, and Anthony found himself closely involved. 'I had just turned 22, and I sort of got roped in to working for Donald.

'In fact it wasn't going well. Money seemed to be tight and there were all sorts of hold-ups. First they were doing a static test and part of the fibreglass body was sucked into the engine, which did all sorts of damage to the impeller blades. Then there was a problem with the boat, with its centre of gravity, which meant it wasn't coming up onto the plane – it was too nose-heavy.

'One morning I was dispatched to the local grocer's shop to get a couple of potato sacks, and then up to the builders' yard to get them filled with sand. The sacks were tied over the back of the boat, with a loop of rope over the fin. And it worked. So we then made lead ingots in biscuit tin lids which we got from my mum at the hotel, collecting the lead form various sources. Donald melted the lead himself with an oxyacetylene torch into the biscuit tin lids, and these weights were drilled and bolted into the stern of the boat, and that's what made the difference.'

What sort of man was Campbell? 'He was an enormous character,' says Anthony. 'One of those people who, when he walks into a room, just has this sort of presence. It's no secret that he was a

lady's man (Campbell was married three times, the third time to a Belgian cabaret star), a bit of a bloody smoothy you could say. They used to throw themselves at him. He was also a very generous fellow, maybe too generous for his own good – one or two people took him for a ride.

'He led by example. He would never expect his people to be slogging away down at the lake all night in the wet and cold. He would be there with them, and he would be the last one to leave.

'He would always go through to the tap room, the sawdust end of the pub, and spend time with the locals. He loved nothing more than coming home at night and sitting round the kitchen table with his sausages and mash. He seemed to prefer that to eating in the formal dining room. He might have seemed a complex character, but I believe that at heart he was quite a simple person, but he had all these things thrust upon him…'

Campbell was 45 in October 1966, and many of the villagers thought he was looking more drawn, less carefree. 'I think he probably was under more pressure on that last visit,' says Anthony Robinson, 'but I was only 22 and I probably wasn't aware enough to really notice.

'He would come and have a couple of brandies in the bar, whereas on earlier visits he hardly drank at all. But he was never a heavy drinker. There are stories that he was drinking heavily at the end, but I saw no evidence of that.'

The night before the final run, Campbell was playing his favourite card game, Russian Patience, and drew an ace of spades followed by the queen of spades. He remarked: 'Those are the two cards Mary Queen of Scots turned up just before she was beheaded. I have the most awful premonition that I'm going to get the chop this time.' After a nightcap with some press men, he went to bed.

So what was the mood the following morning – was there any feeling that something awful was about to happen? 'Far from it,' says Anthony. 'The boat was at last performing as it should. A few days earlier in testing it had been up around the 280mph mark. January 4th, we got up as usual about six o'clock. I'd make tea and coffee and toast, then we'd all go down to the boat house to

> ### 'The attempt started shortly before 9am. Campbell's first run, north-south along the lake, yielded 297mph'

be ready for when dawn came. We had the safety boats already out on the lake, moored at either end of the measured kilometre – small cabin cruisers – and we paddled out to them in blow-up dinghies so as not to create any disturbance on the water. It was our job to act as marshals. I was at the north end, about fifty or sixty yards out into the lake; the timing equipment was on pontoons at the side of the lake. When dawn came up, the lake was absolutely flat calm, clear skies.'

The record attempt started shortly before 9am. Campbell's first run, north-south along the lake, yielded a speed of 297mph. He turned the craft and returned at more than 300mph. About 150ft from the last kilometre marker, when it was decelerating, Bluebird soared into the air. 'I'm going…' were the last words heard from Campbell on the radio link.

'Leo Villa, Geoff Hallawell and me were the closest people to where it happened,' says Anthony. 'It was just a hundred yards away, right on top of us. Then the first thing I can remember is Leo thumping me on the back and saying "Come on Robbo, for Christ's sake let's get going,

let's go and get him."

'You could still see the boat at that moment, lying on its side, but it was sinking fast. By the time we got there, there was no sign of it.

'There were bits of wreckage everywhere – thousands of these little airbags, which had been put into the craft to stop it sinking. And then there were all these bits of clothing – his shoes and socks, gloves, helmet, inner helmet, his mae west, and his little teddy bear mascot, Mr Whoppit.

'It was weird – especially when we saw the helmet and thought we'd found him. Then we picked it out of the water and – in spite of what you hear – there was nothing inside it. The one thing that always puzzled me is we never found one fragment of his blue overalls. The Navy divers told us there would be very little left because of the impact; they likened it to an explosion; everything vapourises.

'We searched around through the wreckage for maybe an hour, then Leo and most of the others went back to the shore. I stayed out on the lake on my own for maybe two hours. It got very, very eerie, and eventually I just came home.

'The divers went down that evening and searched the bed of the lake and the wreck of the boat. Apparently it's intact apart from the nose, and it's still there in the silt, about 140ft down.'

Days after the accident, Donald's mother, Lady Campbell, places a wreath on the lake, Anthony Robinson at her side

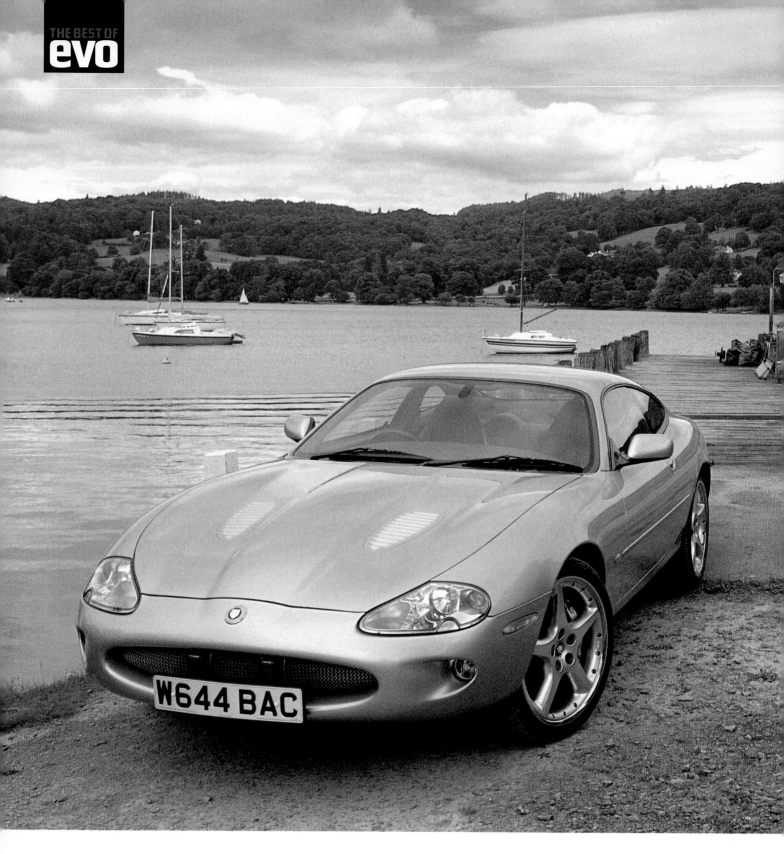

What went wrong? One theory is that Campbell turned too quickly at the end of his first run and the surface was still disturbed when he made his return. Maybe K7's stressed 12-year-old frame finally cried enough. Anthony Robinson suggests another possible explanation. 'One thing that struck me was that there was no fuel around. Had it suddenly run out of fuel? Because you had to lift off slowly – the thrust from the back was keeping the nose down. Or maybe it was a sequence of events. The boat always had this tendency to what Donald called tramping. At a certain speed it

would bounce from one sponson to another.' When the RAF analysed film footage they were able to work out that K7 was doing over 320mph on the return run.

Such was the Campbells' closeness to the Robinsons that Donald's mother, Lady Campbell, lived with the family for two years after the tragedy. When she laid a wreath on the water, Anthony was by her side. 'It was a privilege to be involved,' he says. 'It's inevitable people want to talk about his death, but there are a lot of happy memories too. I knew him for years – as a little

boy I called him Uncle Donald…'

It was on that final visit to Coniston that the Robinson family offered Campbell the use of their bungalow, Sunny Brow, as a bolt-hole. Twenty years later Anthony and his wife, Elizabeth, added an extension and turned it into the hotel – the dining room where we tucked into dinner was actually the lounge where Campbell would have relaxed, or more likely fretted, the night before a run. And sitting outside would have been his E-type.

'He always had Jaguars,' says Anthony. 'On his

Above: Tomalin parks XKR next to the jetty where Bluebird K7 was launched, not realising he's just yards from where Campbell left his E-type before setting out on his final run. Never-before-published picture of Campbell's car (top right) was taken by photographer Geoff Hallawell as he stepped ashore from the safety boat, an hour or so after the accident

final visit he had this E-type sprayed in Bluebird blue. I remember one Christmas, when most of the others had gone home, he asked me if I wanted to drive with him to Kendal. It turned out he wanted someone to go Christmas shopping with him, and to keep him company. On the way back we stopped off for dinner. He said he'd make sure it was all right with my mum – I was supposed to be doing the bar that night. We stopped off at the Wild Boar. It was the first time I'd talked to him on equal terms, sort of man to man.

'The other thing I remember about that trip was there was some switch on the E-type that wasn't working. It had been in the garage and they hadn't fixed it, and he was quite irate. He was angry that the car wasn't working one hundred per cent. That was typical of him.

'He drove the car reasonably hard, but not particularly fast, certainly not recklessly – he wasn't leaving rubber all over the road. He didn't need to impress me. He had nothing to prove.'

Next morning we drive the roads around the lake and up into the surrounding hills. I try to imagine Campbell in his E-type on these roads. They're constantly twisting and climbing, but just once, when the tarmac opens up for half a mile or more into the distance, I keep it flat through the first three gears and feel the thrill of raw speed and hope he would have approved.

Through the serious twists you can feel the Jaguar stiffen its sinews the faster you force it to change direction. Its body control is fist-tight here. As part of the package of R Performance options, the CATS adaptive damping system, standard on all XKRs, was recalibrated, while the springs and anti-roll bars were uprated for increased roll stiffness and the ride height lowered by 10mm. Without losing its natural suppleness, the XK feels locked to the tarmac.

The steering has been retuned too, but while its speed and precision are hard to fault, it remains just a touch inert – there's little variation in its weighting to tell you how heavily the wheels are

loaded, not quite enough detail about the road surface and the attitude of the treadblocks. No complaints about the brakes though – they simply do their job, progressively but with immense power. And if there's a smoother-shifting gearbox I've yet to drive it. The XKR's five-speed auto disguises its upshifts almost to the point of invisibility. Traction control has its limits set high, which is just as well, because when it does cut in it's pretty heavy-handed, slightly more intrusive than the very best systems. You can, of course, switch it off if you want to be a complete Herbert.

The last of the action photography complete, we drive down to Pier Cottage on the edge of Coniston village. There's a slipway here, which is where Bluebird K7 was winched in and out of the water before and after each run. We park the XKR next to the jetty.

It's early evening now. The old wood-decked launches that ply the lake have moored for the night; a few locals are out walking their dogs; otherwise the only sound is Bailie's shutter clicking and clucking as the last images of the XKR are sucked in. It looks sublimely beautiful, aggressive, timeless. It is everything that I love about Jaguars, and I suspect Donald Campbell would have felt the same.

Back at the office I call Geoff Hallawell, the photographer who was with Anthony Robinson and Leo Villa in the safety boat. He tells me he has a shot of the E-type which he took when he came ashore after the accident. When the picture arrives at the office it's another of those spooky moments – we'd parked in virtually the same spot that Campbell had on that fateful morning.

Campbell's nephew, Don Wales, continues to chase speed records in an electrically powered Bluebird car. And sometime next year another Brit, Nigel Macknight, will take his Quicksilver boat to Coniston and attempt to win back the water speed record for Britain at over 320mph. Donald Campbell continues to be an inspiration. The ripples are still there.

A year after this story was published, Campbell's remains and the wreck of Bluebird K7 were recovered from Coniston. K7 is currently being restored.

GET
SHORTY

Fifteen years after the flame-spitting, short-wheelbase Group B Audi Sport quattro finished its final World Championship rally, Richard Meaden relived its last blast in the mountains above Monte Carlo

Photography: Gus Gregory
Archive photography: McKlein/LAT

High in the Alpes Maritime, the weather was up to its usual dirty tricks. Conditions were predictable only in as much as they were totally unpredictable; the roads a treacherous cocktail wet and dry tarmac laced with patches of black ice, slush, deep snow and the occasional swirl of freezing fog. For the drivers and co-drivers about to start the 1986 Monte Carlo Rally, each and every one of the 547 miles of special stages that lay ahead was a far bigger gamble than the longest of long shots placed on the roulette tables of the principality.

One man knew the odds better than most. Already a four-time winner of the season-opening classic, including a hat trick in '82, '83 and '84, Walter Röhrl practically owned the Monte Carlo rally, just as Ayrton Senna would come to dominate the Monaco Grand Prix. No one knew the switchback stages or could read the ever-changing weather like the tall German, and combined with a near-surgical driving style and perfectly metered aggression, it made Röhrl and co-driver Christian Geisdörfer a formidable pairing.

Even so, they started the '86 season under pressure. Their car – the terrifyingly potent but comparatively cumbersome S1 quattro – was beginning to feel its age against the lighter, more modern Lancia Delta S4s and Peugeot 205 T16s, despite having a fire-breathing 500bhp to fight them with. Whether brute power and Röhrl's reluctance to relinquish his hold on the rally

would be enough remained to be seen, but if looks could kill the grotesquely proportioned S1 quattro had the opposition slayed before the start.

As a wide-eyed teenager, months away from his 15th birthday, the closest I got to experiencing the Monte Carlo and Röhrl's fire-breathing quattro was through the pages of *Autosport* and *Motoring News*. Now, in 2001, as an older but still wide-eyed 30-year-old, it's quite a feeling to be storming up the very same roads in the showroom equivalent of Walter's old warhorse. It gives me a buzz just looking at the thing – a decade and a half has done little to blunt the Sport quattro's shock value. It's still cartoonishly ugly from most angles, plain stupid in profile, but the bluff nose, box arches and cotton-reel alloys combine with compelling effect, even to eyes

rendered blasé by prolonged exposure to be-winged Imprezas and Evos. You simply can't resist a lingering glance back at Audi's outlandish homologation special, no matter how much time you spend with it.

We're here to retrace Walter's wheel-tracks, for the '86 Monte Carlo rally was to be the Group B quattro's final fling before spectator and driver deaths prompted Audi to withdraw from Group B competition before the end of the season. We're here in June and not January simply because given the choice between minus 15 and factor 15, sunshine and dry tarmac wins every time in my book. In fact, you don't need wintery conditions to appreciate what Röhrl had to cope with. Winter or summer, these roads are incredible, threading their tortuous way through some of the most spectacular

scenery in Europe. So twisty and narrow that a ten-mile journey can take you the best part of half an hour. Even with caution thrown to the wind, the prospect of attacking them at similar speeds in the snow and ice makes my mouth go as dry as parchment.

To the uninitiated the Sport quattro is just a cooking quattro with 12 inches cut out of the wheelbase. Take a close look and it's shocking to discover just how different the shorter car is from the original. Pretty much all the bodywork is Kevlar-reinforced plastic, from the roof and wings to the bonnet and boot. In fact only the doors remain in metal. With weight saving a high priorit,y the Sport quattro's engine was all-alloy, the new block weighing some 23 kilos less than the old, cast-iron version. A 20-valve cylinder head, much

Above: Walter Röhrl was the master of the Monte in the '80s, but his brutishly powerful Audi (left) was still an almighty handful on snow and ice. Road version was built to satisfy Group B regulations

larger KKK turbocharger and a more efficient induction and cooling system, enabled Audi engineers to extract 300bhp from the 2.2-litre, five-cylinder motor in road trim, with another 200bhp on tap in Röhrl's flame-spitting S1 version. In a formula famed for its excess, the S1 was the mightiest of a warrior breed, so it's fitting that of all the Group B homologation road cars, the Audi Sport quattro was similarly superior.

We've already grown to appreciate the quattro's under-bonnet muscle, having nailed the 1100-mile journey from Peterborough to Nice in one hit, yesterday. For a 15-year-old car, the Audi makes a remarkable long-distance machine. There's plenty of wind noise, not to mention a bit of propshaft vibration, but with a brimmed 90-litre fuel tank and settled at a comfortable, Gendarme-happy 95-100mph cruise, the Audi will run for three and half hours between fuel stops. The ease with which it surges to 125mph with the gentlest stroke of the throttle suggests Audi's claimed top speed of 155mph is well within reach. It's genuinely comfortable, too, thanks to the brilliantly supportive Recaro seats, so Gregory and I clamber out at our hotel on the Rue des Anglais ache-free but hungry for beer and pizza. Nothing new there then.

Back in 1986, the Monte Carlo Rally was a six-day monster that took crews on a gruelling 2474-mile route, 547 of those miles split into 36 diverse special stages. Our considerably abbreviated re-run still includes some of the great Monte stages, from the Col de Turini just north of Monaco, to the superfast Sisteron stage a couple of hours to the north west. We'll also head for stages where Röhrl and the quattro shone brightest,

Right: Sport quattro's extraordinary profile was the result of removing 12 inches from the wheelbase of the regular quattro

including the rally's 36th and last stage between the isolated mountain villages of Loda and Luceram. It's going to be an awesome, eye-opening drive.

After a great dinner and a good night's sleep we meet up with photo-shoot assistant Antony Fraser, 'fresh' off the easyjet redeye from Luton. After collecting a rental Merc A-class that bears more battle-scars than a Gaza Strip minicab, we strike out for Sisteron, one of the toughest stages of the entire rally.

With a huge change in elevation from start to finish, choosing tyres to suit the whole stage was nigh impossible as conditions could range from dry tarmac at the start to black ice and slush on the ascent and deep powder snow at the highest points. Getting the better of surface conditions as fickle as this relied on luck as much as tyre choice, and way before he got to our first port of call, Röhrl had fallen foul of both.

A poor 12th after the first stage, Röhrl snuck into the top six places just twice in the first eight stages. His team-mate, the Swede, Hannu Mikkola, was faring better but not much. Clearly the Audi's power advantage counted for nothing if it couldn't be transmitted to the road, a problem the agile 450bhp, Pirelli-shod Lancia of Henri Toivonen just didn't seem to have. The fight looked lost almost before it had begun – to everyone except Röhrl, who proceeded to take over a minute out of Toivonen's lead on the 10th and 11th stages, elevating the shovel-nosed Audi to a threatening 2nd position. Tyres, as ever, had been the key, and now the Monte

Short wheelbase means Sport quattro feels fantastically alive and darty on tightly twisting Alpine roads, while mid-range muscle of the five-cylinder turbo engine thumps it down the straights. On the limit, below right, it's wonderfully poised. Rally car was as spectacular as they come

'The quattro lifts its vent-peppered nose and punches forward with supercar force'

Meister gathered ominous momentum, his hands circling the rally's throat in readiness for the stranglehold that he would surely apply in the next few stages. Lady Luck had other ideas though, and on Burzet, the longest stage of the rally, Röhrl suffered a puncture. Conditions were good for once, and Röhrl was on unstudded dry tyres, but inexplicably his spare was a studded snow tyre, an error that cost six minutes and any realistic hope of victory.

Fortunately, tyres aren't an issue in our assault of Sisteron. With the sun beating down and crickets chirruping in the meadows, the Sport quattro feels sensational, lunging between bends on a rip-tide of forced-induction thrust. Age hasn't diminished its accelerative punch, and although there's plenty of fluffy, low-compression lag below 3000rpm, when the outsize KKK spools into life, the quattro lifts its vent-peppered nose and punches forward with supercar force. It doesn't thrive on low gears or high revs, the real sweet spot sitting between 4500 and 6500rpm in third and fourth gears. It's here you flex the soulful five-cylinder's muscle most effectively, all 243lb ft of mid-range torque hefting you out of the hairpins, the turbo's final fiery flourish providing the top end to make the most of the straights. Whenever the stage uncoils enough to really uncork the quattro's performance, it devours it effortlessly.

At just over 23 miles long, Sisteron is one of the longest stages on the Monte. For the first ten miles or so it's a riot of clearly sighted second and third gear corners. The tarmac is smooth, and wide, by Monte standards at any rate, though still only two cars wide at best. You climb gently, but as the lush greenery subsides the topography gets more ragged and worrying drops start to fall away to your right. Gnarled armco barriers are now the only thing between you and a seemingly bottomless abyss of fresh air as you blast across frost-cracked asphalt, eye-level with the peaks of 1300-metre high mountains. From here the only way is down, the road plunging into dense forest where without warning it constricts savagely. Barely a car wide and far twistier than before, every corner is blind. It's here that Geisdörfer became Röhrl's eyes, seeing him through the maze of bends and hazards, Röhrl powering on in a literal act of blind faith. At this point, less than two-thirds through the stage, Gus and I stop for photos. Out of curiosity we check the time. We've been driving fast for 20 minutes or so. Coping with snow and ice, Röhrl and Geisdörfer would need only eight more minutes to complete the entire stage. Mind-blowing stuff.

From Sisteron we point the Sport quattro towards St Auban. It's another classic Monte stage, the most memorable section carving its way through a claustrophobic canyon. How anyone built a road through here is beyond me. With a sheer face on one side, a sheer drop on the other, pitch-black tunnels and overhanging rocks it's one of the most hair-raising roads I've ever seen. There's no way we can go quickly through here; it's just too narrow and dangerous, especially as there's traffic coming the other way. Some sections are so scary I have to hoot for comfort before timidly poking the quattro's nose blindly round the corner. For this reason alone it's a memorable drive, despite our lack of pace. Needless to say, our man Röhrl, now driving only to prove what could have been, powered the S1 through here faster than anyone else, no doubt filling the canyon with the five-cylinder engine's spine-tingling war-cry.

After the confines of St Auban, even the sinuous Col de Turini feels spacious. Fast and furious, the road climbs through thick mountain woodland before popping out at the 1600-metre high summit, then jinks diagonally between two restaurants before plunging down the other side. A stone's throw from the Italian border, it's a favourite stage for the most partisan spectators. In 1986 roaring flanks of Lancia and Peugeot supporters lined opposite sides of the stage at the Turini's summit, pelting each other with snowballs and shovelling snow onto the path of the enemy. What they

Meaden and quattro pause for breath on the Col de Turini. Right: detuned road engine produces a mere 300bhp; cabin surprisingly comfortable – car makes superb GT. Bottom right: Röhrl drove like a man possessed after a puncture appeared to put him completely out of the running. The Sport quattro was going out in style...

did to Röhrl is anyone's guess, but the big Audi would have been a handful as it crested the Col, wastegate shrieking and wheels spinning with the force of 500bhp on sheet ice and snow. Broadside through a seething mass of humanity.

All we have to contend with are gaggles of super-fit cyclists, calf-muscles rippling as they pull impossibly high gears up the eye-watering gradient. The Audi also enjoys the ascent, gravity pushing its nose firmly into the uphill hairpins; moist, dense air filling the five-cylinder's hungry lungs. The steering is perfectly judged for this kind of nip-and-tuck work. There's so much feel you know exactly how hard the chunky 225/50 Dunlops are working, each fraction of a turn of lock filled with essential information. You can feel the shorter wheelbase aiding your progress too; an added dartiness when turning into tight corners, an edgier throttle adjustability through the faster curves. It's more aggressive than a standard quattro, but the reassuring feel and balance is still there. Sure it understeers if you carry too much speed or get on the power too soon, but not so much that you can't contain it. It's an Impreza with real feel, an Evo without the synthetic chassis balance. For the vast majority of the time it manages to generate so much

traction from such modest tyres it simply grips and goes, firing out of corners like a champagne cork. More importantly when it does slide you know precisely why, and there's enough information through the steering wheel and controllability in the chassis for you to exploit or remedy the situation without too much drama.

It's on the descent that the quattro feels less convincing. Brakes have come a long way in 15 years, and though vented and clamped by four-piston callipers the disc size is badly compromised by the 15in wheels. To put things in perspective an Impreza P1 WR's discs are bigger than the quattro's wheels. Not surprisingly although the Audi's middle pedal has good initial feel, there's just not the ultimate, repeated stopping power you could find yourself wanting very badly if you charged down the mountain as hard as the engine and chassis encourage you to do.

From the Col de Turini we drive to our last stage of the journey, and the last stage of the '86 Monte Carlo. It's a relatively compact ten miles, and Röhrl, by now back in a safe 4th position thanks to five fastest stage times since his fateful puncture, is still driving like a man possessed. Just 13 minutes and 46 seconds later his point

is proved beyond all doubt, having posted a time nearly 50secs faster than team-mate Mikkola, still the second fastest man through the stage. I have a real crack at this one too, really pushing hard when conditions allow. It's odd, but the quattro feels most at home in moments like this, soaking up the punishment like a sponge. The damping is nothing short of brilliant: soft enough to absorb bumps that would have stiffer cars skittering, but controlled enough to keep the engine's sump from grinding itself into swarf on the unforgivingly undulating tarmac. Gone is the transmission shunt that blights low-speed driving, so too the turbo lag that punishes lack of commitment.

Give it its head and the quattro unleashes a ferocious point-to-point pace that leaves you breathless. Even now, there are very few cars that could attack roads like this with such conviction and emerge with honour (and structure) intact. Fifteen years – half my lifetime – stand between this car and the so-called cutting edge, and yet, right at this moment I'm struggling to think of anything to touch it for its incredible combination of feel and cornering force. The S1 failed to win the Monte, but its road-going progeny remains a uniquely impressive experience. The quattro legend lives on.

Speed
D a t e

When Bentley invited us to drive its Le Mans-winning
Speed 8 in 2003, we didn't think twice. By John Barker

I flick the toggle switch and the raucous engine dies. Muffled voices around me suddenly gain clarity as the left-hand door is popped open. I'm still staring ahead, assimilating the experience, when one loud voice says: 'You looked like you were enjoying that!' Further off, another chuckles: 'Yeah, he doesn't look like he wants to get out!'

I don't. I never imagined I'd be here in the first place, and I'll almost certainly never find myself here again. 'How was it?' asks the Bentley PR lady as I pull my crash helmet off. For a moment I struggle to find a word that adequately sums-up the thrill of my scant four laps.

Sensational? Of course. Awesome? Chee-*sey*.

'Fabulous,' I reply. And I mean it in every sense, as I appreciate more fully later, when I check the definition in the dictionary: '**1** incredible, exaggerated, absurd. **2** marvellous **3** *a* celebrated in fable *b* legendary, mythical.'

Yup, the Le Mans-winning Bentley Speed 8 is all of that, even the last bit since its historic victory in June. The 'absurd' part applies less to the car, more to the very notion that we'd been flown to Circuit Paul Ricard to drive Number 7, the car that was raced to the flag by Tom Kristensen, Dindo Cappello and Guy Smith. Surely a company so acutely aware of its history at this exciting time of re-invention knows that it

would be a brave decision even to wash Number 7, let alone give a bunch of journalists the chance to drive it.

Then, 24 hours before my drive, I learn that although it bears the numbers and names, the car I'll be driving isn't actually the winning car or even second-placed Number 8. And to be honest I'm relieved. It hardly diminishes the experience, because there are only three 2003-spec Speed 8s. This is 004/2, which raced at the gruelling Sebring 12-hours and has born the brunt of endurance testing, racking up some 12,000 miles at racing speeds, including a 30-hour pre-Le Mans test here at the Circuit Paul Ricard. Thus it has played a crucial role in the fairytale that has seen Bentley add its sixth Le Mans winner's trophy to the display cabinet at Crewe, after a gap of 73 years.

And it could be a while before they add another, because just a couple of weeks after our drive, Bentley announced it wouldn't be returning in 2004. No real surprise there. First, the Le Mans programme was scheduled to run for three years and reached its conclusion with this year's win. Second, from a marketing standpoint only an uninterrupted hat-trick would top a solus win, and while that's not

Big carbonfibre hoop dominates cockpit. Getting into the driver's seat requires various contortions. Seat is offset to the right (the regs require space for a passenger seat). Tiny, squared-off steering wheel frames Bosch digital-dash. Gearbox is sequential paddle-shift; there's a clutch, but you only use it when moving off

would top a solus win, and while that's not unattainable, as Audi has shown, even if Bentley won next year, drastic regulation changes would mean building an all-new, more production-based car for 2005. Finally, perhaps most tellingly, they're letting journos loose in one of the three Speed 8s…

Journos with race experience, mind. I've got some but I feel I've barely scraped in when I see that among the lucky ten invitees assembled in the suite above the pits are Phillip Peter, who won the most recent FIA GT race in a Ferrari 575, and the affable Aguri Suzuki, former F1 driver. No pressure, then.

None at all, says suave, five-times Le Mans winner Derek Bell, consultant to Bentley, in his briefing. Our objective should be to get a flavour of the car, he tells us, not set the fastest lap possible; there will be no lap timing because they want the car back in one piece. Fair enough.

Last night we had dinner with Bell and Kristensen, now also a five-times winner, and in a considerably shorter time-frame. 'Took me 26 years. He's done it from eight starts,' said Bell with mock exasperation. Hoping to get an inside line, I ask him how the Speed 8 compares with the other Le Mans cars he's raced. 'Totally

different,' he says. 'In the [Porsche] 962 you'd come into a corner on the brakes, turn and the rear would drift out. Then,' he says, his hands and arms describing twists of imaginary counter-steer, 'you'd pick up the power and apply opposite lock when the rev counter needled flared up.' It always looked to me like the Porsches were guided by Scalextric slots. Seems

like the Bentley approaches that feel: 'The Speed 8 is all about entry speed,' advises Bell. 'The downforce keeps the car pinned to the road and you drive it hard for the apex.'

It's a dazzlingly bright day at Paul Ricard, warm but with a sharp breeze. That's the famous Mistral, which Bell advises us may alter the feel of the car considerably if you're leaning on the

aerodynamics through the long and awesomely fast 'Signes' corner. Clearly this information is not for the benefit of the less experienced, like me, who might confuse downforce with a TV gardening programme.

Standing barely crotch-high in the pit lane, the dark green Speed 8 is both sinister and beautiful, the sort of creature that might have been discovered way down in the inky fathoms of the sea. It's an amalgam of slippery, globular curves and that vast, squared-rigged rear wing. Feeding that wing with a less turbulent flow of air was among the main objectives of the almost all-new 2003 car, along with more front-end downforce to eliminate the understeer that characterised the earlier EXP (for experimental) Speed 8s. Power steering was added so that the extra front grip could be exploited without wearing out the drivers.

Time is tight so batches of journos pile into sumptuous Arnage Ts driven by Bell and Kristensen for single, sedate 'sighting' laps. The first part is easy – out of the pits, under the bridge to turns one and two (L'ecole), a 90-deg-plus right followed quickly by a less-than-90-deg right that connects to a half-mile of the wide Mistral straight. At the brake marker boards, the jovial Kristensen announces: 'You'll be doing 295kmh (183mph) in sixth here.'

Just over the crest, apex unsighted, lurks the butt-puckering Signes right-hander. 'I take fifth but the back can get loose. If you're in fourth and you misjudge it you go straight on, no problem. In fifth you spin into the wall. I suggest fourth.'

Built expressly to win Le Mans, the Speed 8 is surely one of the most dramatic racecars ever created, from its fighter-plane cockpit-turret to its extraordinary rear wing. 4-litre twin-turbo V8 (below left) produces a reliable 600bhp. All-carbon brakes designed to wipe off three-figure speeds over and over again for 24 hours

'I tug back for second early and then press the throttle halfway. *WOAH!*'

Going straight on at Paul Ricard isn't a problem because there are no tall curbs and no gravel traps, just lots more asphalt banded with brightly coloured, arresting strips of high-grip surfacing. The conclusion of the lap is all rather technical, starting with a double-apex right-hander, Beausset. Trouble is, it's featureless as well as being technical, and the view from the Speed 8 is going to be less good than from the Arnage.

Getting into the Speed 8's cockpit requires a high degree of physical flexibility even if you're not much larger than a jockey, placing hands and feet on non-vulnerable parts of the wide sill area before wriggling your legs under the wheel and over the anti-submarining hump of the seat. At Le Mans the driver change time was expected to be a factor in the race with the open-cockpit Audi R8s. As it transpired, the fastest R8 took itself out of the equation when Frank Biela missed the pit entrance and ran out of fuel.

It's snug and a little claustrophobic inside the narrow bubble cockpit. A fat carbonfibre hoop reassuringly encircles the cabin from screen header to floor, while ahead is a small squared-off wheel with metallic paddles, and a small Bosch electronic dashboard. Much of the upper portion of the turret-like, curved windscreen is blanked off but the pill-box view matches that of my crash helmet aperture so visibility is fine. Even so, as Bell explained the previous evening, most drivers prefer open Le Mans cars despite

the wind buffeting: 'You get very hot and sweaty in a closed car and when it rains water finds its way in, so at the end of a stint you're wringing wet. And the windows steam up. Still, when you're upside down at 180mph you appreciate having a roof.'

The 'pre-flight' with Bell ignores the impressive array of dashboard twist switches (which the drivers use during the race to adjust vitals such as fuel mapping), and most of the steering wheel buttons, too. I'm shown how to find neutral, how to re-start in case of a spin, and told that the right-hand paddle is for upshifts, the left for downshifts, and that's about it. 'When you floor it in second you might feel the tail do this,' says a smiling Bell, miming a twist of opposite lock. 'Have fun.'

The door is pressed shut and secured. A mechanic circles his index finger, I press the little green starter button and there's a hollow, metallic ring as the starter motor engages and churns. The 4-litre, twin-turbo V8 catches and assumes a fast-ish idle, its note blustery and tight-lipped, indicating it's a flat-plane-crank design like a Ferrari 360's rather than a thundering trad V8.

I pull back on the right paddle and there's a clattery clonk as chunky straight-cut Xtrac gears mesh like the two halves of a rugby scrum. Thankfully, the massively heavy clutch is only needed to get rolling. After one stall – *ker-chunk*

then silence broken only by the accusing whine of fuel pumps – we're away.

It feels superb: fabulously low-slung but well-sighted, firm but not harsh, and genuinely comfortable. I tug back for second early and then press the throttle halfway. *WOAH!* A smooth, hefty slug of power shoves the Speed 8 forward and it skims down the track, attitude to the road unchanged.

Into the first right-hander and I'm enjoying it even more. The tiny steering wheel turns easily and the nose darts positively for the apex. The Speed 8 is alert but not nervous, its steering light but with a surprising amount of feel, though the clearest message coming through is 'loads more grip, mate'. Once we're pointing straight up the Mistral, I push the throttle to the floor, the rear tyres stay firmly hooked up and the full effect of 600bhp in just 900kg hits home. It's a solid, peak-free delivery, the slam in the back staying the same right through the rev-range. And pretty much right through the first four gears too, the 0.1sec upshifts giving it a virtually seamless feel. This is the thump of any supercar you care to name, plus a bit.

I back off early at the end of the straight, drop a gear, and power tentatively through Signes. As soon as I can see the apex, I realise I've been massively conservative. I up my commitment for the double-apex Beausset, get into the first part nicely, downshift and – oh my God – I miss the

Only three Speed 8s exist, and they'll soon be going into honourable retirement. Although this car wears the number and drivers' names of the Le Mans winner (pictured below right on its way to victory) this is in fact its sister car. But since it's mechanically identical, Barker isn't too worried. Driving thrills don't come any bigger

Specification

Engine	90deg V8
Location	Mid, longitudinal
Displacement	4000cc
Bore x stroke	98mm x 76mm
Cylinder block	Aluminium alloy
Cylinder head	Aluminium alloy, dohc per bank, four valves per cylinder, twin turbos
Fuel and ignition	Bosch 4.2 engine management, FSI direct injection
Max power	600bhp+ @ 7000rpm
Max torque	590lb ft+ @ n/a rpm
Transmission	Six-speed sequential manual gearbox, rear drive
Front suspension	Double wishbones, pushrod links, coil springs incorporating horizontal gas dampers
Rear suspension	Double wishbones, pushrod links, coil springs incorporating horizontal gas dampers
Steering	Rack and pinion, power-assisted
Brakes	Ventilated ceramic-composite discs, 380mm diameter front and rear; ABS
Wheels	9.5x19 front, 12.5x20 rear, forged magnesium
Tyres	265/35x19 ZR front, 335/30x20 ZR rear
Weight (kerb)	900kg
Power-to-weight	677bhp/ton
0-62mph	3.0sec (est)
Max speed	207mph (at Le Mans)
Insurance group	call broker, and pray
Price	c£1,000,000
On sale	you wish

evo RATING ★★★★★

'I get on the throttle earlier and the tail steps out a fraction'

track. It's an embarrassing mistake that goes unpunished thanks to that unique run-off, but a honking great wake-up call for me. What did I do wrong?

I feel my way around the rest of the curves quite happily, thread through the tight right that leads onto the pit straight and floor it. For the first time I notice the shift lights embedded in the top edge of the instrument binnacle and realise I've not yet taken the engine to the redline. I've soon rectified that and I'm up to fifth and around 150mph by the time the countdown boards are looming for turn one. I brake early to see what's in reserve, carbon bites carbon and if I hadn't eased off I'd have been at turn-in speed at about the 100m board. Phenomenal. As with the steering, the surprise is that there's plenty of feel. And the downshifts are superb – crisp and smooth.

I get on the throttle earlier onto the straight and the tail steps out a fraction but correction is a doddle. When I reach the braking area for Signes I'm in sixth, which feels like an overdrive as the revs drop noticeably. Fourth again through Signes but carrying more speed and then I'm lined up again for the Beausset.

First clipping point, downshift, fine. Now turn again, look for the second apex and – cripes! – I have to steer much harder or I'm going straight

on again. The car digs for grip, I feel the g-force build massively but we're round.

It occurs to me that I've just glimpsed the true capability of the Speed 8. I've also discovered that I might be having fun but to pedal one of these really quickly I'd have to get seriously fit – I'm almost dizzy after that 180-deg-plus turn, partly because my duff line has turned into a closing spiral of ever-increasing g-force.

As I tack through the late-apex corners and long fourth-gear curve back to the pit straight again, it dawns on me that although I've inadvertently experienced the Speed 8's potential, in the hands of a professional driver it must be close to that limit in every corner. Obvious, really.

By the time my laps are over, I'm deeply impressed by the Speed 8's sheer driveability, but I need to see what it can really do, feel the pace it was designed to carry through the downforce corners. I need to but I'm also bricking it a bit. And with good reason, it transpires.

Bentley has brought along a hybrid 2001/02 EXP Speed 8 with two seats and, after a suitably long stewing period, I'm strapped into it alongside Bell for a couple of laps at qualifying pace. I've seen Bell's driving in the excellent Duke video *In Car 956* (if you haven't, get a copy

and I swear you'll watch open-mouthed) and also seen the eyes of fellow journos easing themselves out after their laps with him. I have no doubt that the 61-year-old is going to demonstrate the full potential of the Speed 8.

This engine seems coarser but it's just as powerful and the EXP Speed 8 feels as brutally fast. The gearing is a little shorter low down and longer high up, so for Signes Bell takes fourth, and a huge amount more speed. At Beausset, my bogey corner, I think he's got it all wrong. We seem to be carrying massively too much speed and turning in far too sharply, but no – the Speed 8 hangs on like a huge arm has hooked around a lamppost. Bell then actually accelerates mid-corner before braking and turning even harder into the second apex. My head is reeling from the loadings and I've only just recovered before we're into the next, slower turn, Bell muscling the wheel over. This is a hot lap but the second, when the old slicks are warmer, is even faster in the fastest parts. And the braking – at the end of the pit straight it feels like he doesn't hit the pedal until we're upon the 100m board. Incredible.

Two laps of this, with a tang of petrol in the cockpit, is enough for me. Incredibly, at Le Mans this year Kristensen did a stint of almost three-and-a-half hours – twice Grand Prix distance – lapping close to his qualifying time.

My appreciation of the Speed 8's ability has been well and truly cemented. The physical effort required to drive it is no more than that required to drive a supercar like the Zonda or Enzo. You can easily exploit all of the Bentley's straight-line performance and enjoy pushing it in the first and second gear corners, feeling the grip through the wheel and the seat of your pants. In short, the Speed 8 is wonderfully driveable like a modern supercar. But it's a supercar with serious downforce that takes it to another, mind-blowing level. Fabulous is the only word to describe it.

 Words: Colin Goodwin/John Barker/Jethro Bovingdon Pictures: Andy Morgan/Charlie Magee

200MPH
THE ULTIMATE ROAD TRIP

Is it still possible to drive at 200mph on the public road? What sort of car does it take? And what does it feel like? In 2003, we sent three drivers to Germany with a super-accurate GPS-based data-logger and gave them five very fast cars to play with. A few days later they returned, part exhausted, part elated. This is their remarkable story

Ruf R Turbo

We're no strangers to the R Turbo – a 520bhp version with the optional narrow-body and rear-drive competed in our Car of the Year 2001 contest. For this exercise Ruf has wheeled out a bigger gun: a wide-bodied, 4wd example with 542bhp (a very special 582bhp engine is available, too) and Ruf's new front spoiler with cabin-adjustable ride height for driveway ramps, etc. It's also offered with an integrated roll-cage, which seems eminently sensible in a car that will run to the spooky side of 210mph.

SPECIFICATION
Layout: Rear-engined, four-wheel drive
Engine: Flat-six, 3600cc, 24v, bi-turbo
Max power: 542bhp @ 6000rpm
Max torque: 575lb ft @ 4000rpm
Power-to-weight: 372bhp/ton
0-60mph: 3.7sec
0-100mph: n/a
Max speed: 214mph (claimed)
Price (2003): £128,000

Pagani Zonda C12 S

The greatest supercar of the century (so far) and our Car of the Year 2001, the Pagani is a quality item in every respect. It's fabulously well made, from the tip of its front splitter to the Gurney flaps on its dual rear wings, and sensational to drive – it sets the dynamic standard by which all other supercars are judged. We've driven the C12 and this, the more potent C12 S with the 7.3-litre 555bhp Mercedes V12, on many occasions but until now we haven't found the opportunity to keep the hammer down long enough to see how good it feels close to its maximum speed

SPECIFICATION
Layout: Mid-engined, rear-wheel drive
Engine: V12, 7291cc, 48v
Max power: 555bhp @ 5900rpm
Max torque: 553lb ft @ 4050rpm
Power-to-weight: 440bhp/ton
0-60mph: 3.7sec (claimed)
0-100mph: n/a
Max speed: 220mph (claimed)
Price: €481,750

MTM Bimoto

Top speed is all about how much power you've got , which means that the extraordinary MTM Bimoto is more than adequately endowed. On 98 octane pump fuel, each in-line turbo 'four' produces 370bhp, making a grand total of 740bhp. That's over 100bhp more than a McLaren F1, and the unlikely TT has already clocked almost 231mph at the Nardo test track in Italy. It's quite a feat of engineering getting two engines to run together and to synchronise their gearshifts, and probably something that's best not considered too deeply when you're grabbing top gear at almost 180mph...

SPECIFICATION
Layout: Front- and mid-engined, 4wd
Engine: 2 x in-line four, 1781cc, 20v turbo
Max power: 740bhp @ 6750rpm
Max torque: 693lb ft @ 4600rpm
Power-to-weight: 505bhp/ton
0-62mph: 3.6sec
0-124mph: 10.0sec
Max speed: 230.5mph
Price (2003): €250,000

Lotus Esthi 2.4

Only with a twin-engined TT nearby could an Elise powered by a tweaked-up Audi RS4 twin-turbo V6 look almost sensible. It costs more than £70,000, which is a serious amount to pay for an Elise, regardless of its performance. Brandes & Dschüdow have received permission from Malaysia to call the car a Lotus (they are Germany's largest Lotus dealer, which must have helped), but even so, word is that the crew at Hethel are not over the moon about the car. We know why. It's frustration. This is the sort of car that Lotus itself should be building. For the record, guys, you'd like this machine

SPECIFICATION
Layout: Mid-engined, rear-wheel drive
Engine: V6, 2761cc, 30v, bi-turbo
Max power: 414bhp @ 5800rpm
Max torque: 383lb ft @ 4500rpm
Power/weight: 425bhp/ton
0-60mph: 3.75sec
0-100mph: n/a
Max speed: circa 190mph (claimed)
Price (2003): £73,700

TVR Tuscan S

The accelerative abilities of the Tuscan S have never been in doubt. Its combination of a gutsy, normally-aspirated straight-six engine developing 390bhp and a kerb weight similar to that of a Mini Cooper S produces stunning figures. Since launching the Tuscan, TVR has also developed an aero package in the wind tunnel, and last year we attempted to max the Tuscan S on the autobahn. A broken front splitter stopped play. This time we intend to go all the way

SPECIFICATION

Layout: Front-engined, rear-wheel drive
Engine: Straight-six, 3900cc, 24v
Max power: 390bhp @ 7000rpm
Max torque: 310lb ft @ 5250rpm
Power-to-weight: 360bhp/ton
0-60mph: 4.0sec
0-100mph: 9.3sec
Max speed: 190mph-plus (claimed)
Price (2003): £48,800

There's a tremendous crack as a jet fighter blasts through the sound barrier thousands of feet above us in the cloudless German sky. They let fighter-jocks do that over here. Our guys have to fly over the North Sea or Atlantic before they can light the big fire and go supersonic.

In Germany they let you go fast at ground-level, too. That anonymous aviator up there is about the only guy who is going faster than us today, for **evo** is here in Bavaria with a quintet of subsonic speed machines for some serious autobahnwerk. Why? Because one day maybe it won't be allowed. Because there's some interesting new kit about that needs high-speed testing. And because at **evo** we like doing this sort of thing. Anyway, allow me to introduce you to our armoury.

All the way from Blackpool, England, we have TVR's Tuscan S. We're looking at a claimed top end of 190mph-plus from TVR's £49,000 390bhp masterblaster. Next, we have an example

of Alois Ruf's handiwork. This bright yellow 911-based Ruf packs a twin-turbo 540bhp punch and, from the mouth of Alois himself, a top whack of 212mph. Then we have the fabulous Pagani Zonda C12. The projected top speed of the Zonda has yo-yo'd a little, but the word is that the 555bhp S – which, of course, is what we have here – should top-out at about 220mph.

Lastly, we have two eccentric German-grown products. The first is a mk2 Lotus Elise fitted with a mildly tweaked Audi RS4 V6 biturbo in its tail. Mildly tweaked, but good for 420bhp and a top end of 190mph-plus. The second German machine is a completely nutty Audi TT fitted with two heavily tuned 1.8T motors. Yup, you read that right. Two engines. Each has 370bhp, which adds up to 740bhp and a maximum speed of 230mph, which the MTM Bimoto has officially achieved at Nardo in Italy.

Now for the personnel. From **evo** we have two experienced (and ageing) speed-freaks, co-editor Barker and your correspondent Goodwin, along with young gun Jethro Bovingdon (christened during this caper Sir Jethro, Grand Knight of

Speed, for reasons that will be given later) plus sharpshooters Andy Morgan and Charlie Magee. Barker, Magee and myself flew into Frankfurt, and the other **evo** men drove over in the mag's Audi RS6 long-termer.

The plan is to meet at a hotel in Heilbronn just north of Stuttgart, because it's suitably convenient for all parties and, most importantly, because it gives us a choice of several autobahn networks. Road selection will be critical. We need long, long straights as lightly trafficked as possible. To hit the sort of speeds that we'll be reaching in these cars you need a lot of run-up. At over three miles a minute things happen very quickly and a truck that is a sliver of metal in the distance is within a couple of seconds a wall in front of you. The rule is to hit the brakes hard as soon as anything appears in your path. And, of course, passing next to someone in the lane to your right at 190mph is not a good idea.

This is some rendezvous. The MTM Audi TT rolls into the hotel's car park driven by young racing driver Florian Gruber, who Audi tuning specialist MTM has appointed as its 'handy

**'Setting out to do 200mph in a car that has 740bhp split between
two engines will be scary for enough for Bovingdon'**

bloke' for the exercise. Wild machine. You can hear the uneven thrum of the two engines working out of sync. The Elise rocks up next with Lutz Weinschenk and Michael Rosskop, respectively technical wizard and mechanic from Munster-based Lotus dealer Brandes & Dschüdow, who have cooked up what they call the Esthi 2.4 (2.4 refers to 2.4kg per bhp). This Elise wouldn't pass a drugs test as it's pumped with steroids. This is an Elise like no other.

TVR PR/marketing boss Ben Samuelson thunders in with the sexy Tuscan S. TVR owner and mate of Samuelson, Commander Guy Haywood RN, rides shotgun. Good to have a military man along on a jaunt like this. Especially one no stranger to heavy firepower.

Tomorrow we are meeting up with Alois Ruf himself, who will leave the Ruf R Turbo with us. The Zonda will meet us late tomorrow evening as it's on its way across from England. A bloke called Andy Wallace is driving the Italian supercar. Le Mans-winner Wallace will be an invaluable body in this operation as he operates at above 200mph for a living. With him will be his girlfriend Catherine Crawford who happens to be an aerodynamicist. How quick is that? Imagine the pillow talk: 'Darling, can you look at my front splitter tomorrow? I think it's costing us 5mph on the Mulsanne.'

Look, it's not all fun here. Barker has us assembled in the hotel reception at 4.00am sharp, ready to head out to a rendezvous point on the A5 autobahn between Karlsruhe and Mannheim. It is not the quietest autobahn, but it does have many long straight sections. We've shared out driving duties, with Barker to drive

At 4.00am sartorial elegance is low priority (top, left). German eateries are clean but the food isn't always so wholesome. MTM Bimoto joins our long-term RS6 at 'base camp' while Goodwin in the Elise Esthi contemplates the wisdom of trying for 200mph in the dark in a small plastic sports car. It always pays to check the pressures and condition of the tyres, especially when you might need to be braking from 190mph or so to avoid trucks. Warm-up runs in the Esthi were roofless; the top went on for the real thing

the Ruf and Tuscan, Bovingdon to drive the TT (thank God), me to drive the Elise and Wallace to pedal the Zonda with me riding alongside with notebook and nappy.

Sitting in a service area on the A5 waiting for my first shot in the Elise, several factors give your nervous correspondent heart. First, the roads are bone dry; second, there is no wind; third, there are not too many trucks about; and, finally, it's nice and cold so the Audi motor's intercoolers will be gulping nice dense air for top horsepower. It's raw bhp that gives you the big mph numbers. Massive torque gets you there faster, which is, of course, very desirable, but it's bhp we're after today.

The A5 is getting busier by the minute so there's only a narrow window in which to operate. After a few runs to warm up both me and the RS4 motor, we blast up towards 200mph. I've always considered that 150mph is the watershed. Under that speed things happen at a rate which the averagely useful driver can deal with, but above it things start getting surreal. Then there's another step at around 175mph, where the game moves forward in yet another jump. And finally there's the magic double-ton. The crazy zone. Two-hundred, two-o-five, two-ten – they all feel surreal, otherworldly and downright frightening.

At daybreak we fuel up with a ghastly service station breakfast and convoy down back past Heilbronn on the A6, then cut across country on

minor roads through Roth to meet the A9, the autobahn that runs between Nürnberg and Ingolstadt, home to Audi. Audi engineers have previously told us that the A9 is one of their favourites. Alois Ruf, who is meeting us at a services on the A9, prefers a two-laner on the doorstep of his workshop down near Munich. Apparently last night he ran his car to 350kph (about 217mph) just to make sure it was on song.

Alois is on time. Dapper, polite, and a man who understands the concept of having power to spare. You'd like him. I do, not least because he has an example of almost every 911 ever built.

The evo team, ever concerned with not spending our leader Metcalfe's cash, decides to use this service area as a temporary command post and its adjoining Burger King as the mess. Weight, as I'm sure you are aware, is not a factor in top speed. That said, a bellyfull of dopple Whoppers does lengthen considerably the time it takes to achieve maximum velocity.

The photographers busy themselves with catching all the angles while the others neck carbohydrate and caffeine and indulge in serious bench racing, breaking occasionally for a little run up the road in one or other of the cars. We'll wait for the evening before strapping on the gear and going for the really big speeds, but for now we'll stick to 'research' work.

I join Barker for a quick thrash up the road in the Ruf R Turbo. The last Ruf I drove was a big disappointment. Plenty fast enough but unstable,

especially on the brakes. The R Turbo is hellishly fast and effortless with it. Barker and I can talk easily at 150mph while JB gently nudges the car through quick corners. The 550bhp Porsche feels super stable and super competent.

On our return we find young Morgan looking sheepish. He's managed to close the RS6's tailgate on the car's plipper and locked and immobilised the car with the plipper jammed under the bottom edge of the tailgate. We can see it but can't get at it. A sound thrashing for Morgan seems on the cards – the RS6 is loaded with camera gear – until Lotus man Rosskopp performs the work of genius and slides a bit of plastic under the door and opens the car. Years of working on Lotuses prepares you for anything, of course.

About 50 Whoppers later it's time to start some high-speed runs. There's a fantastic section of carriageway that's perfect because it's dead straight and links two junctions that are not too far apart so it's easy to turn around. Barker is up first in the Ruf. You have to be realistic with this sort of exercise. Spend all night trying to eke out the last couple of mph and you are asking for trouble. We're not record breaking here, just running these cars up to big speeds to see how well they cope and how they feel.

Barker returns, looking chuffed with the Ruf. As you can read in a few pages' time, the R Turbo hasn't disappointed. 'There's no question,' says JB, 'that given a little more room the Ruf would

'We're not record-breaking here, just running
these cars up to big speeds to see how
well they cope and how they feel'

Above, from left to right: **forest clearing venue for affixing photographic gear**; Racelogic VBOX datalogging gear uses super-accurate GPS software; Zonda's console; checking tyre pressures on the Tuscan S; Bovingdon fixes digi read-out to Zonda; we only found 'regular gas' for MTM so had to get by with just 740bhp; cool convoy; Zonda ready to rumble; modified Audi RS4 engine in Lotus Elise engine bay; not a race but a photo opportunity

Now for the MTM Audi TT. This will require bravery of the highest order. Bovingdon is too young to know the story of how the late John Cooper nearly killed himself driving a twin-engined Mini on the Kingston bypass in the '60s. I shall spare him that. Setting out to do 200mph in a car that has 740bhp split between two engines and a shape that is fine for an aeroplane wing but possibly not for a high-speed car will be scary enough for him. To sighs of relief all round, Bovingdon returns 20 minutes later looking more than a little shocked.

To conclude the evening's work, Barker and I fit the kit to the Tuscan S and combine the run back to Heilbronn with maxing out the black missile. I like the TVR for its drama and character, but autobahn thrashing is not what the car is good for; its performance is way beyond its sophistication. Above 110mph it begins to vibrate; the wind noise starts to build enormously and the whole plot starts to feel strained. The S is fast all right, but as it nears 170mph it's pretty obvious from the way the whole dashboard and steering column are shaking about that it's far from happy at these speeds. And once we realise this, neither are we.

Just after we arrive back at the hotel, Wallace and Crawford arrive in the Pagani. The wise move – it's about half-midnight – would be to catch some zzzzs ready for tomorrow, but unfortunately Wallace is too good company to be allowed to sneak off to the sack and a few hours are spent at the bar, bench racing with one of the world's best sportscar drivers and one of Britain's most pleasant professional racing drivers. And the best thing of all about Andy Wallace? He loves road cars, and he reads **evo**. The latter is a no-brainer of course, but not all racing drivers like road cars.

Another gorgeous day. Perfect for Morgan and Magee to snap a group shot of all the cars. What a collection. A mechanic in the garage where we fill up is so gobsmacked he rings a mate on his mobile and gets him to nip over for a gander.

Photography over, the group disperses. The Ruf is collected; Gruber leaves in a burst of turbo whine in the MTM; the Lotus men head off in the Elise that doesn't sound like an Elise and Samuelson leaves with Commander Haywood smoking the Tuscan's rear tyres. That just leaves the **evo** team and Wallace, Crawford and the Zonda S. There is unfinished business. Later, at night when the traffic has died down, Wallace and I plan to strap ourselves into the Pagani and go for it. What follows is what it feels like to chase 200mph…

TARGET: 200MPH
TVR TUSCAN S
Driver: John Barker

As I slogged my way down the clotted M11 to Stansted yesterday, the idea of going to another motorway in another country and reaching 200mph, legally, seemed both absurd and unlikely. Now that we're here in Germany where it can happen, the excitement of the meeting when we planned this feature has evaporated, replaced by a tongue-tingling apprehension stoked by the instinct for self-preservation.

'If it doesn't feel right, I'm not going to do this,' I tell Goodwin, who has hopped unbidden into the passenger seat of the Tuscan. He doesn't have to be here; the GPS test gear in his footwell will record everything automatically and the plug-in speedometer suckered to the windscreen will show the real speed in bright red digits.

In all honesty, I'd rather not be here. Maxing the TVR wasn't a job I volunteered for in that meeting – I chose the Ruf R Turbo because I had faith that Ruf could build a car that would take me confidently to 200mph for the first time. The Tuscan is here to take care of some unfinished business, and David Vivian should be driving it. He came to Germany to v-max it a year and a half ago (evo 035) and was foiled when the front spoiler broke at 165mph. Unfortunately (for me) he's busy on another job.

TVR claims '190mph-plus', which on paper makes it one of the slowest cars here. That doesn't mean that it's going to be a stroll, though. The 213mph Ruf should get to 200mph, if not

'I gun the Tuscan up the dark slip-road and the speedo is soon well into three figures'

easily then at least with tangible acceleration in hand, but winding out the Tuscan may well be a more drawn-out affair.

I gun the Tuscan's 390bhp straight-six up the dark slip-road onto the autobahn, the tailpipes blare with a note like a Spitfire, and the digital speedo is soon well into three figures. There are distracting vibrations from below, though. It's hard to know their source – a slight propshaft imbalance, perhaps, or an exhaust mount poorly isolated. 'You do worry that electrical connections and bolts might shake loose,' says Goodwin, matter-of-factly. I check the Tuscan's temperatures and pressures – all fine – note the long arc that the speedo needle still has to travel

before it reaches the final '200' mark, and slot the gearlever into top.

With 150 showing on the digital readout, the thrum of the drivetrain is no worse but the wind noise is at gale force and the instrument pod is shimmying so much the shift lights have blinked on a couple of times. 'It feels like we're attempting re-entry,' I shout to Goodwin.

Over the next brow the three-lane autobahn tracks dead straight for a couple of kilometres and is populated only by a string of trucks on the inside lane. I push the long-travel throttle pedal to the stop and the Tuscan surges forward again. At around 160 it's still pulling well but by 170 it feels like aerodynamic drag is getting the better of it. All three shift lights are illuminated well before 180, including the big red one in the middle, and I'm not sure if there's a rev limiter, but we're so close to 180 I keep it nailed. We've come this far in spite of the noise and vibration, the road ahead is still clear and although it's a slow process, the digits are still clicking over. Finally, after what feels like a fortnight, the Racelogic readout shows 180. I throttle back.

Once we're down to what feels like walking pace (actually 80mph), I say to Goodwin: 'I don't know who's more stupid – me for doing it or you for sitting alongside.' If there was anything left, it was no more than a couple of mph. Goodwin was watching the speedo needle and saw it get within a few increments of 200mph but the GPS logger shows our peak speed was 180.85mph, precisely. More than enough, I reckon.

It looks the part, it sounds the part, and up to a point it performs the part, but the Tuscan S is the least convincing of our contenders when it comes to ultra-high-speed work. TVR claims 190mph-plus, but perhaps not today

LOTUS ESTHI 2.4

Driver: Colin Goodwin

What's so crazy about an Elise with V6 power? Isn't that very much along the lines of what Lotus itself was preparing with the stillborn M250? Crazy? No. Perfectly logical and sensible in our book.

We've got used to German tuning companies doing a thorough job and the Esthi 2.4 is no exception. Esthi? Forgot to ask where the name came from. Sounds like a bloke with loose dentures trying to say Esprit.

The front and rear clamshells are both new and wider than standard with extra vents to channel more air to the radiators at the front of the car and to funnel hot air from the engine bay at the rear. This car is an early development vehicle and has thick, heavy clamshells that will be replaced with lighter pieces, bringing the kerb weight down from the current 990kg to just under 950kg.

The important factor is that Brandes & Dschüdow's engineers have managed to keep the weight distribution 35/65 per cent front/rear, just as it is on the standard car.

The longitudinally-mounted Audi engine is actually not far from standard. Just a special exhaust system, air filter and tweaks to the software that all add up to 420bhp fed through the standard six-speed transaxle.

In truth, I'm a little more concerned with two other items. First, brakes are rather important in a car whose top-end potential has been lifted from sub-150mph to 190mph. This car is fitted with Esprit brakes and an entire Esprit anti-lock system, which also explains its OZ Superleggera 3 wheels that are to the same dimensions as those of the Esprit (they have to be for the ABS system's controller to understand what's going on). The second technical aspect that I'm most interested in is the bodywork. The mk2 generates less negative downforce at speed than the original car, but nevertheless I'm very pleased to see a large front airdam to stop the air getting under the car and a larger than standard aerofoil on the rear deck.

Apart from the noise of a V6 at the back, you'd swear you were driving off in a standard Elise. The light, communicative steering is just the same and the way the car moves down the road identical. Elise and I slowly creep past lines of trucks in the service area. Four-fifty in the morning, more traffic on the autobahn than I'd

have wished for, but hey-ho here we go. The temperature gauge's needle is telling us that the motor is nice and warm – the oil temperature gauge appears to be up the spout – the four-point harness is tight and we're ready.

Out onto the sliproad, squint into the left hand mirror and… woooosh. Bloody hell. The yellow Lotus has suddenly stopped feeling at all standard. No wheelspin, just the scream of the 2671cc motor's two turbochargers and a steady, insistent thrust.

A few years ago I drove McLaren designer

Goodwin used to run an Elise and occasionally saw around 130mph. Today he's planning to add roughly 60mph to that, with help from the 420bhp twin-turbo V6 just behind his back. Created by a German Lotus dealer, the Elise-based Esthi has Esprit-based brakes and no doubt needs them

'No wheelspin, just the scream of the biturbo engine and insistent thrust'

Adrian Newey's 330bhp turbo Elise, which, as it was even lighter than standard, felt even more manic than this one. More manic and quite a bit less driveable. It was a scream, but pretty hard work and terrifying on the public road. The Esthi would be a lot easier to live with.

But right now it's being mad. We're up to 150mph in fifth gear and there's another cog to go. I had an Elsie for two years and I don't

remember ever bettering much more than 130mph. So far it feels fine. That front spoiler and rear aerofoil must be doing their stuff. The Esthi is a few centimetres wider in track than standard but only a fraction longer in wheelbase. I'm very wary of braking seriously hard in case the brake balance is not quite right and the little car tries to 180 on me.

It's so small, so quick. I am Jo Bonnier at Le

Mans in a DFV-powered Lola. Sixth gear, I dare hardly look, but a quick squint at the timing kit's digital readout sees 182mph.

Truck ahead. The brakes are excellent, but it's unnerving feeling the front end dip and the belts bite at your shoulders. It would have been preferable to have got to know the Esthi a little better before running at such high speeds, but whatever, I'm very impressed.

TARGET: 200MPH
RUF R TURBO
Driver: John Barker

'Less than five minutes after being handed the key, I've got to within 7mph of hitting 200mph'

The Ruf felt right almost immediately and sounded marvellous the moment it fired up. 'Ah, yes,' I thought, 'I've chosen well.' I snicked it into gear, intending to move it to where the rest of our cars were parked, and then just kept going, out of the car park, down the slip-road and onto the autobahn. It felt so taut, so firm and positive that I couldn't wait to see what it felt like at speed.

I didn't have to wait long; the midday autobahn was miraculously free of traffic and in a matter of seconds we were cruising at 160mph, effortlessly, Goodwin and I conversing at normal volume. Then I planted the throttle and the speedo needle swept on, eventually reaching 310kph (193mph), the Ruf utterly stable and unstressed. Incredible.

So, less than five minutes after Alois Ruf, boss of Ruf Automobile, had handed me the key to the R Turbo, I'd got to within 7mph of hitting 200mph (indicated). Piece of cake, this high-speed lark. Just last night, Alois had told me, this car had clocked over 340kph (211mph) on the virtually traffic-free two-lane autobahn near to Ruf's Pfaffenhausen HQ. I had every confidence that once it was dark here and the traffic had died away, I'd bag 200.

This R Turbo has a distinctly different feel to the one that was included in our Car of the Year feature a couple of years back (**evo** 039). That example was much more softly sprung, which occasionally made using all of its 520bhp fraught as the rear wheels attempted to ride bumps and transmit all that turbocharged horsepower simultaneously. This one sits lower and its chassis is much more tightly controlled – even in first and second gears it's untroubled by the massive torque produced by the flat-six. And what an engine it is – not just solidly, sensationally muscular, but blessed with a deep-chested, metallic-edged exhaust note that sounds especially good through the underpasses at our turn-around points.

A few hours after nightfall, we're fuelled up and ready to go for it, but it's soon clear that it's not going to be quite as easy as I expected. When we arrive at the long, straight sections, there are always glowing tail-lights in all three lanes. Occasionally we surge up to 180mph, once we get to over 190, but there isn't the space to go for 200.

It feels a little surreal to be ambling along at 160mph waiting for the right opportunity, but ambling is what it feels like we're doing. Into

The Ruf Turbo R is so beautifully, reassuringly engineered that its ability to hit the magical 200mph was never in doubt – it was merely a matter of when the road would be clear enough. Its most impressive party trick is to breeze up to an easy-going 160mph cruise, then pop up to the 190s for short bursts almost at will. Alois Ruf, owner of the company, reckoned to have run this particular car round to 211mph the night before. And this isn't the fastest car Ruf builds...

another straight section and there's only inside-lane traffic. The hammer goes down but this isn't one of the longer straights and we've reached 'only' 193mph before the next brow. I momentarily consider keeping it nailed, knowing there's another straight on the other side, but sense prevails, and we enter the next stretch with 170 on the readout. There are trucks on the inside lane and in the distance two cars in the middle lane. The turbos of the flat-six blow hard, the gradient helps us to over 190 in short order and out of the corner of my eye I can see the digits rolling over until they've reached 196. So close, yet so far. Half a mile ahead, one of the cars pulls out. I keep it nailed for a second more before Goodwin says loudly, 'Er, John'. The brakes go on hard and moments later we're bimbling along behind the overtaking car at 80mph.

There's no point in getting frustrated; it's just a matter of time before the right circumstances fall into place. When they do, an hour later, I'm on my own and there is absolutely no drama, which is as it should be. It takes a little longer than anticipated to get the speed up from 197 because the totally empty straight is on a slight but appreciable incline but eventually the Racelogic speedo flashes up '200'. Thank you, Ruf, and goodnight.

TARGET: 200MPH
MTM BIMOTO
Driver: Jethro Bovingdon

Strapping myself into the MTM Bimoto for the final run in the dark was an intensely lonely and intimidating experience. Everyone new that this was the car that should go fastest but there was also a tangible sense that the twin-engined TT was going to be the wildest ride. I'd felt relaxed up until a few minutes ago but the well-wishers had me twitching. There's nothing like a chorus of 'good lucks' through gritted teeth from your colleagues to send the mind racing with all the dreadful scenarios that might unfold.

Just think about it. Doing 200mph on the road is a risky business, doing it in a car with twice as many mechanical components to go wrong is absurd – add to that the TT's questionable stability and the memory of those high-profile autobahn crashes that forced an aerodynamic rethink, and you're staring fear and blind panic right in the face. Pulling out of the service station and onto the autobahn approach road, I begin to wonder what the hell I'm doing. Maybe traffic will hand me an honourable pardon.

Bizarrely, it's now that any trace of nerves disappears. It's a tight slip road but there's nothing behind as I join the three-lane autobahn and a quick squirt through the gears sends the Racelogic digital display haywire – within what seems like a few seconds the MTM has hit 170mph. An earlier warm-up run has yielded 188mph in moderately heavy traffic, but even so, the ferocity of the Bimoto's performance is still

Believe it or not, this car has seen 230mph at Nardo. Bovingdon (above) settles into the groove of hunting down 200mph+, but keeps a tight grip on the wheel – the MTM's madly quick but has a tendency to meander around a bit at very high speeds

shocking. Later we'll learn that a wrung-out Zonda can't live with the Bimoto even when it's surfing along in sixth.

But despite the frantic acceleration and the venomous hiss of the wastegate just behind my shoulder, I'm totally detached from the mayhem in which I'm immersed. It's odd but I'm utterly relaxed – almost like my brain has switched off some of the reasoning faculties to allow me to concentrate solely on hitting 200mph. A blind brow slows progress but as I crest the hill it becomes clear that it's now or never. Lorries are in the right-hand lane but the outer two lanes are clear. This is as good a chance as I'll ever get.

It's dark and the red tail-lights of slow-moving lorries pick out the road ahead. The Bimoto has pathetic headlights which cast a tiny pool of yellow light only a few feet from the end of the bonnet. For once I'm glad of the traffic, which makes judging distances easier and acts as a vivid reminder that this is the public highway. It's an otherworldly experience – there's so much to take in; I've got half an eye on the digital speed readout and the rest of my attention is focused

on the seemingly stationary traffic in the inside lane and the deviating trajectory of the TT. It weaves alarmingly between gearshifts – even into 6th at 175mph.

Over about 190mph it feels about 10 feet wide as it meanders from lane to lane. You can't make panic corrections at this sort of speed so I simply hang on and guide it as straight as I can.

Fortunately the Bimoto is so fast I don't have to be too patient; 190 becomes 200 very quickly

and I hold on until the display burns 204. At this point the slope is about to bottom-out and there's a lorry fast approaching so I back-off, hoping that the compression doesn't upset the Bimoto any further. The red LED is reading 190 and the lorry disappears from my mirrors like an apparition. That's it: 200mph on the road. Time to head back to base camp.

The return route is snarled up and I'm tickling along at 60 or 70mph. There's no sense of elation

yet. In fact, I'm cursing the congestion. There's a police car escorting a wide load, hence the hold-up – but I clear it at the bottom of the gentle slope that helped the Bimoto scream over the double-ton. The car in front indicates right and in that split-second I decide to do it again. This time I notice the flashes of orange that illuminate the cabin between gears as unburnt fuel ignites in the Bimoto's furious wake.

With the hill against me, quick shifts are crucial and I realise that I'm steering one-handed; the other's resting on the gearlever to optimise changes. Into sixth and hold on. At 190 the pace is slowing and the numbers click up individually. 199, 200, 201… okay, that'll do. 204.8mph in one direction and 201.14mph uphill in the other. That's what 740bhp can do for you.

Only now that I'm writing about the adventure do I begin to realise just how insane it was. Overtaking at over three-miles a minute, guiding a car that bobbed and weaved to over 200mph, even the pangs of disappointment that I didn't get to 210mph. Utter madness, but deliciously thrilling. I'd do it again tomorrow.

200MPH AND BEYOND: Datalogging read-outs from the MTM Bimoto and Pagani Zonda S

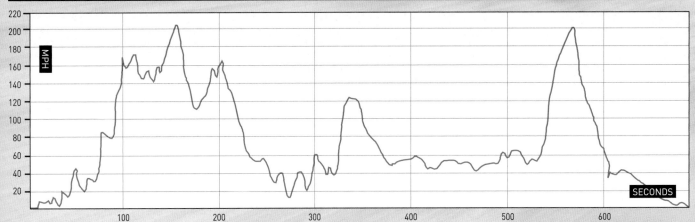

▲ Even in a car as wildly powerful as the MTM Bimoto, finding the space to breach the 200mph barrier requires patience and good luck. Here you can see the peaks where Bovingdon had clear road ahead and could wring the twin-engined car right out. The frequent troughs show where trucks and other heavy traffic hindered his progress for extended periods of time

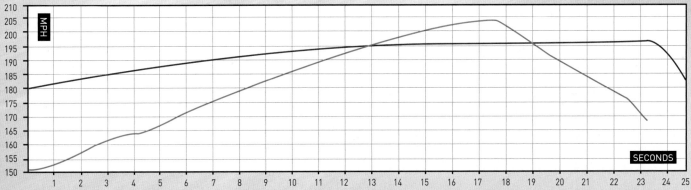

▲ The traces seen here (as with the graph above, recorded using a Racelogic VBOX) show the relative performance of the Zonda S (blue line) and the MTM Bimoto (red line). The Zonda's trace reveals a slow, steady climb to its peak speed, whereas the MTM, over the same time-frame, was able to accelerate from a far lower base and reach a far higher top speed

TARGET: 200MPH
PAGANI ZONDA S
Driver: Andy Wallace

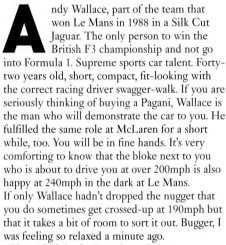

Andy Wallace, part of the team that won Le Mans in 1988 in a Silk Cut Jaguar. The only person to win the British F3 championship and not go into Formula 1. Supreme sports car talent. Forty-two years old, short, compact, fit-looking with the correct racing driver swagger-walk. If you are seriously thinking of buying a Pagani, Wallace is the man who will demonstrate the car to you. He fulfilled the same role at McLaren for a short while, too. You will be in fine hands. It's very comforting to know that the bloke next to you who is about to drive you at over 200mph is also happy at 240mph in the dark at Le Mans. If only Wallace hadn't dropped the nugget that you do sometimes get crossed-up at 190mph but that it takes a bit of room to sort it out. Bugger, I was feeling so relaxed a minute ago.

I have faith in the Pagani, too. It is an incredible achievement, this car. Fresh out of the box it feels sophisticated, predictable, driveable and most importantly for this evening's exercise, extremely stable at speed. We can also trust the AMG-built 7.3-litre Mercedes V12 to not throw a rod or spit its oil out onto the rear tyres.

We have found the most perfect section of autobahn that runs east/west between Mainz and Kaiserslautern. It's very quiet with some very long straights, some with a nice gentle downhill approach that will shorten the time it takes the big car to hit its best speed.

It is the same for drivers as it is for cars. Within a few metres you know that the Pagani is a serious piece of kit just by the way its controls feel and the way it moves across the tarmac even at 10mph. If you've driven with a few great wheelmen you can spot one as soon as he selects a gear and feeds in the throttle. In fact, with a driver of Wallace's talent even the relaxed and methodical way he sits in the car and prepares for the off gives his skill away.

I almost envy the others who are standing in the parking area as Wallace and I drive off onto the autobahn. The Zonda S sounds pretty good from the inside, but from outside it sounds incredible. Just what it will sound like as we pass by them on our run at over 200mph I don't know. Like Armageddon I guess.

The autobahn is quiet, but not empty. It's going to be a matter of cruising at about 130mph then punching the throttles open when we see a break ahead of us. Did I say 130mph? Look again, Goodwin, Wallace has got the Zonda up to a steady 165-170mph cruise. It's noisy alright, but there's also calm inside the cabin. Wallace is concentrating 110 per cent, as if he was on the Mulsanne at night looking for the odd straggling Porsche 911 driven by a slow gentleman-driver.

I have never been around a corner at speeds such as these. One-seventy-five and then full throttle on the straight. The numbers on our digital readout are climbing slowly now. After a few seconds of the big V12 roaring at full throttle the speed readout stops at 194mph then flutters one or two mph either side. The Zonda S has stopped accelerating. We back off and Wallace speaks for the first time in a few minutes. 'I think we'll take the top two Gurneys off.' Oh, that'll be the little flaps that give us extra rear downforce will it? 'Yeah, but the car is so stable – much more so than a McLaren,' says Wallace, 'that I don't think it'll be a problem.' Back at base Wallace unscrews the Gurneys while the **evo** crew stands jawdropped at the back of the Pagani watching those characteristic four exhaust tailpipes glowing cherry-red.

Above left: Le Mans winner Andy Wallace – who better to max the fabulous Zonda C12 S? Below: Goodwin enjoys the ride

Out again and still we can do no better than about 195mph. 'It still feels fine,' says our man, 'so we take off the bottom two Gurneys as well.' Wallace has obviously got the bit between his teeth. Has he just. Even with just the small rear wings the Zonda feels fantastically secure. Now we're going through the gentle bends at over 190mph and I'm mesmerised. I have driven many times at these speeds but never have I seen 190mph with steering lock on. I'll happily sit next to Barker and Bovingdon at these speeds, too, but having Wallace at the wheel is admittedly a huge benefit to my overall karma.

'It's not going to happen,' shouts Wallace. We've been sat at 196/7mph for what seems an age and the Zonda S is all in. We could go on, hoping for a puff of tailwind or a pocket of cold air to give an extra few bhp, but we're playing Russian roulette. Eventually something will happen that even Wallace can't deal with.

I love and respect the Pagani Zonda S even more now. I mean, what would you like? A car that can hit 220mph but is so unstable that it could kill you? Or would you prefer a machine that at 197mph feels as well planted on the ground as it does at 90mph? For me it's an easy one. I can live with the 'shame' of owning a supercar that won't reach well over 200mph.

Colin Goodwin

DMS AUTOMOTIVE
UNLEASHING PERFORMANCE

DMS 997 TURBO
"IT'S EPIC, HILARIOUS AND ADDICTIVE IN EVERY GEAR,
YET DOCILE WHEN CRUISING"
EVO SEPTEMBER 2008

DMS SL55 AMG
"THIS CAR IS STUPENDOUSLY FAST"
PERFORMANCE CAR MAY 2008

DMS 535D
"FROM THE WORD GO, THE DMS 535D FELT AWESOME"
AUTO EXPRESS FEB 2008

DMS 997 TURBO
"MIGHTY IMPRESSIVE. SEAMLESSLY IMPROVES THE
TURBO'S BEST ASSET"
EVO MAY '07

DMS 535D
"LAUGH-OUT-LOUD FAST"
REVIEWED EVO JUNE 2005

DMS 330CD
"NEW ECU MAKES THE CAR SO MUCH FASTER YOU
SIMPLY HAVE TO HAVE IT!"
REVIEWED AUTOCAR OCTOBER 04

DMS 996 TURBO
"STUPENDOUS EXPLOITABLE PERFORMANCE"
REVIEWED EVO AUGUST 04

DMS 996 TURBO
"NOT ONLY IS THERE STAGGERING TORQUE,
THE POWER IS UTTERLY ADDICTIVE"
REVIEWED AUTOCAR JULY 2004

PORSCHE:
997 TURBO » 600+ BHP
996 TURBO / GT2 » 600+ BHP
997 CARRERA S PDK » 400+ BHP
997 CARRERA S » 376+ BHP
997 CARRERA » 348 BHP
997 CARRERA PDK » 368 BHP
997 GT3 UP » 436 BHP
996 GT3 UP » 400 BHP
996 3.6 » 344 BHP
BOXSTER 3.4S » 313+ BHP
CAYMAN S » 317 BHP
CAYENNE GTS » 440 BHP
CAYENNE TURBO 4.5 » 522 BHP
CAYENNE TURBO 4.8 » 578 BHP
CAYENNE TURBO S 4.8 » 600+ BHP

MERCEDES-BENZ:
SL65 AMG » 650 BHP & DE-LIMIT
AMG 55 KOMPRESSOR » 580+ BHP
AMG 55 FULL DE-LIMIT
C63 AMG » 530+ BHP & DE-LIMIT
SL63 AMG » 560+ BHP, DE-LIMIT
RE-MAP & LOWER ABC SUSPENSION
CL600 BI-TURBO » 580+ BHP
S500 2008 » 411+ BHP
SLK55 AMG » 389 BHP
SLK 350 » 328 BHP
200K » 205+ BHP
VIANO CDI V6 » 266 BHP
280 CDI V6 » 257 BHP
320 CDI V6 » 274 BHP
420 CDI V8 » 358 BHP

BMW:
BMW M5 V10 » 548 BHP 205 MPH
M3 E90/92 » 445 BHP + DE-LIMIT
M3 E46 » 370 BHP + DE-LIMIT
M3 CSL » 372 BHP + DE-LIMIT
335I » 370+ BHP + DE-LIMIT
650I » 398 BHP + DE-LIMIT
330D E90 » 276+ BHP
320D E90 » 209 BHP
330D E46 » 260+ BHP
320D E92 » 210 BHP
123D » 252 BHP
X5 3.0D » 278 BHP
X6 35I » 370+ BHP
X5 / X6 SD » 334 BHP
535D / 335D » 334 BHP

EXOTIC & MISC:
FERRARI 599 » 647 BHP
FERRARI 430 » 525 BHP
FERRARI 360 » 440+ BHP
GALLARDO » 546 BHP
GALLARDO LP560 » 600+ BHP
MASERATI GRANTURISMO &
QUATTROPORTE » 438 BHP
AUDI RS6 V10 » 680+BHP & DE-LIMIT
AUDI B7 RS4/ R8 » 439 BHP & DE-LIMIT
AUDI Q7 4.2 TDI » 387 BHP
AUDI A5 30TDI » 282 BHP
RANGE ROVER TDV8 » 326 BHP
R ROVER SPORT 4.2 SC » 450 BHP
R ROVER SPORT 2.7D » 232 BHP
BENTLEY CGT / F-SPUR » 620 BHP
BENTLEY GT SPEED » 670+ BHP

ALL OTHER CARS PLEASE CALL US

SINCE 1990

WORLDWIDE OFFICES AND INSTALLATION
UK » IRELAND » EUROPE » USA » ASIA » AUSTRALIA

+44 (0) 845 850 1845
SALES@DMSAUTOMOTIVE.COM
WWW.DMSAUTOMOTIVE.COM

SPEED
ADDICTS

We've all done it at some time – driven a car as fast as it will go. In 2003 we asked regular **evo** contributors to recall some unforgettable high-speed moments

Roger Green
Vanquishing an M3

It's 9am one sunny Sunday morning in early November. A four-car convoy is making good time along the autoroute between Dijon and Troyes on its way back from southern Tuscany and the tail-end of one of **evo**'s greatest weeks, eCOTY 2001. I'm leading and setting the pace in an Aston Vanquish, barely ambling at a little over 100mph.

The weather is perfect, there's no-one else on the road and the temptation to get my clog down is becoming harder and harder to resist. Just then a flash of gold screams past on the left. It's the M3, which until a few seconds ago was playing rear-gunner. It's now running on the speed-limiter and is quickly followed by the stubby, bellowing rear-end of a TVR Tamora and a full-boost Mitsubishi Evo VII.

Gauntlets on the floor, then. Nothing for it but to show them who's boss and reassert the Vanquish to the front of the queue. Left hand flicks the paddle down to third, right foot mashes pedal to carpet. Aston squats and fires itself at the horizon, the 6-litre V12 delivering thrust and decibels in equal quantities. No car has ever sounded better, and deep into three figures there's no wind noise to dilute it.

As I re-pass the M3 I move back up to sixth gear with a new target: top speed. The Vanquish keeps charging, remaining as stable and as unstressed as it was at a ton. As the speedo needle nudges 190mph there's still a couple of hundred revs to play with and we're still accelerating. But there's a corner in the distance and the point has been proved, so I ease back and allow the others to catch back up. The Aston felt like it could have done it all day.

Brett Fraser
Going like the Devil

The Lamborghini PR man literally threw us the keys to the Diablo SV saying 'enjoy yourselves, see you in a couple of days'. No fuss, no paperwork. Bright red, big SV badges across its flanks, showing signs of being hard-used by the factory boys, the devilish supercar was ours to do with as we pleased.

This was the mid-'90s and we were heading out to the Stelvio Pass on the Italian/Swiss border to do a feature on mountain roads for *Performance Car,* but it was quite a hike along the *autostradi* to get there. And at the time this was the quickest car 'sensible' money could buy.

Even so, concerns about the Italian police kept our cruising speed down to 120mph, until a superbike arrived, aggressively, on our tail. It was one of those occasions when you think, 'I know I shouldn't, but...' Click-clacking the gearlever back across the gate into third caused the Diablo to snort and rage like a crazed bull, and turned the throttle from a pedal into a trigger.

For a short distance the bike dropped us, but as the Diablo hit high revs our two-wheeled antagonist was soon reeled back in. At 150mph the Lambo bellowed past the biker, who raised a finger off the bars in tribute; at 160mph he was a speck in the rear-view mirror and at 170mph he'd disappeared. At about 178mph I noticed the wires protruding from the marker boards in the central reservation that could have been timing gear for a radar trap.

Maybe I should have pressed on; the Diablo still had lots more to give. Afterwards I wished I had. After all, you may as well get busted for going flat-out as for 178.

Richard Meaden
Big-number Porsches

A comparison between Porsche's then-new all-wheel-drive 993 Turbo and Carrera 4 against the legendary 959 for *Performance Car* resulted in the fastest three days of my life.

Having collected the Turbo from Porsche's Reading HQ the previous night, I made a 5am start from my parents house in Surrey next morning for a rendezvous with Gus Gregory and a Little Chef breakfast just north of Grantham. A journey of some 140 miles. The M25 and A1 were deserted, save for a few trucks. 'Don't go balls-out,' I told myself, 'just cool it and settle at a cruising speed the Porsche feels comfortable at.' Very responsible, I'm sure you'll agree.

So imagine my surprise when, having exercised such restraint, I arrived at the aforementioned roadside eatery at 06.30. It began to dawn on me that perhaps my idea of a 'comfortable cruise' might need a little fine adjustment. Somewhat farcically, I then had to wait in the car park for half an hour as the bloody place didn't open until 7.00.

Still, that was nothing compared to driving the 959 across the moors. I'd been following John Barker, who was in the 993 Turbo, and become stuck in traffic. By the time I cleared the last lumbering truck, JB was a high-speed pixel on the far horizon. The road stretched out before me, deserted, no side turnings for miles and straight enough to prompt one of those 'Shall I, shan't I?' moments. Shall beat shan't, and as the cockpit filled with a soundtrack straight from Le Mans, the 959 battered its way to an indicated 185mph before I lost my resolve and backed off. I'm glad I seized the moment then, for it won't come my way again, not in the UK at least.

Left: in the late '60s and early '70s Ferrari's Daytona was emphatically the world's fastest production car, capable of 170mph-plus. Its braking performance, however, left something to be desired, especially by modern standards – a point brought home to Ian Fraser when he drove his own Daytona on the autobahn in the early '90s (see page 137)

the distance in about an hour. That's what we did: 150 miles in one hour. I've never bettered that average and never will. Probably.

We were headed for Maranello to return the car, taking the route along the French and Italian rivieras rather than through the Mont Blanc tunnel, for no other reason than I love this part of the world, and particularly the *autoroute* that runs along the Cote d'Azur.

Above Frejus we picked up a turbo Bentley driven by a toff with attitude. He was well on it, his motor rocking and rolling at close to 150mph. We zapped him at 170, then knocked it back and sat behind giggling at the sight of Crewe's missile flat-out, then we waved goodbye and wound the needle up again and pressed on towards Monaco.

I've sat in McLarens at 210mph, white-knuckled a Diablo SV to 200mph in Sardinia and done speeds at home that are best left for me to remember in old age. That road trip in the Ferrari 456GT was sweetest though, because it was one of my first runs in a Ferrari and the first time that I used a top end of 186mph to really shrink a big country.

David Yu
The big bang

My first Skyline, a dark metallic blue 440bhp R32, which I bought in 1995, bludgeoned its way to an indicated 170mph on the runway at Bruntingthorpe during the filming of the first of Jeremy Clarkson's videos. I could tell there was more to come, but realised it would take more space than a 1.7-mile runway.

The opportunity arose the following Easter when I was given special dispensation to bring the 'noisy Datsun' along on the annual Ferrari Owners Club chateau-visiting expedition. Company that year included a couple of F40s, one of them tuned to an estimated 600-ish prancing ponies.

Having the third most powerful car in the group, I was forever goading the F40's owner into mini-sprints on the wide open French tarmac, and on the return journey on Easter Monday, a couple of hundred miles from Calais, he finally opened up his mad motor all the way in fifth, hitting something like 217mph as I vainly tried to keep up, watching him gradually disappear over the horizon.

The Skyline was maxing out at 180mph with the Brunette and I laughing at the sight of the Ferrari getting ever further away, when suddenly I noticed the oil temperature had sky-rocketed and before I had time to react there was a huge explosion from the engine room followed by the sickening sound of internal parts being sprayed liberally against the underside of the car.

I remember being strangely calm and, with a gentle expletive, slotted the gearbox into neutral and drifted over to the hard shoulder where we came to a halt. It turned out that four of the six con-rods had punched their way through the cast iron block. It was the beginning of a decision to replace the ageing R32 GT-R with a brand new, hence reliable R33 GT-R V-spec. If only I'd known...

Martin Buckley
Classic speed moments

Within the first few weeks of passing my test I got over a ton in my dad's Volvo 240GLT estate which, at the time, was a quick car. Later I remember seeing 126mph out of a Lancia that was only supposed to do 115. I found I could coax really anaemic cars like a 1.6 automatic Sierra and a 900cc Peugeot 205 well into three figures, so by the time I got my hands on my first really quick car, a Renault 5 Turbo, I was well-versed in the delicate art of pressing the accelerator as hard as possible and holding onto a steering wheel while going in as straight a line as possible. I think 135 was the record out of that one.

Driving old cars quickly on a motorway is great because nobody expects you to go past them and somehow you feel almost immune to the law, because they'd never believe what you were driving was capable of highly illegal velocities. The finest hour for my NSU Ro80 was a late-night run from Nottingham to the London end of the M1 in 1 hour 15 minutes, which is a wonderful if expensive way to travel; 9mpg out of a 2-litre engine puts things into perspective a bit.

My personal finest hour should have been 175 (or whatever it is they are supposed to do) in a Lotus Carlton on a German autobahn. I managed 160

until the editor of the magazine decided he should be the one to get the figures for the story, robbing me of my moment of glory. Still, it didn't matter because in 2001 an **evo** trip to the Lamborghini factory gave me the chance for a go in a last-of-the-line Diablo. I wasn't there to 'figure' it but driving between two roundabouts for the photographer's panning shots I saw 175mph several times before a jab of brakes seemed advisable.

Colin Goodwin
Bentley-bashing in a 456GT

We smoked past the gendarme in his Renault 4 at about 175mph and the wake from our Ferrari 456GT wobbled and nearly turned over the little French cop car. But there were no 'phone calls ahead and no difficulties at tollbooths. Perhaps we were travelling so quickly that he didn't take it in.

Whatever, we carried on towards the French Riviera, cruising at super speed. Apart from the odd straggling *gendarmerie* car, the autoroute was quiet. The ability to sustain a cruising gait of at least 150mph is essential in a continental touring GT car. You really can chomp up the miles in a car like the 456GT. It's such a joy to see a sign that says 'Aix-en-Provence 250' and know that you can cover

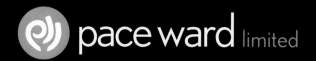 **pace ward** limited

Family Fleet Insurance

About Our Family Fleet Insurance

Family Fleet policies are aimed at Mid to High Net Worth families who own an assortment of vehicles including cars, classic cars, motorcycles and special types such as sports and performance cars generally over group 15.

Policies of this nature can be flat rated i.e. if a further vehicle is added; No Claims Bonus information is not required.

With a Family Fleet policy you can vary the cover on individual vehicles ranging from accidental damage, fire and theft through to comprehensive. Single vehicles with values in excess of £1 million have been covered.

We can also offer Portfolio Insurance which combines Home, Motor, Pleasure Craft and Holiday Home insurance under one policy.

Family Fleet Policy Features

- Agreed value on **ANY VEHICLE***
  (this is an excellent way to protect against depreciation on high specification vehicles)
- New Vehicle replacement cover
- A quality courtesy car for the duration of the repairs (should the worst happen)
- Unlimited cover for replacement of locks following loss of keys with no excess
  (some policies have a £250 or £500 limit, lock sets can easily exceed £800)
- £500 Personal effects cover with no excess to pay
- European Certificates
- Contribution towards security
- Aggregate mileage on a combination of vehicles
- **Track day cover** is also avaliable

We also offer High Net Worth Home Insurance policies
Tailored to meet specific insurance needs.

Ticking boxes or feeding postcodes into a computer does not arrive at these policies. We recognise that every person will present an individual set of requirements and our products reflect this.
Our policy features include:

- Warranty Free Policies
  (No alarm conditions, No Jewellery safe conditions, contact us for more information.)
- Worldwide Contents Cover
- Identity Theft Cover

Track Day Insurance

- Pace Ward can also offer one-off track day insurance for cars.

This cover is very comprehensive, call or visit our website for more details. *Available on application.

For more information or a quote please call us on: 01782 286311
Or visit our website at: www.pw-f.co.uk

Pace Ward Limited • 2 Etruria Office Village, Forge Lane, Festival Park, Stoke on Trent, ST1 5RQ

Email: motor@pw-f.co.uk • Tel: 01782 286311 • Fax: 01782 204707

 **pace ward** limited

Peter Dron
190mph on the hard shoulder

In 1986, I drove to Italy to test Lamborghini's latest Countach, the 5000 Quattrovalvole (without that stupid wing). As usual at Lamborghini, they insisted that I was expected the following week, we had an argument, then testing proceeded.

I was told that for the maximum speed test, to be conducted (totally illegally) on an *autostrada*, I would be passenger, with a Lamborghini test driver (introduced as 'Piero') at the wheel. After a couple of bends, I was impressed enough with Piero's ability to ask if he did any motor racing. Piero replied that yes he did, actually, and had won a Formula 3000 race on Sunday. It was Pierluigi Martini.

For the performance testing it seemed unwise to attach a fifth wheel to measure such high speeds on the public highway, even in Italy, so it had to be done using digital stopwatches and kilometre posts. The top speed figures were disputed afterwards, but nobody ever bettered our standing starts with a Countach.

The speeds recorded (no doubt this will restart the old arguments) were 184.9mph in one direction and 195.2mph in the other, giving a mean of 190.1mph. The speedometer was reading 320kph (199mph), the rev needle well into the red. In the quicker direction, two distant specks rapidly became little Fiats; one pulled out at a critical moment to pass the other, the driver not having checked his mirrors. We zapped them on the hard shoulder at around 190mph. I glanced at Piero. He was grinning from ear to ear.

Ian Fraser
Daytona vs Trabant

Germany's reunification was expensive. Not only did the Americans and West Germans have to pay the Russians a fortune for the acquisition of the communist sector but it also cost me, personally, a horse-choking wad of sterling.

Within a couple of years of the two Germanys coming together again, I happened to be in transit through Bavaria en route to Italy. Settling into a cruise of about 125mph with an occasional burst to substantially more – the Daytona is a 170mph car after all – it became apparent that the much-vaunted *autobahn* lane discipline had gone to pot for reasons I could not grasp. Every so often some gasping Opel or wheezing old Mercedes diesel would, unpredictably and without signals, stray into the overtaking lane which, as everyone in Europe knows, is the preserve of modern Mercs, quick BMWs, 911s and red cars from Modena.

There were moments when I thought I may become a key player in one of that day's more important accidents. While it's true the Daytona still has sufficient performance to keep it in today's supercar league, its stopping power is of another generation. After a sharp joust to 150mph with a 911, a car with brilliant brakes, I backed right off and started reading the minds and number plates of my fellow road-users. It became apparent that many of them were from the old Eastern sector of the country, more accustomed to Trabants than anything else and as unfamiliar with autobahn driving as I am with donkey carts.

Gordon Murray
Accelerating hard at 200mph

A few years ago when we were racing the F1 GTRs in the world championship, I took the opportunity to drive our F1 road car to Hockenheim and back. I'd driven some 6000 miles in prototype F1s when I was sorting out ride and handling, steering, brakes, etc, but I'd never had the opportunity to use the car as a customer would. XP3 prototype wasn't quite up to the very high standard of finish our chaps achieved in the production cars, but it did have the added benefit of being even faster. It was a little lighter than the final car at just 1120kg and the engine was giving about 660bhp thanks to a special exhaust system and the fact that it had always had a more powerful 'old' engine.

The first part of the journey across France and Belgium was pretty uneventful (and slow). I travelled at between 80 and 110mph; the car returned 26mpg.

Germany was a different story – as soon as I could I was having a fantastic time in the top three gears on the autobahn, using the F1 to the max. Speak to the other owners and they will tell you this is sensational stuff – 100mph to 180mph is about 14 seconds! This is where the F1 is in its element; it was not designed as a track car. The suspension is medium/soft, the air-con works, the sound system too (although I far prefer the raucous sound of the intake!).

Some people knew the F1; others didn't have a clue. The 'boy racer' in me surfaced and I responded to nearly all the 'let's see how fast it goes' challenges! Unfortunately, the Porches and Ferraris weren't really a contest, but I did get company from a biker for a couple of hours. He was on something very quick and we spent ages using sign language to communicate things like 'try full throttle in third'. The bike was pretty quick up to 150mph but from 150 to 200mph the F1 just disappeared.

It was quite sobering to find that if you feathered the throttle at 200mph and then banged it open, there was still a healthy push in the back! At these speeds the aero wing made a big difference.

My funniest encounter was with a chap in an unbadged 7-series BMW. We were in the queue to overtake a truck, both being very patient and travelling at about 50mph. Eventually when the line of cars had passed and moved over into the other lanes, we decided to stay in the fast lane. I saw the telltale puff of smoke as he dropped gears and floored it! I stayed a reasonable distance behind as the BMW went rapidly from 50 to 70 then 100, 120 and then more slowly crept up to 150 and stayed there. Eventually he grudgingly moved into the middle lane and the devil in me took over. I pulled alongside, slowed to his speed, looked across, dropped from sixth to fifth, then floored the throttle. The BMW was very quickly a dot in the mirror! Ever so childish but great fun...

Some years later I saw mention of a brake upgrade for Daytonas. So the Ferrari, little used since the trip through Germany, was taken out of storage and given the miracle of new life. It now stops brilliantly and I'm looking forward to a return bout on the *autobahns*. However, I shall have to save up: the upgrade was rather more costly than your routine change of pads. No regrets, but not much surplus dosh either.

John Hayman
Going nowhere fast

OK, I'm ready, let's do it! Time to max out evo's Audi RS6, newly derestricted. Palms sweating, the whites of my knuckles are distracting my sight-line through the letter-box slit of a windscreen. Eyes are dancing between the speedo and the forward view... 100... 130... 150... the rev-counter still climbing with alarming speed... 170... 190...195... 197... 200... 202... 205mph!

The noise bouncing around the cabin is deafening; Christ this is scary! My eyes are locked onto the whited-out vista ahead of me... not even 10 feet ahead of me! Thoughts of loss of life are scrambling through my head. What if? What if a bearing overheats and seizes? What if a tyre blows? Christ, I'll be through that wall at 205mph...

Very quickly it's all over. The rev limiter is doing its stuff and stuttering away. Done it! Time to slow down and shut the bonnet. I've never had so much fun on a rolling road before...

David Vivian
The hire car

Seeing how fast a fast car will go on a ruler-straight German autobahn – purely out of curiosity – is fine. In a sense, if the opportunity presents itself, it has to be done. But there are no material benefits, no obvious set of consequences, apart, maybe, from temporarily enhanced levels of spatial awareness and concentration.

Seeing how fast an ostensibly slow car will go on a twisting, writhing Italian *autostrada* when you've missed the last Ryanair flight out of Bologna and need to catch the last Ryanair flight out of Pisa is a different matter. It has an acute real-world dimension. The cast of attendant emotions includes fear, dread, panic, whatever it is that causes absurd rictus grinning and, yes – as you drag yet one more whole mile per hour from an engine so terminally over-extended it can only be operating in a state of quantum uncertainty – elation.

True, photographer Morgan and I had experienced elation just hours earlier inside the cabin of the

fastest production car.

It was dark and we were heading south in the McLaren F1 after a long and exhilarating day on the North Yorks Moors. On one unusually smooth stretch of B-road we came onto an arrow-straight stretch of at least a mile.

The F1 came onto the straight in third gear, so that magnificent 6-litre V12 was digging deep. For passengers riding 'sidesaddle' to the centrally placed driver, the sound of the V12 climbing up the torque curve is incredible because the air intake is right by your head. The throttle stayed wide open, the slow, almost metallic clack-clack! of chunks of air being ingested quickly speeding up until the V12 had begun to howl. Virgin passengers sometimes join in, for this is when the engine gets a hold of the F1 and starts to slam it forwards. Then there's another unbelievable surge as it hits a sort of VTEC cam- phase at 5500rpm.

The 7500rpm limiter isn't long coming after that, and there's still plenty of straight left. Is our driver up for it? Oh yes. He snicks the lever crisply into fourth (at 125mph) and the V12 resumes its savagery. Moments later he engages fifth (150mph) and although I've felt the force many times today, the fact that the acceleration seems barely diminished as we close on 7500rpm in fifth is simply awesome. Simultaneously we hit the limiter and a surface/gradient change that probably barely registers if you're doing 60mph but which induces a severe compression at three times that. Our driver eases off; enough.

Richard Porter
Mini to the max

I remember the intense rush of the wind past the windscreen pillars. I remember the scream of the engine just in front of my feet. I remember the thrilling sensation of a machine working at the very extreme of its ability and the sheer effort of concentration as the wheel shifted and writhed in my clammy palms. The one thing I don't remember is realising that I was a lanky student with stupid hair and a heavy right foot and I shouldn't have been howling along a downhill stretch of the M6 in a mate's 1275cc Mini doing an indicated 100mph. If that had occurred to me maybe it wouldn't have been in such bother when, soon afterwards, we arrived at the back of a very big traffic jam. Not a problem for a horsepower-heavy Italian sex-wedge with equator-sized discs and callipers like baseball gloves; rather more of an issue for a piddly little Noddy car pushing its luck somewhere near Keele.

I remember hoofing the brakes as hard as I could. I remember the front wheels locking and smoke curling prettily over the front wings. At some point I remember switching on the hazards, perhaps reasoning that it'd make it easier for the emergency services to find the wreckage. I remember we came to a halt just inches from the back bumper of the immobile Astra ahead. But most of all, I remember learning a valuable lesson: the thing about going fast is that at some point you're going to have to stop. ∎

violently accelerative and noisy Edonis supercar we'd come to northern Italy to feature. Probably too much. That's why we missed the flight. And that's why we now had to find out exactly how fast our payload-burdened and hitherto resolutely sluggish 1.6-litre Renault Megane Estate hire car would go.

Andy felt that as I had only recently been piloting the 650bhp Edonis, the responsibility should be mine. It was obvious the Megane's life thus far had been desperately tough and we wondered if this might finish it off. Then, when we joined the autostrada south, something rather unexpected happened. We discovered that although the Renault's acceleration was as mild as Fairy Liquid, it showed every sign of lasting just as long. Our jaws loosened as, on the first decent straight, the speedo needle crawled past the 120mph mark and kept on going. Patience and a right foot jammed hard into the carpet was rewarded with a further 10mph.

Suddenly we were mixing it with 5-series BMWs and E-class Mercs. The autostrada snaked through valleys and punched through mountains and incredibly, an hour later, we were still part of this mostly German high-speed convoy. In fact, the only thing that had overtaken us was a weird evolutionary regression where our foreheads narrowed and receded from our brows, our jaw bones acquired a Coulthard-esque prominence and gauge and we started bouncing up and down in our seats, hitting the steering wheel and dashboard and screeching. Our reasoned gameplan to conserve speed at any cost – never lift, slipstream, take all bends flat – had been subsumed by the primal thrill of the chase.

We made it not with minutes but over an hour to spare. To this day, neither of us quite knows how. But our appearance has, more or less, returned to normal.

John Barker
Riding sidesaddle

If he'd changed into sixth, we could probably have hit 200mph; there was a chunk of straight still to go. That said, we didn't know we'd hit 180mph until we checked the gearing. We hadn't even intended to clock some massive speed, it just sort of happened, as it does in the world's

No matter how large or small!

Has you covered

VentureShield Paint Protection Film is the latest in advanced clear coated urethane technology

VentureShield Paint Protection Film has the largest network of manufacturer trained installers in the World

VentureShield Paint Protection Film is race proven within the pinnacle of Motor Racing Series on both two & four wheels

VentureShield Paint Protection Film is the only choice when it comes to protecting your investment from the damage caused by stone chips, environmental damage and minor abrasions

VentureShield Paint Protection Film can be professionally installed to your vehicle from as little as £299

Call 0845 050 6536
for details

WWW.VENTURESHIELD.COM

JAGUAR XJ13

It had a thunderous mid-mounted V12 engine and one of the most beautiful bodies ever created. And in 2006 the XJ13 was restored to fully functioning glory

Words: John Simister | Pictures: Andy Morgan

One vital ingredient was missing in Jaguar's competitions department at Browns Lane in the 1960s. Superstition. Maybe it would have blended badly with the objective science of race-car construction, but not even the most rational individual can think it was a great idea to call a car XJ13.

Oh, how Jaguar's mid-engined vision of beauty suffered for its name! As if failing to be ready for Le Mans before rule changes outlawed it wasn't bad enough, in 1971 it was all but destroyed in a massive crash, launched from the banking at the Motor Industry Research Association's test track. Rebuilt two years later, it lived a life of demo runs and destroyed one of its two available engines. Then, in 2004, it fell off a high kerb in Copenhagen while being unloaded for an exhibition, destroying its sump and cracking the casting above.

From Le Mans dream to static exhibit, the unlucky Thirteen was at rock bottom. So it remained until last year, when the Jaguar Daimler Heritage Trust took a deep breath and decided to restore this unique piece of history, for which Jaguar was once offered £7.5m, back to raceworthy trim.

As you can see, it looks fabulous: smart and shiny but still patinated with stories. The mechanical parts, including its 5-litre, 502bhp, quad-cam but 24-valve engine, are in similarly good shape. For the first time in decades, the XJ13 can be driven as intended. And I have.

What, then, is the XJ13? Experimental Jaguar 13 was built in 1966 to take on the might of Ford and Ferrari, and maybe rekindle Jaguar's 1950s Le Mans glory days. Sir William Lyons was far from convinced his company should return to racing, but others thought differently and the XJ13 was created in secret. The catalyst was Jaguar's still-experimental V12 engine, designed by Claude Baily and later to reach production in 1971 in single-cam-per-bank form. The chance to create a rival for Ferrari's V12-engined sports prototypes, painted in British Racing Green, was just too tempting to pass up.

But time was against the XJ13. It was completed in 1967 but too late to be tested and ready for that June's Le Mans, in which first- and fourth-placed Ford Mk IVs, with monstrous 7-

Tail-lights were shared with the E-type (along with that unmistakable Jaguar DNA). Right: intake trumpets topped Lucas mechanical fuel injection system

litre V8s, bracketed the second- and third-place Ferrari P4s. And Jaguar never found out if the XJ13 would have been on the pace, because the FIA changed the prototype rules for 1968 and the XJ13's engine was considerably bigger than the new 3-litre limit. All that effort, all that hope and expense, for nothing – except that it did result in one of the most beautiful racing cars ever built.

As with the D-type racing car and E-type road car before it, the XJ13's curves were the work of aerodynamicist Malcolm Sayer. So despite an engine position entirely new for a Jaguar, the XJ13's genes were instantly recognisable. It's a delicious mix of form and function, the curves and the flared-out wheelarches crossed by lines of rivets and battalions of louvres, the rounded tail finished off with E-type tail-lights. Spoilers and trim-tabs are notably absent; who knows how the XJ13 would have looked in final racing trim once it had some serious test mileage under those fat, squat Dunlops?

We do know the XJ13 is quick, though. Whether it would have broken 200mph on the Mulsanne Straight with the right gearing will remain a matter for speculation, but it did set a new UK circuit lap record at MIRA during testing: David Hobbs averaged 161.6mph around the tricky circuit with its three flipped-up banked bends, and reached 175mph on the straights.

After its racing plans evaporated, to Sir William's relief because to have been uncompetitive would have hurt deeply, the XJ13 went into hiding until the production V12 engine was ready for launch in the E-type and the XJ12 saloon. So it was that in 1971 the XJ13 was dusted off and taken to MIRA for some promotional filming.

Jaguar's veteran test driver, Norman Dewis, drove. Towards the day's end he went for a final rapid run on the banking. The official story is that the right-hand rear wheel collapsed, pitching the Jaguar down the banking and into the infield where it dug in, flipped end-over-end twice, rolled twice and finally stopped the right way up. Dewis, by now cowering under the dashboard, was miraculously undamaged, but the XJ13 was wrecked. Strangely, though, there are photographs showing the wreckage sitting with all four wheels apparently intact. So what really happened? History goes fuzzy here; suffice it to say that the bits were swept up and gathered dust for the next two years.

In 1973, the XJ13 was comprehensively rebuilt with nearly every panel recreated. It earned a living at various public appearances, its engine terminally over-revved at one of them to the detriment of a cam-lobe and a cylinder head. The other surviving engine was duly installed but one of its pistons had been welded, which meant it couldn't be driven in anger. And that's how its life continued until that ignominious incident in Copenhagen.

Now it's back to full health, a process that I was privileged to follow closely. The body had its dull, scuffed paint flatted, reprimed as needed and refinished by XK Engineering, a Jaguar restoration company run by ex-Jaguar people. It was strange to see half an XJ13 in the bodyshop, but the sheet-aluminium structure terminates just behind the cockpit and the rear

Cockpit is cosy – and hot, with exposed oil and water pipes. Sheet aluminium structure clearly visible

'It's a delicious mix of form and function, the curves crossed by lines of rivets and battalions of louvres'

XJ13's curves were drawn by aerodynamicist Malcolm Sayer, who also designed the C, D and E-types

'Whether it would have hit 200mph will remain a matter for speculation'

suspension is bolted directly to the engine, just as a contemporary Cosworth DFV provided the rear strength of a Lotus 49.

The engine had its heads refurbished by Chesman Engineering and its crankshaft reground and pistons machined for new, wider rings by the Coventry Boring and Metalling Company. Engineers at Jaguar's own Whitley technical centre put it all back together, using the steel 'sump' (it's a dry-sump unit) from the over-revved engine and welding the block's cracked bedplate back together. The welded piston was X-rayed and found to be perfectly usable, so all that past pussyfooting turned out to have been unnecessary.

Why not just use the other block and pistons, though? Because that over-revved engine, lost for many years but recently unearthed, was in too poor a condition to make it preferable to the engine Jaguar already knew. The two engines are the only ones out of the seven prototype four-cam V12s to have gear-driven camshafts: four straight-cut gears per bank, the first in each geartrain driven by chain from the crankshaft.

The block is similar to those of later production V12s apart from its smaller bore (87mm instead of 90mm). The stroke is the same short 70mm, resulting in a 4994cc capacity. The intake trumpets are set between each head's camshafts; Lucas mechanical injection squirts fuel straight into them, outboard of the throttle butterflies in typical racing practice, and the distributor uses Lucas Opus electronic ignition.

THE RESTORED XJ13 DIDN'T make it to the 2006 Le Mans parade, but it did run, in anger, at the Le Mans Classic shortly afterwards. Nicely run-in and with the new paint authentically blackened around the two exhausts, the unique Jaguar then returned to MIRA where, almost unbelievably, I was able to drive it.

The doors are ultra-light, the cabin is cosy and hot with its exposed oil and water pipes, the steering wheel is almost vintage with its wooden rim. Two toggle switches activate ignition and fuel pump, a further prod of the ignition switch triggers a savage eruption behind my ears. The V12 settles to a noisy, chattery but steady idle

and I move the five-speed ZF transaxle's tiny, right-hand gear lever into first.

There's nothing difficult about driving the XJ13. Its new clutch is smooth and doesn't drag, so gearshifts are clean. Peak power arrives at 7600rpm, but Jaguar's Richard Mason, who masterminded the rebuild, would prefer I didn't venture much above 5000. Not to worry; that crank speed arrives bombastically quickly as I point the shapely snout around the MIRA handling circuit's fast bends, intake trumpets snorting on each exit and four lots of three-into-one exhausts bellowing across Warwickshire.

Slow speeds make the engine fret but it's glorious when roused. Peak torque is 382lb ft at 6300rpm, but there's plenty below that speed and the XJ13 weighs just under a ton. It turns with the inertia-free immediacy typical of a mid-engined car, yet feels uncannily, well, *comfortable* on those little 15in wheels and squidgy Dunlops. Perfect for 24 hours of Le Mans racing in fact, but it was a dream unfulfilled. Jaguar's XJ13 will forever be the most famous British racing car that never raced.

SCARLET FEVER

These are the greatest supercars that Ferrari has ever made. In 2004 we brought them together, drove them hard for two days, and then decided which was the best of all. The result came as a surprise...

IOO GTS

Considering that we haven't had breakfast, we're a surprisingly chipper bunch milling around the car park of our Welsh hotel early on this chilly, damp Tuesday morning. Then again, the view is spectacular, and I don't mean mist-shrouded lake Bala below us. Our party arrived in dribs and drabs late last night and only now can we see what we've managed to pull together – Enzo, F50 and F40, three of the greatest Ferrari road cars ever, their dramatic, distinctive shapes sheened with bobbles of water, their red paintwork glowing almost luminously in the thin light. They're ours for two days and they're just waiting to be fired up and driven.

The excitement is tangible. I'm reminded of a long-held idea for a range of alarm clocks for people like us. Instead of an irritating, ever-louder beep-beep, how about a bedside clock that begins waking you with the starter motor whine of your favourite supercar and then builds in volume with the sound of the exotic engine catching and bursting into life. Still not awake? After a period at a fast idle, it shifts up to haul-your-sorry-ass-out-of-bed-NOW volume with savage throttle blips and a bellowing standing start, complete with the squeal of tortured rubber.

I'd buy one, and any second now the rest of the hotel's guests are going to get an idea of just what it might sound like. The alarm call they didn't ask for begins gently, because first we have to move the cars we've used to box-in our precious trio – a mere £60K Audi RS6 and £100K Aston Martin DB7 GT. The still air is soon pulsing with the soft throb of the Audi's V8, and then the Aston's V12 joins in with a whooping flourish. That will have jolted the light sleepers from the Land of Nod. The rest will soon follow when the minimally silenced Enzo gets going…

The F50 gets in first though, its 4.7-litre V12 barking into life and idling with a glorious, deep, hollow howl that makes the Aston sound like it's got socks stuffed up its tailpipes. Then the Enzo erupts, its 12-cylinder crackle ripping the air, its quartet of tailpipes spewing great plumes of vapour like a massive kettle. We look like a bunch of kids who've just left a banger in a milk bottle on someone's doorstep.

Best not to hang around, then, but which to take first? It would be fascinating to drop behind the wheel of the earliest car and then work up to the Enzo to see how the ultimate Ferrari road car has evolved over the last 20 years. I can't though, because that's the drop-dead gorgeous 288 GTO, the fourth car we've managed to source for this unique test, and it won't be along until lunchtime.

So what'll it be: 478bhp F40, 513bhp F50 or 650bhp Enzo? Decisions, decisions…

I plump for the F50, figuring things will just get better and better. It's the only one of the four that hasn't been given a five-star rating in The Knowledge section of the mag, though that's up for review say Meaden, who drove it here, and Bovingdon, who drove another example in fast convoy to Spa and back a couple of months ago. As I open the door, Dickie fixes me in the eye and says: 'It wheelspins in fourth.' Righty-ho, then.

Up to this point my total experience of the F50

is a stolen half a lap of Ferrari's Fiorano test track some six years ago, so by the time I reach the end of the hotel driveway I'll have almost doubled my mileage. My lack of F50 experience hasn't gnawed away at me. This stems partly from the positive but slightly guarded reception it received from the press when it was launched in 1995. Ferrari permitted only very limited driving, just a few laps of super-smooth Fiorano, which precluded definitive judgement. If journalists had been allowed greater access, including some road driving, it might have been compared more favourably with the F40, which many – me included as we start this test – still believe to be the best driver's Ferrari ever made. The next 48 hours should finally provide all the answers.

There is another reason why I've not hankered after driving the F50, and that's the way it looks. I accept that this is entirely subjective, but for me its soft, extravagantly swoopy lines and convertible roof undermine the credibility of its uncompromising engineering. I'm open-minded, though, and more than a little thrilled to be clambering into a very rare 202mph Ferrari that has over 500bhp, weighs little more than 1200kg and doesn't have power steering, traction control or anti-lock brakes.

'I'm more than a little thrilled to be clambering into a very rare 202mph Ferrari that has over 500bhp and doesn't have traction control'

F50 might not be the best-looking Ferrari ever but with a V12 derived from a Formula 1 car, carbon chassis and race-style suspension, it's a serious driver's supercar

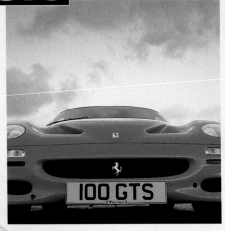

F50 is the only open-top car here – it actually looks much better with hardtop in place. It was first Ferrari production car with full carbon 'tub'. Normally aspirated V12 is bolted directly to it; produces over 500bhp from 4.7 litres. Tyres are specially-developed Goodyear F1 Fioranos

It's a wide car, the F50. The deeply sculpted seat has a sort of low, flat armrest that's level with the wide sill and helps you shuffle your backside across and into the seat proper. The floor-hinged, aluminium-faced pedals appear strongly offset to the right, but as soon as your feet find them you realise it's an optical illusion. At the apex of the seat I find a knobbly aluminium wheel like a Ferrari fuel filler cap and crank the backrest to the ideal angle, and although the classic three-spoke Momo doesn't adjust, it doesn't need to. This feels good, really good.

Just about everywhere you look in this simply styled cockpit you see shiny carbonfibre – even the gearknob is fashioned from it – and the tub trembles to the complex idle of the V12. There are rubber floor mats and strategically placed rubber strips to prevent scuffing, manual window winders and the simplest of heater controls, while the stereo and speakers look like the after-thought that they are. The message coming through loud and clear is that this is one seriously focused Ferrari.

The F50's stated aim was to deliver 'the emotion' of Formula 1 on the road. It was Ferrari's first fully carbonfibre monocoque road car and featured inboard, pushrod-operated suspension and that fabulous V12, mid-mounted and bolted to the tub. The world had already marvelled at a not dissimilar concept a year earlier when McLaren launched the F1 and instantly established many new supercar benchmarks. However, the F50 demonstrated an altogether rawer take on the idea; its engine was derived from the naturally aspirated F1 3.5-litre V12 that Ferrari had designed to suit the new regulations at the end of the turbo era in 1989.

The new 4.7-litre unit didn't use the racer's pneumatic valve actuation or rev to 14,000rpm but, as in the F1 car, this much reworked and (to a degree) civilised engine is a structural, load-bearing component. You certainly know you're sitting in a tub that's fixed to the engine; there's quite a commotion as the four-cam, 60-valve V12 climbs the lower slope of its torque curve, every shade of vibration discernable through the seat of your pants. Yet the ride is surprisingly supple, which adds a compensating level of civility as we thread our way through the town of Bala and out onto the open roads we know so well.

It's not raining but the single wiper is flick-flacking across the screen as water begins to stream off the bonnet. Ahead is the squared off rump and outrageous hoop spoiler of the F40 and beyond that the almost alien-looking Enzo. The F50 is loud but when Meaden cracks open the Enzo's throttle I can hear it above the loping, rhythmic pulse of the V12 at my back. The F40's tail hunkers down a little and it charges forward in comparatively noiseless pursuit. I ease the F50's firm throttle pedal down an inch or so down and the car snaps forward instantly, the V12's note deepening and hardening. I can't help laughing out loud at this incredible million-pound convoy.

Even though the oil that the cogs are spinning in has yet to come fully up to temperature, this is one of the finest shifts I've ever tried – precise, perfectly weighted and mechanically satisfying as only an open-gate Ferrari shift can be. I've yet to venture past 4000rpm – less than half its rev range – but there's a tremendous amount of grunt on tap, its effect magnified by the F50's light build.

I've just about warmed it through by the time we arrive at our first photo location and it'll take a few more miles to get really comfortable with the weighty, unassisted steering and to bring the initially numb brakes up to full working temperature. Although our challenging route hasn't yet taken in the road to Damascus I'm already thinking that the overall poise and demeanour of the F50 are something special.

The day is gradually brightening but the roads are still rain-slicked. I ought to take the Enzo next, it being the only one with traction control and anti-lock, but the F40 needs brimming with Optimax so I selflessly (ahem) volunteer and leave the others to get on with the photos.

The F40 is much more compact than the others – the Enzo looks huge standing next to it – and there's a stark purposefulness about it. The detailing is no-frills, the panel fits of the Kevlar-enhanced composite body are gappy but, hell, what a shape. If you've never been up close with an F40, simply buy a 1:18 scale Bburago model and bring it closer and closer until it appears full-size. The reality isn't much different – what you see is pretty much what you get.

Ferrari created the F40 in little more than a year, its gestation accelerated by the use of two of only five 288 GTO Evoluziones as development hacks, and in 1987 it was unveiled as a car to celebrate 40 years of Ferrari. Some commentators reckoned the F40's sole purpose was to restore Ferrari's pride by getting one over on the Porsche 959 which had upstaged the 288 GTO, and in classic Top Trumps fashion the F40 did just that, claiming a top speed of 201mph, four mph more than the Porsche.

It couldn't have been more different from the 959. In a very German way, the Porsche was built with the utmost technical integrity and endowed with the most sophisticated 4wd system yet seen, electronically adjusted dampers, anti-lock brakes and even tyre pressure monitoring. It was built

and trimmed to the same high standard as any 911, and it raced at Le Mans and rallied in the Paris-Dakar.

By comparison the F40 looked like a hastily tidied-up racecar (even though it was never intended to race), and its technical highlights were, well, the most extensive use of carbon/Kevlar yet seen in a road car. Yet whatever the cynics thought of the motivation behind its creation, it was quickly hailed as a great driver's car, probably the best that Ferrari had ever built. Even though it cost £160K – £15K more than the fantastically sophisticated 959 – it sold like hot pizza. Porsche moved 283 959s while Ferrari set out to build 400 F40s but then left the line running for a couple of years until some 1300 had been made. That means there are more

F40s around than 288 GTOs, F50s and Enzos put together.

Being the most common car here doesn't make it any less special to be around. A pseudo-racer it might be, but the deep-dished, centre-locking, split-rim alloy wheels, Naca ducts and that high-rise wing push all the right buttons. The theme continues on the inside with proper racing bucket seats, a non-reflective, padded felt facia and minimal fixtures and fittings – the interior door catches are operated by drawstrings.

It's clearly a car from an earlier generation than the F50. There's no high-quality, high-gloss curvy carbonfibre here, just simple panels of yellowish, matt-finish carbon joined with what looks like bright green bath sealer. It's not actually a full carbon tub – beneath it is a tubular steel chassis to which the stressed composite panels are bonded. At the time, Ferrari said the construction was three times stiffer than a conventional steel monocoque.

Wriggle into the high-back, deeply scalloped seat, tug the Sabelt harness tight and you feel right at the heart of things. Turn the key, thumb the starter button and the sound of the V8 on show in the glazed bay behind is considerably plainer and quieter than the F50's V12. Being a flat-plane-crank V8 there's no woofle, the firing order effectively producing two perfectly synchronised fours, its note light and smooth with an underlying depth.

The F40 isn't the raw, wild, jarring experience the visual pointers might lead you to expect. The steering wheel is tilted back rather more than I'd

'The F40 isn't the raw, wild, jarring experience the visual pointers might lead you to expect'

F40 looks every inch the racecar, inside and out, yet its stripped-out cabin is remarkably comfortable. Tubular spaceframe lurks beneath bare carbon panels. Twin-turbo 2.9-litre V8 pumps out 478bhp

like, but after the F50 it feels like it's power-assisted and has an encouraging, easy directness, while the ride is remarkably supple. You have to concentrate on the shift, working the heavy clutch sensitively and palming the tall gearlever around the open gate with deliberate precision, adding a throttle blip for snickety downshifts. But then getting it right is one of the rich pleasures of the F40.

Not that you have to use the gears much. The 2.9-litre twin-turbo V8 backs up its 478bhp with a thumping 425lb ft of torque at a handy 4000rpm – considerably more than the F50's V12 musters. You don't need a master's degree in applied mathematics to work out what happens on a wet road when you select second and add that sort of turbocharged torque to a mass of just 1100kg and

divide it between two plump Pirelli P Zeros. WHOA! I grab a half turn of lock to catch the slide, steady the throttle and then ride it out until wheel speed and road speed match. Easy? Well, it's not as hard as you'd imagine because the twin IHI turbos spool up progressively, the steering is light enough to allow rapid, accurate correction, and the F40's chassis is poised and faithful. Any driver comfortable with power oversteer wouldn't be intimidated by what it does, just by how much it costs.

Slot third gear, *squeeze* the throttle and you can enjoy most of the F40's thrust without provoking the tail. This isn't a *fizz-bang!* turbocharged engine; once it's on boost you can meter out the thrust with satisfying precision, conducting the ebb and flow to match the road as it unfolds before you.

The chassis feels more agile and biddable than the F50's, even though it requires a fraction more lock for the same radius corners, but it feels at its best on flowing A- and B-roads.

Tighter corners expose what little lag there is – after a sequence of fast sweeps you enter a sharper turn and find that you've already thought yourself up the road away from the clipping point before the boost has arrived. If you're feeling right at the top of your game you can anticipate this and gas it before the apex but this is truly committed stuff that's best practised only if you're a confident owner. It's certainly not advisable if the F40 isn't yours and its owner is sitting beside you. Did I mention that generous owner Len Watson was in the passenger seat? No? I must have been too absorbed…

Enzo is packed with technology, looks like nothing else, goes like nothing else – even in the wet, thanks to highly effective traction control. Carbon-ceramic brakes are astonishing and anti-lock assisted. No outrageous rear spoiler needed thanks to underbody aerodynamics

Refuelled and weighed down with crisps and sandwiches, we rejoin the main party, just in time to see Jeremy Cottingham from DK Engineering arrive in the 288 GTO. Oh. My. God. It's so rare to see one in the metal that you forget just how stunning it is. Pininfarina's 308 is one of the most beautiful cars of all time, no question, but for me the Group B-inspired 288 GTO preserves its curvaceousness and adds serious, you-want-a-piece-of-me? intent.

I want to jump in it right now but Bovingdon hands me the key to the Enzo and says: 'You need to try this.' I'm not going to argue; we're heading off on one of our favourite loops, starting with the most exhilarating leg.

At first I wasn't a fan of the Enzo's edgy styling but the more I see of it, the more I appreciate the way the almond-shaped centre section melds with the individual pontoon-like wheelarches. Pretty it ain't, aggressive it is, and brutally effective. No outrageous rear spoiler is needed to keep the tail planted at high speed, only a nifty flip-up lip; it's mostly taken care of by under-floor air management – witness the venturi sculpting below the rear numberplate.

Pull down the beetle-wing door and it gets more intimidating, the leather Sparco race-seat slung low, the side windows high on the shoulder, the

deeply curved windscreen stretching far beyond arm's reach. The facia is a collection of small, shiny carbonfibre pods – it's as if the skin and soft padding have been stripped away in an acid dip to expose the substructure. You can see wiring and steering column knuckles between the wheel and the two-dial instrument cowl, while daylight filters down through a gap beyond it so that your feet work away in their own little atrium.

The steering wheel is an F1-inspired multi-function affair with an exciting array of colour-keyed buttons and a row of up-shift lights subtly embedded into its flat carbon top. Enhancing the wow factor, the scale of the white-on-red rev-counter goes to 10,000rpm and the biggest number on the smaller speedo next to it is 400. That's kph, equal to 250mph, give or take. OK, so 350 would have done (that's 218mph and Ferrari claims 217mph+) but, hey, 400 looks neater, and you never know when you might find yourself going downhill with a following wind.

I know what's coming as my finger pushes the bright red starter button but the bark of the V12 still prickles my nape. It's how a supercar should sound – not quite as loud as this, perhaps, but a fabulously rich and complex rumble that promises mighty, pulverising performance. It's an all-new V12 and at 6 litres a chunk bigger than the F50's,

and with modern variable cam timing and induction length management it develops monster torque as well as huge power – no less than 485lb ft at 5500rpm and 650bhp at 7800rpm.

You can sense that structurally the Enzo is uniquely stiff yet the ride is quite absorbent and the car always feels planted. Once you've adjusted to the incredibly direct steering you find a chassis beneath you that is wieldy and alert without being nervous. There is a sense of being somehow disconnected, though, and that's probably because you're not required to guide a gear lever or modulate the clutch. This is probably the best F1 paddle-shift I've tried – smooth and crisp-acting

– yet somehow you feel you should be required to work a bit harder, to earn the right to access the performance.

I know this fast, wide, undulating B-road unfurling ahead of me, and just a couple of miles after firing up the Enzo I've got the traction control warning light flickering. This is, indeed, a mighty engine; docile and willing when you're sauntering but ever-ready with a massive, electrifying slug of acceleration, whatever the revs. From tickover to 8000rpm is a fantastic rush, the thrust pinning you against the seat, the bellow of the V12 mutating from a heavy rumble into a spectacular howl.

'From tickover to 8000rpm is a fantastic rush, the bellow of the V12 mutating from a heavy rumble into a spectacular howl'

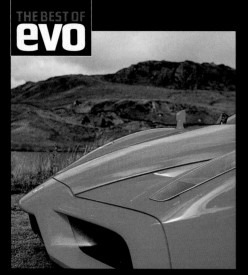

Glossy carbonfibre dominates Enzo interior. Steering wheel festooned with buttons, F1-style. 6-litre V12 develops 650bhp and humungous torque, fed through paddle-shift 'box, which means only two pedals (the 'third pedal' is a reflection of the throttle in the chromed scuff-plate)

As you'd hope, the carbon-ceramic brakes are more than equal to the task. They deliver sensational bite and haul off 30 or 40mph in an instant, as you flick the left-hand paddle to request a couple of blip-perfect downshifts before tucking the nose into the next apex. It's crazy, intoxicating stuff, your pace seemingly limited only by your bravery, the occasional intervention of traction control, and the bigger bumps and sharper ridges which are a stern test of suspension travel and have you wincing in anticipation of expensive Italian carbonfibre being duffed up by unyielding Welsh asphalt. The damp patches are a concern, too; you're never quite sure how hard you're pushing.

When we reach our destination there's a drizzly mist. Snappers Morgan and Gregory go off to recce nearby and a smiling Bovingdon ambles over. 'It's fast, isn't it?' he says with deadpan understatement. Oh yes. 'It felt mega-fast on the run to Spa with the F50,' he continues, 'but there's a bit of a difference between nailing the throttle on a wide *autoroute* and summoning the courage to unleash the full 650bhp here. When you do it's borderline terrifying – it must be the angriest, most manic road car I've ever driven.'

Meaden has just stepped out of the gorgeous GTO and is wearing a look I've seen before. 'That,' he says, nodding at the GTO, 'is fantastic. I was truly surprised by the performance. I know DK Engineering has fettled it to the rudest health

but it was staying in touch with you lot. I bet those modern Michelins it's on help a lot but the balance and poise are superb.'

The F40 ought to be even better but Hayman looks a bit nonplussed. 'That was hard work,' he says, reaching for a Marlboro. 'The steering, brakes and gearshift are heavy, and when the turbos spool up all hell brakes loose – it goes sideways even in a straight line! Scary.'

We are surrounded by an incredible collection of shapes. Nineteen years separate the GTO and Enzo, and they might as well be light years. It

seems incredible that there are only three years between the F40 and GTO. Clearly the influence of aerodynamics took a firm hold in those years, the upswept nose and tail of the GTO contrasting with the ground-hugging profile of the F40. There's a surprising amount of shared design DNA between the Enzo and F50, though; the extraordinarily long front overhang, the positioning of the front and rear wheels, the nostril-like vents for the front-mounted water radiators, and the cockpit window line – even more so when the F50 is wearing its hardtop.

'It doesn't feel any slower than the F40, its twin-turbo V8 driving the tail into the tarmac and flinging it up the road on a swelling, whooshing flood of torque'

The 288 GTO is the least supercar-like in the modern sense but no less attractive for that. It was inspired by the then-new FIA International Group B regulations, as was the Porsche 959 along with the maddest, baddest rally cars ever seen – Peugeot 205 T16, Lancia Delta S4, Ford RS200 and Metro 6R4 – and its architect was Ferrari's F1 designer, Dr Harvey Postlethwaite. The GTO was never seriously raced; what it did was demonstrate Ferrari's grasp of the latest technologies to create the ultimate roadgoing supercar of the day.

You can see the donor 308's roof and glass area but little else remains. Under Postlethwaite's direction, the transverse V8 was turned through 90 degrees to allow the fitment of twin turbos, which lengthened the wheelbase by 4.5in. The V8 was also reduced from 3 to 2.8 litres to give an FIA turbo equivalency rating (multiply by 1.4) of just under 4 litres.

Pininfarina painstakingly reshaped the 308, incorporating the more shovel-like nose, kicked-up rear deck and more bulbous arches for the 4in wider tracks and broader rubber needed to deploy 400bhp and 366lb ft. Effecting these changes was easier than it sounds because early 308s had glassfibre bodies. The 288's incorporates Kevlar and carbonfibre and is mounted to a tubular chassis as opposed to the 308's semi-monocoque, helping the 288 weigh in some 110kg lighter. To keep the overall length similar, 2.5in was chopped off the tail, and gills were added beyond the rear arch as a reference to the 250 GTO of the early '60s. Only 200 examples were needed to homologate the car in Group B but in response to demand Ferrari eventually built 272. Even so, that makes it the rarest car here.

Photography-wise, there's nothing doing, so we're heading back down the loop. I bag the GTO's key and set off with Hayman behind in the Enzo, followed by Bovingdon in the F50 and Meaden in the F40.

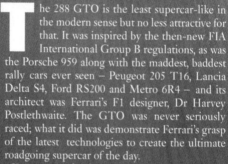

What luxury there is in the GTO. It has carpets and electric windows, a facia trimmed in a velvet-like cloth and classic perforated leather seats (set a touch too high). Apart from a trio of auxiliary dials above the centre console, it appears quite similar to a 308, but no 308 ever went like this. It'll fizz its rear tyres in first but thereafter remains remarkably well hooked-up to the tarmac, and it's so poised, so balanced, so easy to drive very quickly indeed.

I was expecting the Enzo to be all over the back of the GTO but its annoying Xenons flaring in the rear-view mirror don't appear to get any closer. I can feel why: the GTO is sailing over this tricky surface, barely acknowledging so many of the lumps, bumps and compressions that test the travel of the Enzo and F40. Then there's the unassisted steering – direct, feelsome and marvellously weighted. This is clearly a very tight, sorted original, and helped by modern rubber, but it delivers, and the tougher the road, the better it gets. It doesn't feel any slower than the F40, its twin-turbo V8 driving the tail into the tarmac and firing it up the road on a swelling, whooshing flood of torque.

Soon there's a bit more of a gap to the Enzo and when we stop I ask Hayman if he was really trying

or if he'd backed off to prevent road chippings peppering the Enzo's nose. He confesses that he was going as hard as he wanted to. 'On the steering wheel there's an ASR button with a cross through it. I took heed of that. I wasn't going to venture into the realm of unaided traction, no way matey, not with the little yellow light flashing away furiously every time I floored the throttle, not in something this fast, this wide and costing £400K!'

Bovingdon appears to have had an almost religious experience in the F50. 'I stayed back to avoid the gravel and debris the Enzo's venturis were throwing up, but also to concentrate on the road and the F50. It was absolutely mesmerising. Everything just clicked. It bombards you with information and demands your total attention without ever becoming recalcitrant or tiresome. Perfect gearchange, superb brakes, steering that filters out everything you don't need to know and amplifies the important stuff, and an engine that's a work of art.' If we don't keep an eye on him he'll be nipping into the nearest tatooists to get a heart with 'F50' inside.

Meaden is rather less glowing about the F40 after their first date. 'Everything I've read suggests it's a savage animal of a thing. I was

GTO is arguably the prettiest
Ferrari of all time. Evolved
from the 308, it uses Kevlar
reinforcement in vital areas and
has a 2.8-litre twin-turbo V8
good for 400bhp. Superb
chassis makes the most of it

Cockpit of GTO is positively luxurious compared with those of its stablemates, featuring carpets and electric windows. Twin-turbo 2.8-litre V8 is mounted longitudinally and stretches wheelbase by 4.5in compared with 308; tail chopped by 2.5in to maintain visual similarity

expecting a quick-witted, no-nonsense car that demands your attention yet rewards confidence, but the delivery is broadly similar to the GTO – this one's not quite as punchy, actually – with a soft-edged throttle followed by a swell of forced-induction power and torque. The steering feels a bit slow, which seems to exacerbate a feeling of reluctance to turn in. It's quick, certainly, but there's little of the rawness and steely-edged tactility I was expecting.'

I could take it for the run back to the hotel but I'm keen to get more under the skin of the F50. Meaden has hopped back in the GTO and isn't hanging about, so I've got my work cut out even with an advantage of more than 100bhp. I quickly discover that earlier in the day I'd barely scratched the surface of the V12's ability. Keep it nailed beyond 4000rpm and it suddenly hits its stride, the delivery ramping up in urgency like some sort of mega-VTEC engine, complete with an incredibly rich, spine-tingling note. That's in both the literal and metaphoric sense, because as well as hearing the V12 work its way onto cam, you can

feel its efforts through the seat; the shudder as the twelve cylinders begin to drive hard towards peak torque at 6500rpm, the lighter zizz as revs and cam timing optimise at peak power – an incredible 8500rpm.

First gear is very leggy but once you're on your way the ratios of the six-speed 'box are perfectly spaced, and the shift is sublime. It's perfectly loaded across the gate, positive and precise as the lever snicks between the aluminium fingers before slotting home with a satisfyingly lip-smacking *sher-clack!*

It's a fantastic sight tailing the GTO into corners in the twilight, its round brake lights aglow, two-foot-long flames shooting from its blunderbuss-style tailpipes on the overrun. The F50 has the measure of it, and it's not all down to the V12's devastating top end. There's agility, poise and a stream of detailed feedback that allows you to push hard and to know just how hard you're pushing. It's beautifully balanced, a smidgen of understeer letting you know you've got it loaded, and if you've got the engine in the

sweetest spot, between 6000 and 8000rpm, you can neutralise it with a measured amount of throttle so that the F50 feels right on its toes. Totally absorbing.

Away from a T-junction there's a smooth, deserted straight. There's only one thing that's going to happen here. I let the GTO go and then gun the F50 through the gears, keeping an eye on the rear view mirror to see what the Enzo behind has got in hand. Three snap shifts later and I've got the answer – not a lot.

'The GTO has the most wonderful steering, as laden with feel as an Elise's'

Back at the hotel, Hayman describes what it felt like in the Enzo. 'I was shouting, "Come on!", but for a long time I just wasn't gaining on you.' This reflects well on the F50 rather than badly on Ferrari's latest hypercar, because there is no argument that what the Enzo has in abundance is sheer head-spinning speed. 'It's not just the engine that batters your senses into a muddled mess,' reckons Bovingdon, 'that jolting F1 'box adds to the feeling that the Enzo is in even more of a hurry than you are, and the speed with which it reacts to steering inputs can actually be a little unnerving. You have to recalibrate your eyes, hands, everything to drive the Enzo quickly.'

The F50 is more organic in feel, and mightily accomplished, too. Further exposure has made Bovingdon an even bigger fan, and Meaden is smitten, too. 'When I collected the car its owner asked what else would be here. I told him and he handed me the key with a look that said 'prepare to be surprised', and I am. The engine is an absolute monster. Its note builds into a brutal, Diablo-like bellow and it then revs way beyond any Sant 'Agata V12. You feel awed when you let loose in second and third; there's a real sense of big, big power in a relatively lightweight package. I've really got dialled-in to the chassis too, and I know this sounds absurd, but you really can drive it like an Elise.'

This morning the F50 was the underdog of this test and the F40 was, if not top dog, then certainly a strong contender for the top slot. It hasn't lived up to the expectations of my colleagues, though. I've driven F40s on a couple of occasions and they've always left me deeply impressed. I remember driving Nick Mason's example some ten years ago and being blown away. I couldn't believe that the world's first 200mph supercar – with 478bhp, rear-drive and no traction control – could be so controllable and driveable, even on puddled roads.

Meaden, Bovingdon and Hayman have waited a long time to try it for themselves. 'It's certainly not the savage animal that you might think it is,' says Meaden. And Bovingdon concurs. 'I approached it with a mixture of one part excitement and nine parts fear. It's always been my ultimate Ferrari – probably my ultimate car, full stop – and I hoped it would suck me in with raw feedback and even rawer power. I wanted to be a little bit intimidated, I wanted it to be loud and difficult to master, I wanted to emerge exhausted but elated. It didn't quite happen.'

The GTO, on the other hand, has charmed everyone. This is slightly odd because although it looks ten years older than the F40, in truth only a few years separate them. The F40 should come across as a more focused GTO; faster, harder, grippier. To a degree it does, but the margins aren't as big as the dramatic styling and stripped-out interior lead you to expect, and the GTO has the most wonderful steering. 'It's incredible,' grins Bovingdon. 'As laden with feel as an Elise's but more delicate once lock is wound on. Even in the wet you can sneak up on the limit of the front tyres' grip.'

Its supple ride is a real asset on these roads, too, as Hayman found when he chased it in the Enzo. 'I wasn't having an easy time keeping up,' he says, 'because I know too well where all the dips and troughs are that would smash out lumps of expensive carbonfibre.' Meaden quickly got into a groove with the GTO, too: 'It flows with such ease that you can relax into enjoying the prodigious performance in a way that the lower, wider, harder and altogether more skittish Enzo never allows. I guess it's because ultimately the limits are lower and more clearly telegraphed, but if the end result is a more tactile, driveable car that makes you feel like you're getting more out of it, then where's the progress?'

Next morning I slot myself into the Enzo with the phrase 'where's the progress?' bouncing around inside my head. Does having traction control empower me or diminish my contribution? Should I welcome the F1 paddle-shift because it gives more time to concentrate on steering, braking and lines, or rue it because it requires less skill and takes away a layer of interaction?

Considering the Enzo's near-220mph potential and the amount of power that's under my right foot, it's remarkably tractable, comfortable and supple as we thread through town. I reckon I could pull away from rest with fewer attention-grabbing revs in a conventional manual, and the composite brakes *shush* noisily even with light applications, but once we're out on the open road the gearshifts are quick and smooth and the Enzo feels nicely planted through the long sweeps that takes us out towards Ffestiniog.

I'm following in the spray-laden wake of the GTO and keen to see its pace, but when the first decent straight presents itself and the F50 and F40 scoot away, the GTO appears to be napping. I flip the Enzo down a gear, wait close behind for a few seconds, decide Bovingdon wants to hear the Enzo blat by, and nail it. The thump in the back is immense, the traction control light flickers and the acceleration falters momentarily, and then the shove resumes and we howl by. Chalk-up one for ASR. However, peeling into the succession of curves there isn't much feel through the assisted steering to judge the surface by and I end up treading gingerly through the turns and wringing out the fabulous V12 on the straights in an effort to catch the others.

When the GTO meets up with us at the first photo location Bovingdon looks worried. The car's not running right, but it transpires that the V8's hesitancy is down to damp electrics – it's clearly more used to overnighting in a warm, secure garage than in a blowy, wet car park. Given that it's worth almost £200K, perhaps one of us should have given up our room.

We were lucky with the weather yesterday but up on the hills today the low cloud and drizzle never lift. Morgan and Gregory busy themselves with individual cars and the rest of us take turns to hold brollies or slip off in the spare cars to, er, refine our opinions. Sunset should be about 4pm, but a couple of hours before then it's so gloomy and the rain is so heavy that further photography is pointless. All that remains, then, is to decide which is the greatest supercar Ferrari has ever made…

Initially none of us can decide which we'd take if we were offered the keys to just one. Fact is, of course, that there isn't another car maker that could field four supercars of such calibre, and to own any of them would be a dream come true. But as the debate rumbles on, some kind of consensus begins to emerge, and lowest on the scale of desirability is the F40.

I know, I know. It's the Ferrari I'd like to see when I lift the door of my dream garage. As Meaden says, 'no road car before or since has managed to look so racerish and uncensored'. Yet on these roads, in this company, it hasn't struck the right chord with my colleagues, none of

Four of Ferrari's finest, spanning two decades, from the GTO of '84 through to today's Enzo. They have over 2000bhp between them and together are worth well over £1m. They're all outstanding drivers' cars but we have a clear favourite…

whom had driven an F40 before. It wasn't quite the uncompromising car they were expecting.

'It's a legendary car with the aura to match,' says Meaden. 'It looks like much more of a weapon than the GTO – all the subtlety and curves have gone – and it's quick, certainly, but there's little of the rawness and steely-edged tactility the F40's reputation suggests it should have. The GTO does the iron-fist-and-velvet-glove act more convincingly, while the F50 and Enzo are so much more vibrant and aggressive. The F40 seems to be caught between two eras.'

I can see what he means. You don't expect the F40 to be quite so comfortable, but it has superb seats and a compliant ride that makes it an easy companion for long distances. It's not deafening when you wring it out either, thanks to the dampening effect the turbos have on induction noise. Dynamically, though, the expectation is that it'll feel like the F50, not the 288 GTO, and the GTO lands a punch on this particular F40 by having even better steering.

'It's still one of the great motoring experiences,' says Bovingdon. 'The elasticity of the delivery is its great strength: once you've ridden the spike as the turbos spool up, there's a wide powerband to work in, making the F40 a very fluid companion. I still want one, but a couple of others have elbowed it down my ultimate wish list.'

Surprised to find the Enzo, Ferrari's 21st-century supercar, our third most favourite? It takes current car dynamics to their ultimate

conclusion – more stiffness, more ultimate grip, better electronics than anything else to make it the most effective tool possible. It is an incredible car, like nothing else, and there's no contradiction between how it looks and how it goes.

'Its immense structural rigidity gives it an arcade-game quality,' says Bovingdon. 'The world rushes towards you and all you have to do is steer, brake and accelerate.'

Ultimately it's this lack of interaction that keeps it off the top slot. As the driver you should be more involved. The Enzo does the full-on ten-tenths drive like nothing else here, aided by spectacularly effective brakes and, when necessary, finely-judged traction control. It's surprisingly happy to burble around town too. The gripes surface when you're somewhere in between; the lack of steering feel or a gearlever and clutch to master make it unsatisfying.

'Once the the initial absurdity of its pace fades,' continues Bovingdon, 'you're left with the nitty-gritty details that matter, like steering feel, of which the Enzo has none. And even a good paddle shift isn't as satisfying as a manual.' Meaden agrees: 'There's just not enough to do other than hang-on tight and concentrate on your braking points. That might be fine for F1, but a road car should offer more involvement. In another 20 years the Enzo will still be a startling snap-shot of cutting-edge early-21st-century technology, but I fear it will seem painfully old-fashioned.'

Are we seriously saying we'd take the 288 GTO

over the Enzo? If we hadn't had them nose to tail on the same roads I wouldn't have believed it either, but the GTO isn't only an exquisitely beautiful Ferrari, it's also an incredibly effective road car, too. I've absolutely no doubt that an Enzo would pulverise a GTO around Fiorano, but on a wide, fast, writhing A- or B-road – on a driver's road – the GTO shows that the Enzo has perhaps spent too much time going round the same smooth circuit.

The real world has lumps and bumps, cambers and compressions, and the GTO takes them all in its stride. Although it doesn't deliver quite the accelerative hit of the Enzo or F50, by any other standard it is supercar quick, and it makes that performance count, which makes it almost uncatchable. That's not all: the GTO has feel, feedback and interaction in wonderful abundance, and we love it for it.

'You become immersed in the experience,' gushes Bovingdon. 'The delicacy of its feedback, the rush of its turbos and the supple chassis really got under my skin. That all this comes wrapped in a compact, beautiful package is a big bonus.'

'It's the right size for these roads and very fast on any road. So it doesn't do the supercar thing of looking and feeling like an event. So what? It does everything else,' says an emphatic Hayman.

Meaden is also won over by its effortless effectiveness: 'Of all the cars here I felt most free hustling the GTO, even in the wet. If you flex the low-gear muscle rather than jab at it, you can really get on top of it. It's the car you feel most confident about controlling and gathering up, to the point where you even begin to provoke it – something you certainly wouldn't do in the F50 or Enzo. In pure emotional terms the GTO is my favourite by quite a margin.'

Has any magazine, UK or otherwise, ever driven an F50 hard on decent roads? If they have, we missed the report, because we've never read how exceptionally good its dynamics are. It rarely features in Ferrari 'top tens', probably because so few people have discovered its ability, and the reason for that is probably because it isn't the best-looking supercar Pininfarina has ever penned. An F40 with the F50's hardcore nature and inspired handling would be to die for.

It might sound odd, but in many respects the F50 is a 'Club Sport' Enzo – a purer, even more focused version stripped of all aids including power steering, brake servo, anti-lock and traction control. A version that has been honed to connect with the driver and put the driver in control, not least through a manual gearshift of outstanding quality which somehow makes the power of its V12 seem more real. You don't simply jump into the F50 and go fast. You have to work at it, take more notice of the feedback and get it to flow, but the satisfaction of driving it well is immense. Today, Ferrari probably wouldn't countenance the levels of vibration and harshness induced by the 60-valve V12, but it's all a part of the unique experience the F50 delivers.

Meaden can't understand why it has gained a reputation as a chestwig chariot: 'Contemporary road tests suggest it's a bit soft, a pale imitation of the rip-roaring F40. That's cobblers really.'

Hayman hates the way it looks (so Miami) but once he'd hopped in he quickly warmed to it. 'Everything feels right – ergonomics, steering, pedals, gears. Then there's that engine. Thunderous, never-ending power, tractable at tickover, bonkers at the red line. Utterly superb.'

Bovingdon agrees. 'Of all the magic moments I had over two days, the F50 provided the most brilliant sequence – chasing the Enzo and GTO. You can lean so hard on the thing it's amazing, and it rewards on so many levels when you up the pace – the gearchange is perfect, the brakes are strong and trustworthy, the engine is a work of art. It's a proper old-fashioned supercar made useable.'

'I certainly had my most memorable and committed drive by far in the F50,' adds Meaden. 'It's tactile enough to make you feel part of the process at all times, with an excess of power and performance that leaves you feeling like you've got close but not quite touched the outer limits of its ability. I found it completely absorbing.'

The last word goes to young Bovingdon: 'The Enzo is more sophisticated and arguably a greater achievement, but Ferrari perfected what we think of as a supercar when it made the F50. It's the most engaging physically and emotionally, which is why it's the best supercar Ferrari has made.' ∎

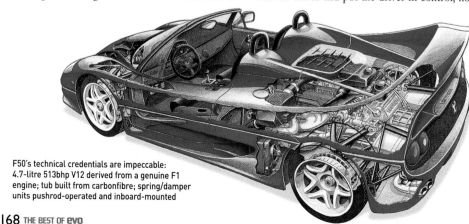

F50's technical credentials are impeccable: 4.7-litre 513bhp V12 derived from a genuine F1 engine; tub built from carbonfibre; spring/damper units pushrod-operated and inboard-mounted

Many thanks to Len Watson for the loan of his F40, and to Jeremy Cottingham at leading Ferrari specialists DK Engineering for sourcing the 288 GTO

	288 GTO	F40	F50	ENZO
Engine	90deg V8	90deg V8	65deg V12	65deg V12
Location	Mid-mounted, longitudinal	Mid-mounted, longitudinal	Mid-mounted, longitudinal	Mid-mounted, longitudinal
Displacement	2855cc	2936cc	4699cc	5998cc
Bore x stroke	80 x 71mm	82 x 69.5mm	85 x 69mm	92 x 75.2mm
Compression ratio	7.6:1	7.8:1	11.3:1	11.2:1
Cylinder block	Aluminium alloy	Aluminium alloy	Aluminium alloy	Aluminium alloy
Cylinder head	Aluminium alloy, dohc per bank, four valves per cylinder	Aluminium alloy, dohc per bank, four valves per cylinder	Aluminium alloy, dohc per bank, five valves per cylinder	Aluminium alloy, dohc per bank, four valves per cylinder
Fuel and ignition	Weber-Marelli electronic injection/ignition system, twin IHI turbos, twin intercoolers	Weber-Marelli engine m'ment and fuel injection, twin IHI turbos, twin intercoolers	Bosch Motronic 2.7 engine management, sequential multipoint fuel injection	Bosch ME7 engine management, sequential multipoint fuel injection
Max power	400bhp @ 7000rpm	478bhp @ 7000rpm	513bhp @ 8000rpm	650bhp @ 7800rpm
Max torque	366lb ft @ 3800rpm	425lb ft @ 4000rpm	347lb ft @ 6500rpm	485lb ft @ 5500rpm
Transmission	Five-speed manual, rear-wheel drive	Five-speed manual, rear-wheel drive	Six-speed manual, rear-wheel drive	Six-speed manual, sequential paddle-shift, rear-drive, lsd, tc
Front suspension	Double wishbones, coil-over dampers, anti-roll bar	Double wishbones, coil springs, dampers, anti-roll bar	Wishbones, inboard coils actuated by pushrods and rocker arms, variable electronic dampers, ARB	Wishbones, pushrod links, coil springs incorporating horizontal gas dampers, anti-roll bar
Rear suspension	Double wishbones, coil-over dampers, anti-roll bar	Double wishbones, coil springs, dampers, anti-roll bar	Wishbones, inboard coils actuated by pushrods and rocker arms, variable electronic dampers, ARB	Wishbones, pushrod links, coil springs incorporating horizontal gas dampers, anti-roll bar
Steering	Rack and pinion	Rack and pinion	Rack and pinion	Rack and pinion, power-assisted
Brakes	Vented discs front and rear, 306mm front, 310mm rear	Vented discs front and rear, 330mm front, 330mm rear	Vented discs front and rear, 356mm front, 335mm rear	Vented carbon-ceramic discs, 380mm front, 380mm rear, ABS
Wheels	8 x 16in front, 10 x 16in rear	8 x 17in front, 13 x 17in rear	8.5 x 18in front, 13 x 18in rear	9 x 19in front, 13 x 19in rear
Tyres	225/55 VR16 front, 265/50 VR16 rear, Michelin Pilot Sport	245/40 VR17 front, 335/35 VR17 rear, Pirelli P Zero	245/35 ZR18 front, 335/30 ZR18 rear, G'year Eagle F1 Fiorano	245/35 ZR19 front, 245/40 ZR19 rear, B'stone RE050A Scuderia
Fuel tank capacity	26.4gal/120 litres	26.4gal/120 litres	23.1gal/105 litres	22.2gal/100 litres
Weight (kerb)	1161kg	1100kg	1230kg	1365kg
Power-to-weight	350bhp/ton	441bhp/ton	424bhp/ton	484bhp/ton
0-60mph	4.9sec (claimed)	3.7sec (claimed)	3.7sec (claimed)	3.5sec
Max speed	189mph (claimed)	201mph (claimed)	202mph (claimed)	217mph (claimed)
Price when new	£72,999	£193,000	£342,700	c£420,000
Value in 2004	£190,000 approx	£130,000-£200,00 approx	£290,000 approx	c£420,000++

evo RATING ★★★★★   ★★★★★   ★★★★★   ★★★★★

MASERATI

R&D Factory Team

The edge of reason

In 2006, Richard Meaden took part in the gruelling Nürburgring 24 hours

There's no bigger challenge or spectacle in motorsport than the Nürburgring 24 hours. Held on a special circuit that combines the legendary Nordschleife with the modern GP track to make a lap of more than 15 miles, attended by 200,000 fanatical race fans, and contested by no fewer than 220 cars driven by professionals and amateurs alike, it is the world's ultimate endurance race.

It's hard to imagine a bigger honour than being invited by Maserati's R & D Factory Team to join the marque's historic return to this fearsome venue – a place that saw Fangio deliver the finest race of his glittering career behind the wheel of a Maserati 250F. It's also a prospect of daunting magnitude.

The R & D team has been formed especially to compete in the 'Ring 24 hours, as a means of testing engineering ideas, and to prove the reliability of Maserati's road cars. A special 'Laboratorio' version of Maserati's GT3 Light FIA racer has been entered in Vitaphone livery, to be driven by works drivers Michael Bartels, Andrea Bertolini and Eric van de Poele, while the car I'm to drive is a more standard GranSport Trofeo, painted in the evocative red and yellow of Maserati's famous works racers of the 1950s. I'm sharing it with three other drivers: American Patrick Hong, a journalist from *Road & Track* magazine; Gianni Giudici, an Italian

What have I got myself into? Right: Meaden's in good company, though, with Maserati co-drivers including former F1 star Jacques Laffite (left) and former ITC Championship racer Gianni Giudici (right)

gentleman racer who has extensive experience of the Nürburgring, and a certain Jacques Laffite, French F1 hero of the '70s and '80s.

We're competing in the SP8 class, which is a production-based class for cars with engine capacity of between 4 and 6.2 litres. That puts us up against some terrific machinery, including a V8 Dodge Viper, Lamborghini Gallardo, Audi RS4, Weissman, Aston Martin V8 Vantage (driven by Aston boss Dr Ulrich Bez and test drivers Chris Porritt, Wolfgang Schuhbauer and 'Ring ace Horst von Saurma) and, er, a Mercedes 500SEC that started its racing career with 250,000km on the clock and has completed countless 'Ring 24-hour races since. Such variety is the spice of this event.

Signing-on isn't due to start until Thursday, but Patrick Hong and I arrive on Monday so that we can attend a rookie training event, organised by the Nürburgring Motorsport Akademie. It's here that we learn about the vagaries of this unique race, and get to lap the circuit for a whole morning, with the help of expert instructors, including Ron Simons, boss of the excellent 75 Experience (www.75Experience.com). I'm treating it as a quick reminder of the circuit, but for Patrick it's his first experience of the place. He doesn't so much have a learning curve to climb as a sheer cliff, but by the end of the course he's well on his way to learning the track, albeit with a sense of deep foreboding!

After nerve-wracking daytime and night-time practice sessions on Friday, we all complete our statutory two timed laps. The pressure is ramping up, but the final few hours' build-up to the 3pm

start on Saturday is like a carnival, and provides a welcome distraction. The pit straight is awash with excited fans, stressed team personnel, nervous drivers, grid girls and brightly coloured cars. I feel odd, detached almost. Seeing my name on the roof of the Maserati is just plain surreal.

Because there are so many cars, the race has to be started in groups of 70 or so, each group forming their own grid and led around the green-flag lap at three minute intervals by a safety car. It's a confusing process, but once all the cars have completed their first racing lap, the timekeepers compensate for the three- or six-minute delay so all the cars effectively start the race as one.

Jacques Laffite starts for us, as he has far more

Right: pitlane a hive of activity prior to the race – perfect for distracting nervous drivers (Meaden, below left) from the task ahead. Below: party atmosphere surrounds the track; smoke from barbecues can be detected from the driver's seat. Far right: Laffite and Meaden pose for photos with fourth co-driver, *Road & Track* journalist Patrick Hong (centre)

experience and, let's face it, is a much bigger media draw than a lucky hack that no-one's heard of. Besides, the thought of piling into Turn One alongside 69 other pumped-up drivers fills me with dread.

The sun beats down as the field powers past the flag. Air horns blare, banners wave. It feels strange watching the cars barrelling around the GP circuit before shimmying over the crest to join the gnarly old Nordschleife for the first of countless laps. It's like authorised anarchy.

We've agreed that the next driver in the line-up should be in the pits, suited and ready to go, in case the driver out on the circuit has a problem. So, when Patrick Hong takes over from Monsieur Laffite, I don my overalls and wait in the garage, nervously scanning the screens, dreading my first stint, but hoping beyond all hope that the car doesn't suffer a premature failure and deny me a drive. Such conflicting emotions, it seems, are part of racing here.

Patrick's doing well, staying out of trouble and lapping the massive circuit that, until just a few days before he'd only driven on a PlayStation, in around 11 minutes. The team's plan is to put each of us in the car for six-lap stints, both to get a handle on fuel consumption and to make sure we each get at least one go in the car before dark.

We suffer an early setback: Jacques misinterpreted the 'IN' signal on his pitboard to mean come in immediately, via the emergency pitlane, rather than through the conventional pitlane entry at the end of his next lap. We lose a lap as a penalty, and coupled with Patrick's understandably steady pace it means we're running in a rather lowly 155th place by the end of the second hour. A team member cheekily suggests that I need to bring the car back in 100th place at the end of my stint. I smile, but privately think that I'd settle for simply bringing it back in one piece.

I get the nod. Patrick's completing his last lap. Time to push the radio earpieces into my lugs, pull on my balaclava, HANS device, helmet and gloves and go to stand in the pitlane. My stomach bubbles with anticipation, the responsibility of bringing the car back fighting with the desire to haul us back up the order. And then it appears, the satin scarlet bodywork and bright yellow noseband followed by the sharp, revvy tone of a Maserati V8. This is it. No going back.

The team springs into action. Air jacks hiss, wheel

wrenches chatter, the air fills with high-octane petrol fumes. Patrick hops out, eyes wide, face speckled with sweat. I fold myself up, drop through the roll cage and into the seat. As I'm strapped in and the radio is hooked-up to my helmet, I watch the guys work on the car. The bonnet comes down, the screen is sprayed and cleaned of rubber smears and dead bugs, the staccato *click-click* of the torque wrench providing a reassuring percussive beat to the soundtrack as each wheel-nut is checked. It's a mesmerising process, but a bang on the bonnet snaps me to. Flick the ignition toggle, start the engine, pull back on the right-hand paddle for first, then watch intently as Paolo scans the pitlane for approaching traffic, before waving me out on my

way. Christ, it feels like my head is going to burst.

The radio fizzes into life as race engineer Fabio Tosi calls an important reminder. 'Richard, Richard. Remember, 60km/h in the pitlane, repeat, 60km/h in the pitlane.' A quick look at the speedo confirms we're OK. Just. Wait for the green light at the end of the pitlane, then boot it. Revs flare and the tail squirms as brand new Pirelli slicks submit to 425bhp. Jesus, don't get carried away, Dickie. There's still 22 hours to go.

It takes most of the GP circuit to get some heat into the tyres. I feel a bit lost, jumpy, tense and struggling to focus. Fortunately I've emerged into a clear section of track, and manage to complete the GP circuit without being ambushed by quicker cars. But the Nordschleife awaits, and I'm as nervous as hell.

The track's change in character is immediate and overwhelming. The graffiti, the air horns, the bumps, kerbs and cambers. It's almost overwhelming. The run through Hatzenbach is a real wake-up call, the car dancing on the cambers, the proximity to the

barriers massively intimidating. All your attention is focused through the windscreen. Picking your line, scouring the marshals' posts for flag signals. And then, after who knows how long, you glance in the rear-view mirror and it's full, and I mean *full* of yellow and green Porsche. Shit! It's the leading Manthey car, lights ablaze, bright blue strobe pulsing in the windscreen denoting its Top 20 qualifying pace. It's positively crackling with aggression and urgency, and I literally jump out of the way, picking up what feels like 10kg of marbles – the detritus that gathers off-line – on my fresh slicks in the process, as the awesomely quick Porsche punches past, the second-place Altzen 997 GT3 tucked into its wake.

After that baptism of fire, a bizarre state of calm washes over me. I've been lapped by the fastest cars on the track, and made it past countless slower cars, all in the space of ten minutes. Other than torrential rain, which was my biggest pre-race fear, traffic was my main worry, but now that I've been both lapper and lapped I'm really beginning

to relish the experience. It's a buzz of unmatched intensity.

The remaining five laps pass without incident, although each time round I can see the remains of massive accidents, even at this early stage. Confidence growing, both in myself and the car, my lap times begin to tumble, settling comfortably between 10min 05sec and 10min 15sec for the whole stint, which if you ignore the time spent on the GP circuit, equates to a best Nordschleife lap of around 7min 45sec. I return to the pits and hand over to our fourth driver, Gianni Giudici. I emerge much as Patrick did: hot, sweaty, buzzing, relieved. Proud too, as we're now in 101st place…

Disaster strikes the Vitaphone car. A backmarker has turned across Eric van de Poele's bow. With nowhere to go, EvdP hits the rear corner of the Golf hard, the VW barrel-rolling into the air and hitting the roof of the Maser, before finally coming to rest, capsized, on the barriers. From the helicopter view shown on the TV screens it looks bad, but the mechanics prepare a new nose, door and rear wheelarch, along with a fresh front subframe and suspension, in the vain hope that the car can drag itself back to the pits. It can't, and I catch a glimpse of Bartels, face smouldering with anger and disappointment, as he powers away from the paddock on his scooter. All Maserati's hopes now rest with us.

My first night stint beckons. The sky is just changing from inky blue to velvet black when Patrick returns to the pits. There's a big, burnt rub mark on the passenger door, scars left by a Viper that barged its way past. It's almost 11pm. Cars scream by in the darkness, the frantic fury of the Manthey 911 tearing strips out of the muggy night air. My nerves are jangling. If someone came

up to me, put their arm around my shoulder and said 'It's OK, Dickie, I'll drive this stint', I'd run back inside. But I know that's not going to happen, and the feeling of inevitability is nauseating as I wait in the pit box. The pitlane is bathed in light, gantry after gantry illuminating cars as they refuel.

Back into the car. The GP circuit feels like nothing now, a wide open space that serves only to allow you time to fill your lungs before plunging into the depths of the Green Hell, now rendered a smothering, impenetrable black by the cloak of night. Jacques is right, the lights are terrible. I'd always wondered why seasoned ADAC 24-hour cars had seemingly cross-eyed spotlights pointing left and right, but now, chasing a narrow pencil of light, I know. Without them it's impossible to see the kerbs, while the cresting nature of almost every corner renders the conventional main beam largely useless. Imagine driving along a hilly country lane at 120mph with only your sidelights on and you'll have some idea of what it's like. I feel like a blind man who's lost his guide dog.

At Hohe Acht, the highest point of the circuit, the crowd is partying. Smoke hangs in the air like thick fog infused with the smell of sizzling sausages. Flash guns pop in the darkness, airhorns honk, music thumps. I can even hear the inebriated bray of drunk German fans. Having been up here earlier in the week, I'm petrified of breaking down out here, for the crowd are a primitive bunch, stripped to the waist, sunburnt and fuelled on

Nürburgring 24 hours sees an unrivalled variety in its 220-car line-up, including everything from Minis (above right) and Mantas (above left) to mighty GT3 Porsches. Right: where else would you see a Mercedes 500SEC with over a quarter of a million kilometres on the clock sharing track space with a Gallardo?

potent lager. It's like a zoo. No, strike that. It's like *Jurassic Park*. We were told before the race to carry plenty of Euros in our overalls, for many of the fans can be persuaded to siphon fuel from their cars. The rules don't allow outside assistance, but no-one ever complains, apparently.

At just after midnight I'm overjoyed to be back in the pits with car and myself in one piece. With Giudici, Laffite and Hong between me and my next stint, I head back to my room in the vain hope

of a little sleep. Fat chance. I manage snatched catnaps, but every five minutes I jolt awake, scared I've overslept. By 1am I give up, get back into my overalls and wander back to the pits, sick with nerves and fatigue.

When I return, Patrick is in and driving, but as I go to check-out the pit garage, Jacques returns to the hospitality area, eyes blazing, face flushed with uncharacteristic anger after his first fully dark stint. 'Zat was unbelievable! I could not see a f---ing thing. Zee lights are sheet. Un-be-live-vable. I am not driving again in ze night. F--- zat!' I make my way to the pit garage via the toilet.

Fabio has started to stretch our stints a little further, his colleague Massimo Portiolo having calculated each driver's fuel consumption and relative pace. With my second night stint fast approaching he's happy to stretch the tank of fuel to eight laps, but has suggested reducing our pace to around 11mins, both to save fuel and the car. Eight laps equates to 122 miles of flat-out driving, with compromised visibility, on the toughest race-track in the world. The nerves return with a vengeance as I drive down the pitlane.

Every lap I've faithfully radioed Fabio to say that I'm entering the Nordschleife, as our radio signal fades soon after. Every lap he's replied with a simple, short, 'OK. OK.' At night his voice becomes a lifeline, one final piece of reassurance before plunging into the turmoil. I notice that with the darkness has come an addition to his

Left: racing continues through the night, with drivers and crew grabbing moments of sleep between bursts of activity. It's terrifying out on track, so Meaden opts to do a double-stint... Bottom right: Meaden and Hong cheer team-mate Gianni Giudici home as the GranSport Trofeo crosses the finishing line after completing almost 2000 miles in 24 hours

jolts of adrenalin through my system.

I find another partner – a Honda S2000 – and though it's slower than I'd ideally like to run, I just want to survive this low ebb of energy. All is well as we skim along the endless Dottinger Hohe straight, the crisp VTEC bark of the Honda audible over the Maser's rich V8 growl, relaxed on three-quarter throttle. Through the Tiergarten kink we go, braking comfortably for the final twists before the pit straight. But then something very odd happens. The Honda, once calm and controlled, locks-up and spears over the kerbs, launching itself almost head-on into the barriers before clattering back into my path, crippled engine screaming, steam, and fluid spilling onto the track. It's a dramatic scene, played out before me like a video game. I'm stunned at what I've just witnessed, but relieved to have cleared the carnage.

As I pass the pits, Fabio's voice fills my ears. 'Richard, you have one lap left, then pit. One question. Do you think you could do another stint? Repeat, could you do another stint?' I reply before I have a chance to change my mind: 'Pit after this lap, then complete another stint. Yes. OK.'

The stop goes without a problem. New front Pirellis go on to cure the vibration caused by pick-up stuck to the tacky rubber, plus another tank of fuel. The briefest of moments to grab a suck of water from the in-car drinks container, then thump off the air jacks and away we go again.

What follows is one of the most memorable 60 minutes of my life. The darkness had begun to lift towards the end of my last stint, but now the sun is beginning to crawl above the horizon, a spirit-lifting ball of burnt orange heralding what every endurance racer regards as the ultimate experience: racing into the sunrise.

I catch glimpses of mist hanging in far-off forests, the Eifel Mountains providing a serene, tranquil backdrop to this most crazy of races. The sun lifts above the trees, and as we plunge down the rollercoaster flat-in-sixth Fuchsröhre (Foxhole) it's blinding: so bright I can barely see where I'm going, steering between vivid flashes of red and white curbing and the odd glint of Armco. So bright too, that I can't see anything in my mirrors, the first hint of being lapped by the Zakspeed Viper being the feral gargle of its engine as the big red bonnet lunges down my right-hand side into the Adenauer Forst chicane.

The noises from the transmission are still a

message: 'OK. OK. Take care, Richard.' I feel like an Apollo astronaut passing around the dark side of the moon.

The track seems quieter now. Dozens of cars have retired already, many after violent accidents, and as I pick my way around the first lap, shadowy debris lurks at the side of the track, testament to some sickening shunts. Perhaps because of the darkness and the skewing effect it has on my senses, I'm more aware of the Maserati and the noises it's making. The engine still sounds beautifully bassy, emitting a tremendous V8 snargle as it powers through the mid-range, but there's a worrying clatter from the transmission. The shifts are still clean, but it feels and sounds tired. Hardly any

wonder, with around 90 full-bore shifts per lap.

My first two laps are bang-on 11min, but it's hard to drive so slowly. In the end I settle on letting a car by, assessing its pace and then following it at a safe distance. It works well enough, apart from the time I let a clearly confused Opel Corsa driver pass me, only to sit behind him twiddling my thumbs before he waves me by. Eventually I hook-up with an M Coupe that's running a comfortable 10min 35sec pace. His lights are good too, so I use him as a pathfinder for three enjoyable laps. Then the frontrunners come by and separate us, the sudden solitude hitting me hard. Tiredness is taking its toll, too. Concentration is getting harder by the lap, little mistakes creeping in here and there, releasing

'The car has made it through the night. Still eight hours to survive…'

concern, so I decide to upshift at 6500rpm rather than the 7500rpm redline. I also decide to try and take corners a gear higher, again to reduce the wear on the car. It feels good: smooth, relaxed and just as quick. By the end of the second stint, I'm lapping faster than I was before, but using less fuel in the process: the ideal endurance racing combination.

It's 7am when I get out of the car, just minutes short of the two-and-a-half hours maximum any driver is allowed to run without a break. I've driven 14 laps – or 214 miles – without a break, but I swear it feels like I was in the car for just 20 minutes.

Everyone is elated that the car has got through the night. We're solidly into the top 50 cars now, but it's hard to believe we still have eight hours left to survive. My last stint comes at around midday. After the worries of last night the car actually feels better, but you can't afford to relax for a moment. Every lap I encounter the aftermath of an incredible crash, each seemingly bigger than the last. Now more than ever, the race is about survival.

I try to savour my last lap. On the exit of Steilstrecke, some Union Jack-waving fans give me a honk of air horn and the thumbs-up, while further along some Italians wave the Tricolore before the Karrusell. I wave back, proud to be driving a Maserati, elated to have survived this incredible race.

Back in the pits I hand over to Giudici for the last 90 minutes. Most of the mechanics gather

in the pit box, leaving the tireless Fabio on the pitwall as the last laps are reeled off. Alongside me is Maserati boss Karl-Heinz Kalbfell, as desperate as I am to see the last hour pass. It's a tortuous time, the hands of my watch crawling around with treacly torpor. With a lap to go we spill into the pitlane, Patrick and I climbing the retaining fence to wave Giudici home. It seems to take an age, then the red and yellow nose spears into view. After 24 hours 9 minutes and 44 seconds, 126 laps, 1927 miles and more than 11,000 gearshifts, the Maserati GranSport Trofeo crosses the line, 36th overall and 5th in class. Everyone shouts and hollers, hugs and smiles. It's a euphoric moment. What a car. What a race. ∎

LAP OF LUXURY

Driving a race car round the Ring is one thing; back in 2003, Harry Metcalfe tackled the Nordschleife in a V12 Maybach limousine...

Pictures: David Shepherd

One minute the inner lobby of Stuttgart's Imperial Hotel is bathed in early-morning summer sunshine; the next minute it's as if God has accidentally knocked the sun's dimmer switch. Something very large has come to a halt just outside the hotel, throwing the lobby into shade. I believe the Maybach has arrived.

If you've never seen a Maybach in the metal, I can promise you this: it's at least twice as big as you thought it was. Honestly, nothing else comes close. If you parked one next to a tacky American stretchy, it would be like comparing a giant Sun Seeker with a British narrow boat. They come in two sizes too: extra large (I'm really quite well-off) and jumbo (I'm seriously rich). Ours is a jumbo — the 6.17-metre-long Maybach 62 — and it's arrived with a besuited driver called Hanns, so I'll be able to enjoy both driving and passengering. All I have to do is explain to Hanns where we want to go…

The Maybach's styling has always been contentious, but something it has never lacked is presence. As we fill the boot/loading bay outside the hotel, a growing crowd of seriously impressed 'suits' give snapper David and me a rare taste of celebrity status. If only they knew.

As we leave the urban crawl of Stuttgart, Hanns is struggling to get his head round the idea that we want to take this near-three-ton monster to the Nürburgring. Hanns would much rather show us to some nice old buildings he knows, park the Maybach next to them, take some nice photos. Instead we want to take it to the most challenging racing circuit in the world and drive it round as fast as it will go. Thinking about it, he may have a point.

But hey, what we have here is the most powerful road car this side of a Ferrari Enzo. Residing somewhere up front is a 5.5-litre twin-turbo V12 pumping out a ridiculous 542bhp and a seriously useful 664lb ft of torque at a very leisurely 2300rpm. Even in something the size of small bungalow, that should make for some fairly exciting laps. As we head for the Eiffel hills, we'll find out soon enough.

I do feel a bit of a fraud lounging around in the back of the Maybach. Normally I'd head straight for the driver's perch, but the thought of guiding well over 20ft of Maybach through Germany's morning rush-hour isn't particularly appealing, so I snuggle down into the most cossetting passenger seats ever produced; there isn't a corporate backside yet created that won't get comfy in here.

I've never felt this pampered in a car before. My colleague Mr Shepherd isn't such a fan of the extending footrest that

[Maybach at the 'Ring]

telescopes out of the seat, though he is rather taken with the down-filled, super-soft suede pillows attached to the headrests. A hundred miles just slide past.

Hanns snaps us out of our slumbers by giving the accelerator an extra squeeze as we pass a delimited autobahn sign. In a flash the roof-mounted speedo (perfect for spying on what your driver's getting up to) is showing 200kph. Where did *that* come from? There wasn't a hint of protest from the engine room, no growling exhaust, no wheezing as twelve overworked pistons rushed for the redline, just seamless thrust. This is a very, *very* quick car and, after this stunning demonstration of horsepower, I decide it's time to pull rank on Hanns. I want a go.

As I settle into the captain's chair, I'm a little underwhelmed by the cockpit. The surroundings seem a little too familiar. Maybe the wood is a few notches up on the shiny scale, and there are a few extra buttons beside the auto selector, but otherwise it's Mercedes S-class standard issue.

Something I've not experienced before, though, is the king of navigation systems, Dynamic Navigation. Not only is the whole of Europe covered by the DVD system, but thanks to a tie-up with both Trafficmaster and local radio stations, traffic jams are also shown on the screen. It doesn't stop there either, because the system works out the quickest route to your destination using all of this info. So it will route you round the hold-ups if it's quicker, taking in actual traffic speed in the jam and expected speed by the time you'd get there. Seriously clever.

It's a two-hour drive to the Ring and we fall into a near-silent cruise, close(ish) to the prevailing 130kph limit. This is a bit weird, though: take your foot off the accelerator and you're still doing 130kph, the car seemingly unfussed by the 90mph headwind. Something to do with the near-three-ton kerb weight and relatively slippery shape I reckon, as we continue to blast through central Germany.

Hanns tells us that some parts of the German autobahn system are now continuously limited to 130kph thanks to the rise of the Green party, these days a powerful political force in Germany. Fortunately they don't control the whole motorway system and soon another derestriction sign looms into view.

As the accelerator is firmly mashed into the thick Wilton, the big V12 sighs, then huffs and the

Nürburgring Nordschleife one of the few things longer than the Maybach 61. Left: rear passengers get roof-mounted speedo, clock and outside temperature gauge. Utterly brilliant satnav has Ring's 73 corners fully mapped

Maybach sculpture attached to the end of the bonnet bounces into the air as if it was attached to a springy diving board as the speedo needle does a quick-step round the outer reaches of the dial. In a trice, 140 becomes 200 and 200 becomes 240 before traffic brings us back down to 220. This is silly – there's no noise, just a slight ruffling of airflow around the C-pillars together with this feeling of complete and utter effortlessness – but then I've never driven a three-ton hot-rod before. Lord knows what it would run to if the 250kph limiter wasn't there. A reputable German magazine has already timed the Maybach 62 at 13sec dead to 100mph and 80-100mph in 4.2sec, which puts it into M3 territory.

It does feel a bit remote, though, the steering wheel purely a guiding device, but then the whole car has been designed to cosset the passengers rather than pamper the driver; feelsome steering wasn't exactly a priority during the design process.

As we reel off the autobahn towards the Nürburgring on a gently curving slip road, the car gives me a sudden reality check: I've only driven this beast in a straight line so far and this cornering stance doesn't feel very nice. True, I've got the suspension on full comfort mode, but the roll angle is approaching 2CV proportions (I've been there and I wouldn't recommend it). Right now it's like being in one of those comedy custom cars

that leap about on their adjustable suspension legs, and the two on the port side are fully extended. Right now I can't quite believe we're about to lap the Nordschleife either. The Maybach appears to be not only excessively overweight but allergic to corners, too. It occurs to me that this could all end in tears.

To calm the nerves we go off and check the action from one of the viewing areas scattered around the track, but a few minutes of watching camouflaged cars burst through the trees, pro drivers hurling them from apex to apex only

makes me feel worse. There's even a Carrera GT lapping here today – the sound of its V10 alone is worth the trip – along with a thunderous C55, a revised X5 and a baby X3. No-one's going to notice the Maybach going round with this lot out there, are they?

We're on in thirty minutes so it's time to pop the brave pills and buy a ticket. How many laps shall we have? Two, perhaps? We should get further than that before something expires. On the other hand, ten might be pushing it too far. I settle for six – about an hour on track for just 76 euros.

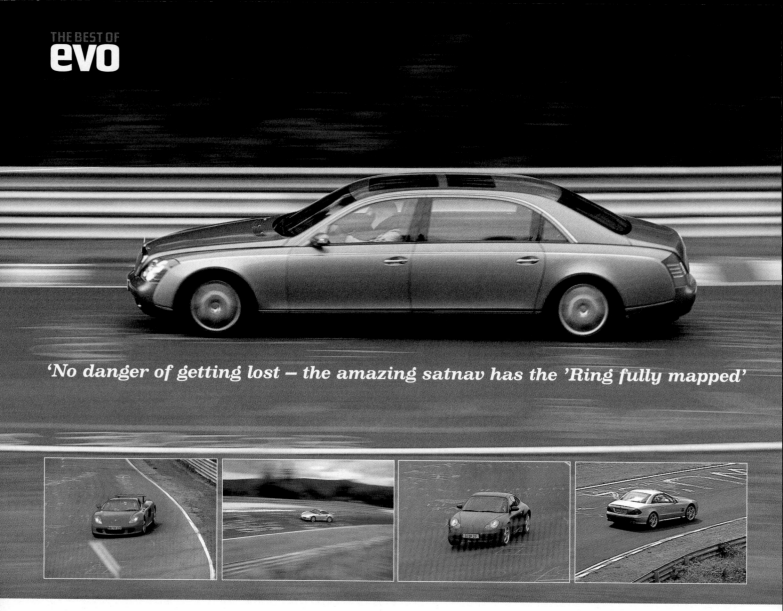

'No danger of getting lost – the amazing satnav has the 'Ring fully mapped'

When I get back to the paddock, there's a crowd around the Maybach. Judging by the knowing smirks on their faces, I get the feeling that they think I'm on day release from the asylum. Hanns is doing an excellent job of keeping them entertained with some fascinating Maybach facts: 600watts of music power with surroundsound for every seat in the house; rear lights that house 528 separate LEDs rather than conventional bulbs; a 0.5sqm solar panel above the driver to power part of the ventilation system, circulating air even when the car's parked; seven separate electric motors in every seat; aluminum rear doors that can be power-closed via a switch in the roof… The list just goes on.

And now there's nothing else for it. It's time to

don the helmet and venture out of the now-crowded paddock. Oh God this is embarrassing – I can't get out. It was empty when we arrived, but we've been hemmed in by various 911s and the like. Good old Hanns gets them to shuffle out of the way and at last I escape the throng and line up at the barrier. I choose position three on the damper control (comfort, normal, and 'Ring perhaps?), poke the ticket into the machine, and the barrier rises to let me through. Next obstacle – they've laid out some cones to stop you racing away, but they're arranged for cars somewhat smaller than the Maybach. One final wriggle and I'm finally on my way, hoofing down the straight to the sound of David giggling in the back.

No danger of getting lost on the 13 miles or so

Above: 20ft-plus Maybach makes an amazing spectacle on the hallowed tarmac of the Nürburgring Nordschleife. On the day we visited, cars out testing included Carrera GT (far left) and MercLaren SLR (above right). Oh, and a Bentley Continental, whose driver now wears a permanently puzzled expression

of twisting, swooping tarmac – the amazing satnav has the Nordschleife fully mapped, so I even have a crib sheet in the middle of the dash to work from. After just a few corners, my concern that we may have bitten off more than the Maybach can chew starts to melt away. The leviathan pulls itself together and settles into a rhythm that's considerably faster than I was expecting, the initial lurch as we pitch for the apex much calmer now that the dampers are stiffer, while the distant rear seems happy to take its lead from where the front is heading, which is excellent news.

We're taking up an awful lot of track, though, as we power on towards the far side of the circuit. Fortunately there doesn't seem to be much other traffic about. As we arrive at the famous Karussell and dive into the concrete ditch, the car judders as the power seemingly disappears. Turns out I've left the ESP on and the Maybach can't work out what's going on. Understandable really. You don't often fling a car into a ditch on purpose. I decide that since the Maybach actually appears to *handle*, we can do without the safety net of ESP from now on.

Metcalfe takes in the full enormity of what he's just done. Below: the full enormity of the Maybach's 5.5-litre twin-turbocharged V12

After all the twists that make up a lap, it's almost a shock to arrive at the long start/finish straight. The car slips into a higher gear and simply devours the space between us and the pull-in that leads back to the barrier. We swing round and find an excitable Hanns, who's been timing us with his watch. 'You've only been gone eight minutes!' he shouts. Maybe a *tad* optimistic, but it was a whole lot quicker than I'd have thought possible.

David jumps out to take some shots from trackside and I line up for another go. I blast off down the first straight, quicker this time, and into the first fiddly section. The Maybach could understeer for Germany, especially on the downhill sections, but it picks up so much speed on the straights that corner entry speed requires serious concentration.

I can't quite believe I've still got brakes either. I'm desperately trying to give them an easy time, but three tons takes a lot of stopping. Fortunately the Maybach has monster stoppers, 376mm discs up front, fitted with *two* four-pot callipers each side. They give you amazing confidence, though it helps to scrub off speed by unsettling the car through trail-braking into the corner. Tyre squeal is available in any variety you like, from a polite squeak from the run-flat Michelins to full-on, tortured howling as chunks of rubber try to break loose from the overworked carcasses.

It's difficult to avoid clipping the kerbs with a wheelbase of 12ft, but the suspension copes so well with the sudden compression that I start to do it more and more. A few bikers catch me up and pull terrific wheelies as they go pass, yet the Maybach holds them briefly through the corners. This is too much fun! I make myself more comfortable by switching the seat coolers on before activating the 'pulse' function on the driver's seat to get a gentle massage throughout the lap. Schumacher, eat your heart out.

As I line up for the barrier again, a pre-production Bentley Continental GT is going through the gate. Now this could be fun. Just then the dash pings up a warning of overheating brakes. No! Not now! The pedal feels fine but I have to take it easy, using more engine braking than before and pitching the car even harder into the corners. I catch the Bentley just as the brake warning disappears from the dash; it's as though the car knows what's going on. I pull out to overtake as we plunge through the Flugplatz section: 542bhp, 2855kg and a downhill slope are a powerful combination, too much for the Bentley as we power past through the compression and up the other side. God knows what the driver's thinking as he flaps around in the Maybach's wake, but we disappear and pull out the length of the final straight by the finish.

One lap to go. Do I pootle round to cool the brakes, or go for one more hot lap? Well, what would you do? Once again the brake warning light is on (it's the hauling down from 140mph on the final straight that does it), once again it disappears a few minutes in, yet the power never fades so I conclude the warning is a bit premature. Once again I'm amazed at the car's ability. It really is quite a tidy handler, nicely balanced, if a little hard to read through the lifeless steering. Far from being a nightmare, it's been a privilege to bring a Maybach to the 'Ring.

Hanns take the wheel for the drive to the airport – we're on a tight schedule to make the return flight, but Hanns knows the way and isn't scared to use the horses. David and I discover a bottle of champagne in the fridge, and set about demolishing it before we reach the airport.

Confession. Before today I thought the Maybach was one of the most hateful cars there's ever been: ugly, crass and pointless. As we spear down the autobahn at 230-250kph, sipping the cooled fizz, I'm not so sure. This is a truly amazing way to travel. The ride has reverted to 'comfort' now and there isn't a ripple to be felt. The big reclining seats may be a bit naff, but they're a damn sight more comfortable than the Rolls's rear bench over long distances. I've even become used to the car's looks. It may not be to British tastes, but think where the car is most likely to be sold and it starts to make sense.

And then there's the surprising turn of speed. Maybach conquers the Green Hell. Can I make a late nomination for Trackday Car of the Year? ∎

MAYBACH 62

○ Engine	V12, 5513cc, twin turbo
○ Transmission	Five-speed automatic
○ Max power	542bhp @ 5250rpm
○ Max torque	664lb ft @ 2300-3000rpm
○ Weight (kerb)	2855kg
○ Power-to-weight	193bhp/ton
○ 0-62mph	5.4sec (claimed)
○ Max speed	155mph (limited)
○ Price (2003)	£281,380
○ On sale	Now

O N
D A Y S
L I K E
T H E S E

In 2004 this was the stuff of dreams – two Pagani

Zondas, one of them the then-new Roadster, on deserted Italian mountain roads...

This time I'm going to be ready when Mr Pagani unleashes his V12-powered sonic assault. We're about to dive into another tunnel on a fast-flowing stretch of Italian autostrada, me in the latest Zonda Roadster, Horacio Pagani ahead driving a fixed-roof C12S. A few minutes ago we entered the first tunnel and Horacio nailed the accelerator – for no other reason than to enjoy the consequences of the howling 7.3-litre V12 being given its head – and it felt as though the air was literally being ripped apart.

The Zonda's engine is fabulously loud at any time, but from where I was sitting it was an utterly surreal, almost deafening sound that must have triggered seismographs across southern Europe. The sheer intensity of noise erupting from the blunt end of his fast disappearing Zonda had to be heard to be believed.

Now I'm just feet away from Horacio's glowing quad exhausts, which are pointing almost directly at my equally hard-charging open-topped Zonda.

This time there won't be just one V12 doing the damage inside the tunnel. This could just be the greatest cacophony ever heard.

Tunnels and supercars seem to have been made for each other, like gin and tonic, or bacon and butties, and if man ever gets around to building a V24, 14.6-litre, 1100bhp supercar , then I only hope it sounds as exquisite as this matched pair. Right on cue, Horacio bangs the accelerator to the floor, but this time I'm ready, poised in third gear, and a fraction of a second later I do the same. The naturally rich, velvety undertones of AMG's fabulous V12 creation soon metamorphose into a rising snarl that's more animal then mechanical as the tacho needle swings past the 5000rpm mark. The sound is now assaulting me from in front and behind, those 24 pistons hungry for more revs. The noise level doesn't subsiding one decibel before an even angrier finale over the last 500rpm or so, just before the 7200rpm limiter is breached. There's no thrash, no strain, just pure aggression bellowing from eight exhausts, assaulting not just my ears but my whole body thanks to the sheer number of decibels that are now bouncing in all

Above: Zonda Roadster leads C12S coupe through some suitably epic mountainscapes somewhere south of Rimini. Sound of two 7.3-litre V12s is enough to turn grown men into grinning idiots; the Sound of Music had nothing on this. Below right: Harry's in heaven (in a Zonda Roadster)

directions off the confines of the tunnel walls. It's almost a relief as we storm out from the tunnel exit, the warm Mediterranean air rushing over my exposed scalp at some 220 clicks or so, adding yet another layer of pleasure to the almost overwhelming sensory experience in which I'm immersed.

Welcome to the extraordinary world of the 200mph Pagani Zonda Roadster, surely one of the most extreme sports cars the world has ever seen. You've joined us as the car's creator, Horacio Pagani, and I are blasting down the autostrada running south from Rimini. We're heading to an area some 400km south of Modena, from where we set out earlier today. I've only read about our destination in a little-known guide book (even Horacio hasn't heard of the place), but it holds the promise of some of the quietest roads in Italy, combined with some pretty special scenery.

'No thrash, no strain, just pure aggression bellowing from eight exhausts'

The utterly feeble pretext we're using for heading down here in the first place is to discover if the outwardly delectable Zonda Roadster is actually a bit of a softie, a bit compromised when compared with the stupendous C12S coupe we know and love. Owners, it seems, are having problems deciding between the two, because of the eleven Roadsters built so far, seven of them have gone to existing owners of Zonda coupes. And those coupes haven't been part-exchanged for a shiny new Roadster, oh no. Those seven lucky owners now have both a closed-top *and* a Roadster sitting in their garages. That's a brace of supercars worth £700,000 or so. In fact we could be doing future buyers a big financial favour if we can decide which is the better driver's car. Well, that's my excuse…

First, though, we have to find a hotel for the night, so we pull into a sprawling town called Teramo to do just that. Predictably I soon find myself with the Carabinieri on my tail and in an instant the fairy lights are ablaze on top of their Alfa 156. I'm just about to pull into the hotel car park so they follow me in. Fortunately, this being Italy, all they actually want to do is look

at the car, so there's no tedious document-checking needed on this occasion. Instead Horacio quizzes them about the hotel we're about to book into and where to find the best restaurant in town – it turns out to be hosting the local olive oil competition tonight. What a civilised country Italy seems to be at moments like this when compared with our own Gatso-infested land.

Over dinner, I ask Horacio about the goals he set himself when he began to create the Zonda

back in 1995. He tells me that he wanted to fulfil a dream he'd had since he was a boy, to create something beautiful but very personal, something handcrafted but with no sacrifices being made in terms of quality anywhere in its construction. He cites Patek Philippe watches and Riva powerboats as having the same sort of standards in terms of manufacturing that he has sought to achieve. But above all he wanted to make a car that was both fantastically fast but also safe for owners to use.

This question of safety comes up again when I ask him about the need for such a zealous traction control setting on current Zondas. He insists it's the right thing to have, adding that any 550bhp mid-engined supercar is a potential weapon in the wrong hands. He wants his car to be safe for even inexperienced drivers to enjoy, though he does point out that you can turn the traction control off if you want to…

He also relates a chilling piece of automotive folklore – how a certain performance icon from the 1980s has so far killed over 200 drivers and passengers as a result of its explosive power delivery and propensity to spin off into the scenery at high speed. He doesn't want his car to gain the same sort of lethal reputation sometime in the future. He may have a point.

The current supercar that Horacio admits to admiring the most is the Porsche Carrera GT, because it seems to him to be a very pure, beautifully built GT car in a similar vein to his Zonda, even though it was planned to be produced in much bigger numbers. He likes the way it has remained a manual too, rather than adopting the electronically controlled clutch and paddles that seem so popular at the moment. He believes that removing the clutch from a supercar takes away something important from the driving experience and decreases the driving pleasure to be had as a result.

There's another reason he's taking a close interest in the Porsche Carrera GT – it's just eclipsed Pagani's long-held fastest lap of the Nürburgring in a road homologated car, set in 2002 when the German magazine *Sport Auto* recorded a lap of 7min 44sec in a standard C12S. Horacio was told that the damp conditions on the day probably cost around 7 seconds, and he fully intends having a crack at the Carrera GT's new record of 7min 32sec next summer, once a few tweaks have been introduced on the car.

We finish dinner and Horacio glances at his watch. It has two faces, one showing Italian time, the other the time in his Argentinean homeland. He makes his excuses – it's time to ring his father in his baker's shop in Argentina.

Next morning we're up before dawn to give us a chance of getting to the target area, some 70 miles away, just as the sun breaks cover over the horizon. The Roadster has taken on a mystical look overnight with a myriad of shimmering dewdrops now clinging to the highly polished,

'We've chanced upon some of the most magical roads you could wish for'

Purple Daze

In this world exclusive, we were first to drive
the 610bhp Caparo T1 on the road – and put
some figures to its mind-blowing performance

Clockwise from above: Catchpole (left) and T1 development driver Phil Bennett; the Caparo emerges from its trailer; not your usual attire for on-road driving; Henry in the hot seat. Below: interior of this test car isn't to production spec, but in what is surely the closest thing you can get to a race car for the road it feels far from out of keeping

'I was going to be the first journalist to drive the Caparo T1 on the road'

really don't like Clarkson sometimes. There I was, returned to the Catchpole family home for the weekend, and whilst mother Catchpole was concocting something hearty on the stove, the curly haired Vectra lover popped up on the screen in the corner of the room with the Caparo T1 in all its 610bhp, 600kg glory. I'm sure you've seen the skit: he has half of Surrey and Hampshire's emergency services on hand and then proceeds to say that it is undriveable at both low and high speeds and will kill all the Premiership footballers who buy it.

My parents fairly quickly caught on that this was the self same car that I was meant to be driving the following week and, whilst I'm not sure she would bemoan the loss of the odd Rooney or Terry, this was not the sort of jaunt that a mother wants to hear is in store for one of her offspring. It took quite a lot of persuading to convince her that it was merely Clarkson being a ham-fisted numpty and that I'd be fine. I didn't bother to tell her about Jason Plato.

A few days later the insurance disclaimer pinged into my inbox. Stipulating a helmet seemed fair enough, but full flameproof overalls,

boots and gloves? It didn't actually mention brown underwear, but...

Then, just two days beforehand, carefully laid plans started changing. Originally I was going to be the first journalist (and probably the second person ever) allowed to drive the T1 on the road, getting my chance to take the wheel while the car underwent testing in Wales. But then there were some cold feet; Caparo wasn't completely happy with how the car might ride on the road. Instead they'd decided that I could only ride in it as a passenger. This didn't exactly lift my heart and fill me with joy, because whilst I'd psyched myself up for controlling my own 922bhp-per-ton destiny, the idea of simply sitting there whilst someone else grappled with the car seemed rather unpleasant.

It's with this thought tumbling around in my mind that I wake up to a particularly miserable-looking Wales on a Thursday morning. The soggy sheep I pass on the way to the chosen test road look about as morose as me, but then I am in a KTM X-Bow, looking out through droplets streaking over my visor. When I arrive the weather hasn't improved and we find ourselves in the middle of a moist cloud that's fogging-up the hillside. Everyone agrees that there is nothing to be done in the way of photography

or driving, so I jump into Phil Bennett's Clio 197 and we go off in search of sun.

Phil has worked for **evo** in the past, but he is better known for his Touring Car and Sports Car exploits and setting a lap record round the Nürburgring in a turbocharged Radical SR2. He's very fast and knows absolutely no fear. For the last year, though, he has been working with Caparo on the T1 and it's enlightening chatting to him about it as he left-foot-brakes his way across the misty moors.

'They shouldn't have let it out so early,' he says of the early press exposure, 'but they rather sweetly thought the world's press would understand it was a prototype and cut it some slack. We've spent the time since then sorting things out, durability testing and honing the ride and handling. It is now a car that you can simply get in and drive without having to worry about it. That's what makes it more attractive than buying a second-hand F1 car.'

I ask Phil about the *Top Gear* piece.

'Well, I drove it around the track and it didn't understeer in the way that Clarkson said it did,' he says. It seems the trouble was that he of the '80s stonewashed jeans would boot the car in a straight line, be flabbergasted by how quick it was, then realise that there was a corner coming up rather rapidly, so he'd hit the brakes, wipe off too much speed and then try to accelerate the whole way through the corner. And of course if you do that then it's going to understeer – as would any other car.

The fact that Clarkson said it was unsafe was what really rankled Caparo, though, because one of the principal innovations that designer Ben Scott-Geddes is proud of is the safety aspect of the carbon tub – the same technology that protects F1 drivers so spectacularly. So why all the protective gear, you might ask, and what about the Jason Plato incident? Phil reiterates that the cars were still in development when the world's media started driving them, that Caparo was flattered by the attention, so it naïvely let them drive the prototypes. And though the car is now effectively finished, we're still gatecrashing a test session. I doubt any supercar goes through its development without crashing or breaking, it's just that car companies usually keep it all behind closed doors.

In front of us a valley has unfolded. Carpeted in snooker-table-green grass and ecclesiastically purple heather, it's being lit by shafts of sunlight breaking through the grey clouds above. Perfect. We fetch the others and return in convoy.

As it emerges from the trailer like a huge insect I'm shocked at the size of the Caparo. It makes it all the more impressive that it

weighs just 598kg dry (672kg with fluids and a half-load of fuel). Eighty per cent of the T1, by weight, is made by Caparo, if you include the engine developed and built for the car by Oxfordshire-based Menard Competition Technologies. The gearbox casting supports the suspension, F1 style, and houses Hewland racing gear sets, which along with dampers, battery and tyres (Michelin Pilot Sports – just like those on the KTM) accounts for the 20 per cent of the car that is non-Caparo parts.

Phil hurtles off up the road to check everything over, then drives some more for the benefit of Stuart Collins' camera lens, then it's time for my passenger ride. I don't provide much wind resistance if I stand sideways, which is just as well because the T1's passenger seat is tight. It's also set back slightly, so you get the same view of the steering wheel as if you were looking over someone's shoulder trying to read their newspaper on a crowded train.

My first impression of the Caparo is a fairly obvious one: it's fast. Then I realise that I'm not being shaken to pieces. The ride is actually very good; not plush, but not vertebrae-jarringly hard either. Even Phil is pleased by how well it's performing on public tarmac. It certainly bodes well for the planned assault on the Nürburgring, where they want to go for Bellof's 6min 11sec outright record set in a Porsche 962 in 1983.

'The ride is actually very good and bodes well for the assault on the Ring record'

Above: T1 is a showcase for the technologies Caparo can offer. Bottom left: Caparo group has a division that specialises in brakes. Below: glass canopy is available as an option, but not in the UK

INSIDE THE COMPANY BEHIND THE T1

Imagine you wanted to produce a new car. You'd need a vehicle design team, someone to build you a prototype, companies to handle the production engineering and tool making, then others to manufacture the bodywork and powertrain. Getting all those parties to work together could be challenging, so now imagine if there was one company that could do it all. Well there is. It's called Caparo.

Caparo has a massive global manufacturing capability, with factories in India, Europe and the USA, and over 5000 people delivering a £1bn turnover. It makes most of the parts for the Tata Nano, the brakes for Land Rover's Defender and engine blocks for Aston. In fact it can make just about anything you could want in a car except the tyres and stereo.

At the 'pointy end' of the organisation is Caparo Vehicle Technologies (CVT), providing cutting-edge design and analysis. With a small team of 12 highly talented engineers, it blends skills from aerospace, materials engineering, production and motorsport, and is guided by Ben Scott-Geddes, the ex-McLaren F1 and SLR design guru – and creator of the Caparo T1, the ultimate showcase for the advanced technologies developed by the company.

Pondering the relevance a car like the T1

has to the man on the street, I ask Ben if exotic materials such as carbonfibre will be commonplace in a car of the future. 'I think that in 10 to 15 years' time customers will notice their car is no longer made of metal,' he says. 'Composites will become mainstream, but only when the technology is re-engineered for mass production. So yes, things like carbon will be more common, but they will be very different from today's materials molecularly. Here, we're starting a new relationship with one of the world's biggest chemical companies in order to develop these new materials.'

Today composites only make commercial sense at the two extremes of the car world – saving weight on supercars and (used sparingly) enabling small cars to get good crash performance out of a small space. More affordable composites will enable more cars to benefit from their weight-saving properties, and reducing weight is a virtuous circle: brakes and suspension can be scaled down, saving on the all-important unsprung weight and improving performance, then the engine and transmission can be shrunk, saving even more weight and reducing emissions.

But what about metals? After all, Caparo owns a number of alloy casting companies and supplies engine blocks to NASCAR. 'Metals will continue to have an important role to play,' reckons Ben, 'particularly in things like the engine and possibly outer body panels, but many small metal parts can be integrated into a composite moulding, improving performance and reducing the number of nuts and bolts.'

Another part of the Caparo group is AP Braking, which provides a major outlet for braking innovations, such as the uprated monoblock setup for the Aston Martin DB9,

which gives a whopping 24 per cent reduction in stopping distance and improves pedal feel. According to Caparo, today's race-style carbon brakes will remain only on exotic cars, but other technologies will replace them, possibly integrating electric motors/generators into the brakes for the next generation of hybrids.

To get a feel for what's possible with the technologies Caparo has to offer, I ask Ben what he thinks he could get the weight of a luxury 4x4 – which can currently tip the scales at up to 2700kg – down to. 'I think we could realistically achieve between 1500kg and 1800kg, maintaining the same performance and refinement,' he says.

CVT also makes fully working concept cars for clients, and although many of these vehicles will never be seen by the public due to their confidential nature, some projects are more open. For instance, Caparo is currently working with Lotus, Jaguar Land Rover and MIRA to develop a 'green' limo.

It's not just cars, either. The team has worked on diverse applications including a structural roof on a building, and we may even see a Caparo America's Cup racing yacht in 2011.

From a company that started out in the '60s making bent tubes, it has grown and spread into a wealth of complementary fields, which all add up to a very powerful and innovative organisation whose influence will touch most of us in one form or another.

Ralph Hosier

'With an engine revving to 10,000rpm strapped to your back, sounds in the T1 are felt as much as heard'

There's more photography. The police turn up to have a look. More photography. Then just as the light is turning distinctly eveningy, something remarkable happens.

'You really should drive it if you're going to write about it,' says Phil. 'Just pretend that you haven't!'

Simply sitting in the driver's seat is immensely exciting. We often talk about bucket seats but this is the real deal, with your bum lower than your feet and your legs stretched out on a level with your chest as you lie back. It's a wonderfully secure feeling with the sides gently pressing your shoulders, like lying in a narrow bath. There's no elbowroom to your right, but it doesn't feel restrictive.

The chaps from Caparo are quick to point out that this isn't a customer-spec interior, but I have to say I like the slightly raw, used feeling of this test car. The wheel is pure race-car and doesn't even make a pretence at being round, although the red button does activate a horn, which I doubt you'd find on Kimi's car. The rows of LEDs are shift lights and the lovely blue anodised dial beneath the screen is for the adjustable traction control – all the way to the right for fully on, turn left in 25 per cent increments to progressively loosen the leash.

Ignition, starter, lights, adjust the mirrors (electrically!). There are three pedals, all requiring a reassuring weight of pressure, but you only need the clutch to get off the line. There's a big thump as the sequential 'box engages first gear, yet the clutch doesn't bite viciously so it's not too difficult to get away without stalling. Short-shift to second, visor down as another bug meets its end splatting into the forehead of my Arai. (UK windscreen regs allow for a small aeroscreen, but anything bigger requires a wiper, which in turn needs a glass screen because plastics get scratched too easily, so the full plastic canopy is only offered in foreign climes.)

Traction control to 100 per cent and squeeze the throttle all the way. With an engine revving to 10,000rpm strapped to your back, sounds in the T1 are felt as much as heard. From the outside it sounds like an elephant screaming in pain. The figures that John Barker will record later (see p202) will give you some idea of how bonkers quick the T1 is, but the wonderful thing is that it isn't actually scary. Admittedly, it's so fast it makes you hold your breath until your brain has switched to a higher level of processing, but somehow you feel secure. The snug, low driving position

means you're not buffeted unbearably by slipstream, and because the whole of the Caparo feels like it was designed to go this fast, I feel much more at ease than I'd expected.

At first the steering feels disconcertingly light just around the straight-ahead, but as soon as you turn the wheel it weights up in your gloved hands and you can push the wide front track into the corner with confidence. The monobloc calipered steel brakes wipe off speed as astonishingly as you'd hope, but it's the car's stability that gives you the confidence to keep going deeper into the pedal each time. You'd think it would feel skittish and twitchy but it doesn't. I even risk turning the traction control down – something which I need to do when turning round at the end of the road just to give the very shallow steering lock a helping hand.

I have five or six runs up and down the road. The first few are with Phil pacing me in the KTM. He says he was flat out and I'm sure he was, but the ease with which I could yo-yo up to his bumper and drop back was absurd. By the fourth run I'm imagining what it would be like if the Targa Florio, Pescara or Reims still existed for modern LMP1 or F1 cars. It is an extraordinary sensation, because for all the world you feel like you are in one of Henri Pescarolo's finest (and they reckon it's as quick), yet I've just driven across a cattle grid and, as I swoop down the hill (a bit like Eau Rouge in reverse), the deserted road is diving off through

'I'm tingling with excitement as I take off my helmet'

Above: doing the numbers at Bedford and Bruntingthorpe (see over the page). Left: rear lights are neatly integrated into the uprights for the spoiler. Right: engine was originally developed to meet Indy 500 regs, where it would have run on methanol, but it was never used for racing and instead further developed for road use

a beautiful wilderness of a landscape.

As I pull up next to the lay-by where everyone's waiting, I dip the clutch, thumb the black button on the wheel for neutral and kill the ignition. I'm tingling with excitement as I loosen the belts and take my helmet and balaclava off, finding it hard to believe what's just happened. The only useful criticism that I can think of is that the paddles are a bit bendy (they're very, very thin carbonfibre) and that the dash could be better, both things that it seems Phil wants to change, so he is glad to have someone else concur. Whilst still grinning, I ask if I can write about driving it. We told the truth when it was embarrassing on the launch so now it would be lovely, I say, to tell the truth again and let everyone know how good it is. You can work out their answer.

So, is it a road car? Well, you can certainly drive it on the road. When you stand next to its shark gills and wings, everything rational in you screams 'This is ridiculous!'. Yet on this evidence the only thing that really makes it less of a road car than the KTM is its huge turning circle. So just avoid mini roundabouts. And speed bumps. If you can afford to buy one of the 100 planned cars then I'm sure you could get a minion to transport it up to North Wales or the west coast of Scotland. Then you could helicopter yourself in. I promise it would be worth it.

CAPARO AGAINST THE CLOCK

PERFORMANCE
CAPARO T1

0-30	2.2
0-40	2.8
0-50	3.4
0-60	3.8
0-70	4.3
0-80	4.9
0-90	5.6
0-100	6.2
0-110	7.0
0-120	7.8
0-130	8.9
0-140	10.1
0-150	11.6
0-160	13.3
0-170	16.1
0-180	20.1

1/4 MILE

sec	11.0
mph	143
Conditions: dry	

We're just halfway down Bruntingthorpe's two-mile runway and all of the shift lights are lit up in sixth gear. That's 180mph. Not for the last time today the Caparo is delivering figures I wouldn't have believed had they not been recorded by our data logger. It's the smaller numbers we're more interested in, though. Caparo's initial and arresting claim of 5.7sec to 100mph was calculated for a slick-shod car, one-up. Today the T1 is on P Zero Corsas and, to get a fair 'two-up' figure, Phil Bennett has wriggled into the passenger seat. He reckons the optimum start revs lie between 4000 and 6000rpm.

Clutch down, right-hand paddle tugged, revs lifted into the region… I drop the clutch and after an initial lunge the Caparo falters, its V8 off-cam… and then picks up, and then I'm steering into a slide as it soars on-cam. A dreadful start but even so 100mph comes up in 7.2sec. First gear goes to over 80mph and upshifts feel instantaneous and utterly seamless. Next time I use more revs and seem to be steering left and right for hundreds of yards before the tyres hook up: 0-100mph in 6.8sec. After a few more goes, a part-bog, part-spin launch bags a beaut: 0-100mph in 6.2sec. Faster than any road car we've ever tested. Thing is, it could be faster still – 0-30 in 2.2 is tardy. With optimised traction control it could be half a second faster. And so to Bedford.

I didn't quite believe Bennett when he said he expected the Caparo to be around 10 seconds a lap faster than anything else around the West Circuit. Or perhaps I didn't want to. The current record holder

is the Gumpert Apollo (1:19.4). The idea that anything on road tyres could take ten seconds out of that seems absurd, yet my tentative first lap to warm up the tyres is a 1:22.4. The next is a 1:17.8, almost two seconds under the Gumpert's record. I don't know this, however, because Bennett isn't in the passenger seat with the VBOX – he made himself scarce when I pulled on my helmet. Can't say I blame him.

Lap three is a 1:14.5, lap four a 1:13.6, and it isn't done yet. The staggering, unreal acceleration, the instantaneous gearshifts and the downforce-enhanced cornering make it feel more like guiding a missile than driving a car. Understeer? Nah. In the slowest corners there's a little push but back on the power it's the back sliding that you need to worry about. The T1 feels neutral and nailed through all the fast turns, though, apart from the last one with its unfavourable mid-turn camber change. On lap five it power oversteers more than on previous laps and I travel half the length of the pit straight backwards, wreathed in tyre smoke. Time for a pit stop to gather thoughts.

At Bennett's suggestion I wind the traction control up from 25 to 50 per cent, and it helps. There's less drama and even more speed, and after a couple more laps my hands are starting to ache through the fastest turn, the exit of Palmer Curves, taken at 120mph and pulling up to 1.8g, as the VBOX later reveals. And the best lap? 1:10.8sec. Staggering. Even two-up it would have obliterated the current record.

John Barker

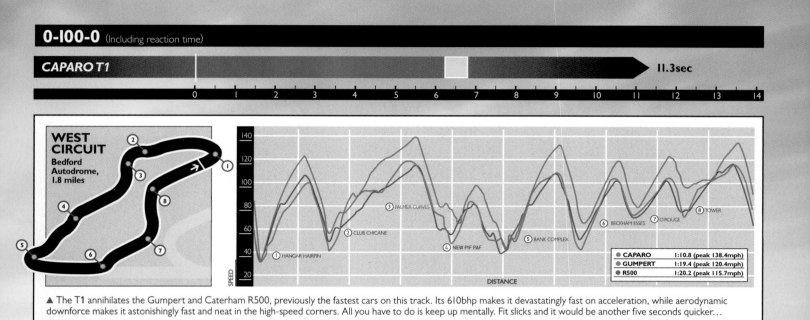

0-100-0 (Including reaction time)

CAPARO T1 ━━━━━━━━━━━━━━━━━━━━━━━━━━━━➤ **11.3sec**

0　1　2　3　4　5　6　7　8　9　10　11　12　13　14

WEST CIRCUIT
Bedford Autodrome, 1.8 miles

SPEED — 20 40 60 80 100 120 140

① HANGAR HAIRPIN
② CLUB CHICANE
③ PALMER CURVES
④ NEW PIF PAF
⑤ BANK COMPLEX
⑥ BECKHAM ESSES
⑦ O'ROUGE
⑧ TOWER

DISTANCE

● CAPARO	1:10.8	(peak 138.4mph)
● GUMPERT	1:19.4	(peak 120.4mph)
● R500	1:20.2	(peak 115.7mph)

▲ The T1 annihilates the Gumpert and Caterham R500, previously the fastest cars on this track. Its 610bhp makes it devastatingly fast on acceleration, while aerodynamic downforce makes it astonishingly fast and neat in the high-speed corners. All you have to do is keep up mentally. Fit slicks and it would be another five seconds quicker…

'It feels more like guiding a missile than driving a car'

Dino

'I am convinced that when a man tells a woman he loves her, he only means that he desires her, and that the only perfect love in this world is that of a father for his son.'

These words were written by Enzo Ferrari in 1961, five years after the death of his son, Alfredo, known affectionately as Dino.

Dino's tragically short life – he was just 24 – was soon woven into Ferrari folklore, while a series of racing cars and road cars were named in his honour, the most famous being the gorgeous Dino 246 GT.

But what was Dino, the man, really like? And does the 246 GT deserve its iconic status? Peter Tomalin went to Modena for answers and was granted rare access to the people and places at the heart of the Ferrari legend.

This, then, is the story of Dino Ferrari and the cars that carried his name

Pictures: David Shepherd

Dino 246 GT looks as pretty today as ever. Some owners added Ferrari shields, but a totally original 246 has only Dino badges

Boy, it's warm in here. Warm and very noisy. Just a few miles south of the Ferrari factory, the road climbs rapidly into the hills, stringing together the sleepy villages of Montagnana, Montardone and Serramazzoni. The tiny silver sports car howls between the corners, its V6 engine revving close to 7000rpm before each upshift. To my left, in the driver's seat, owner Massimo Cecchi is clearly enjoying wringing every last drop of speed from his wonderful little Dino. 'It's a great engine, no?' he shouts above the raucous exhaust note and the rush of the wind – both side-windows are fully down to draw some air

into the cockpit, yet our shirts still cling to our backs when we pause, elated, in a lay-by a few minutes later. Massimo grins and points a finger at me. 'Now your turn.'

It's always slightly nerve-wracking, driving someone else's supercar, especially when they're sitting alongside, and even more so when it's as achingly beautiful and totally pristine as this gorgeous Dino 246 GT. And I want so badly for it to be great, because this is a car I've loved since I was a boy. For me, this is so much more than just another road test.

In fact this story is something I've been wanting to write for years, ever since I read Brock Yates' biography of Enzo Ferrari, which

includes a number of evocative passages about the young Dino: how he became wracked by a mysterious illness before dying at the age of just 24, how his father came almost to deify his memory, and how he inspired a series of 'baby Ferrari' racing cars and road cars.

I wanted to drive a 246 GT on the roads around Maranello. I wanted to ask the people at the factory whether we would ever see another Dino road car, as has been rumoured in sections of the press. Most of all, though, I wanted to know what Dino the man was like, and to try to get to the truth of some of the stories about him. Did he really design the first Ferrari V6 engine, the first engine that would

'It's nerve-wracking driving someone else's supercar, even more so when it's as achingly beautiful and totally pristine as this Dino'

carry his name, or was that all part of Ferrari mythology?

Dino's short life was dogged by debilitating illness, but he did have one blissful means of escape. He forged a close friendship with a young test driver at the factory, Sergio Sighinolfi, and the two of them would spend hours ripping along these very hill-roads above Maranello in whatever was the latest Ferrari model – a 212 Inter, perhaps, or a fearsome Mondial.

The Modena region in summer can be stiflingly hot, the temperature frequently in the mid-30s; it's only late-April now, but already it's in the high-20s. As Massimo brings the howling 246 GT to a halt in the next sleepy village and we swap places, still grinning, it's not very hard to imagine what it must have been like for Dino and Sergio. I blip the throttle; the revs fly again. Italian hill-roads, Ferrari sports cars, baking sunshine – some things seem almost eternal.

REWIND TO THE MORNING, and the quiet, leafy back-streets of central Modena, 15 minutes up the road from smaller Maranello. Modena is where the Scuderia Ferrari was formed, where the Ferrari family lived – and where they were laid to rest. We've been brought here by Ferrari press officer Roberto Casolari to meet a man who was as close to the family as perhaps anyone has ever been.

We park near an imposing, stone-built 19th century apartment block; Roberto thumbs a numbered button on the intercom panel, the door clicks open and we step off the pavement into a cool, marble-floored hallway. Two flights of stairs up, we're greeted with a warm handshake by an elderly man who seems strangely familiar (only later does it click that I must have seen him in numerous photos with Enzo Ferrari). 'Peter,' says Roberto, 'May I introduce Franco Gozzi…'

Inside the apartment it's dimly lit, the windows mostly shuttered, but we're ushered into a small sitting room which is flooded by

Left, from top: Franco Gozzi at home, surrounded by
Ferrari mementoes; nine-year-old Dino with his dad;
Gozzi makes a point; Dino cuts his engineering teeth;
lunch at the Montana with Massimo Cecchi

soft late-morning sunlight, the high-ceilinged walls covered in photos and memorabilia. Everywhere you look is Ferrari.

Franco Gozzi's life first became entwined with Ferrari in 1958 when, fresh from university, he secured a work placement at Maranello. He must have made an immediate impression, because one of his first assignments was drafting the thesis that won Enzo Ferrari an honorary degree in engineering. In 1960 he joined the payroll, initially as assistant to the sales director, later as head of the press office, in which role he was for many years Enzo's filter, spokesman and confidant. For several years he was also director of motorsport (it's all there in his book, Memoirs of Enzo Ferrari's Lieutenant). Basically, Gozzi was at Enzo Ferrari's side for three decades and was still at the heart of the company when Luca di Montezemolo began his reign. Franco Gozzi *is* Ferrari's history.

But there's more. By one of those almost spooky twists of fate, Franco Gozzi was born in 1932, the same year as Enzo's first-born. The young Franco actually went to school with the young Dino Ferrari.

So I ask him to tell me about Dino. Some reports suggest that, even as a small boy, he was frail and sickly. Not so, says Franco. 'I knew him from school, we were classmates, and he was a normal boy till he was a teenager. Tall, average build, active, just another boy…

'After we were at secondary school together, he went to technical school while I studied humanities. When I saw him later he was quite different. Very stiff and awkward in his movements. By the time he was about 19 it was obvious something was not right…'

Dino, it would transpire, was showing the classic symptoms of muscular dystrophy, a genetic condition that causes muscle-wasting, resulting in increasing weakness and disability. 'For many, many years nobody really understood why he died,' says Franco. 'Muscular dystrophy wasn't really understood. But I have no doubt that's what it was. Later Mr Ferrari made many donations to muscular dystrophy research.'

There seems to be no question that Enzo was genuinely devoted to Dino. In fact the boy influenced his father's life even before he was born. Enzo had vowed he would give up motor-racing if he had a son, and he was as good as his word. When Laura Ferrari gave birth to a boy on January 19, 1932, Enzo called time on his driving career, turning instead to team management, first with Alfa Romeos (under

the Scuderia Ferrari banner) and, after the war, with his own cars. The boy was named Alfredo, after Enzo's late brother, though everyone called him Alfredino (little Alfredo), which was later shortened to Dino.

The family lived in a tiny two-bedroomed apartment over the Scuderia at 11 Viale Trento Trieste in Modena. They weren't wealthy, but Ferrari made sure Dino had the best schooling available. After high school and technical school, he studied economics at Bologna then mechanical engineering at a Swiss university. In fact, although he gained a degree, it was only a two-year course, Ferrari perhaps being mindful of his son's failing health. 'In Italy to have the title of engineer would take five years,' says Gozzi, 'but for the father, this was enough – enough to call his son an engineer. The father was so proud of the son…'

And with good reason. Dino was certainly bright, passionate about cars, and with a good eye for styling as well as an aptitude for engineering. Even after he started work in the engine design department at Maranello, he also spent many hours at the Scaglietti coachworks, which was just across the road from the factory, and he is widely credited with the design of the pretty 750 Monza, one of the definitive mid-'50s sports-racing Ferraris.

Of his involvement in the design of the engine that would be named in his honour, there is more doubt. Ferrari legend has it that as Dino's health deteriorated and he spent more time confined to his bed, he would sketch engineering concepts that he and his father would later discuss with engineer Vittorio Jano. One of these, towards the end of his life, was for a 1.5-litre V6 engine.

Franco Gozzi, having spoken to most of the people who were around at the time, thinks it unlikely that Dino actually designed the engine. But did he have some input into the design? A long silence. 'It's… possible. He was involved in the discussions, yes, but how much was his idea we'll never know for sure.

'What is certain is he had a great passion for engines – everyone I spoke to told me this. He was like his father in this regard. Ferrari himself was only interested in the engines, never chassis and bodywork. I remember he would speak of Dino as his *technical* son. My technical son…'

Despite his illness, Dino put on a brave face for the world. Franco Gozzi's wife, Gabriella, also knew the Ferrari family well – her father, Antonio, ran the barbershop that Enzo Ferrari would visit first thing every day, for a shave and to catch up on all the Modenese gossip (old man Ferrari was an inveterate gossip). Gabriella doesn't speak English, but through Franco she tells us how she would visit Dino when he was confined to bed, either at the apartment above

Tomalin enjoys the
246 GT on the old
Ferrari test routes.
Below: a teenaged
Dino at the wheel of
a 166 Inter, which
had a 2-litre V12.
One of his greatest
pleasures was driving
these same roads

'The little Dino is wonderfully light on its feet… and bursting with energy'

the Scuderia or at the local hospital. He was, she says, always smiling, always positive.

I ask Franco how Mr Ferrari remembered Dino when they spoke of him. 'He was already an icon, a myth. There were pictures of Dino in the factory, in his office, everywhere. I remember he asked me to write that Dino was his *total* son. Total son. It seems strange now, although for a long time of course it was not widely known that there was a second son…'

It would emerge only years after Dino's death that Ferrari had another son, Piero, by his long-time mistress, Lina Lardi. Born in 1945, Piero Ferrari is now 62 and has long since taken his

place in the Ferrari company hierarchy – today he is vice president of Ferrari and retains a 10 per cent stake in the company. It's highly unlikely the two brothers ever met, says Gozzi. 'Dino died in 56, and until 1960 it was absolutely secret that there was a second son. In 1961 Mr Ferrari brought Piero to me to find some work for him…'

It's said Enzo planned and hoped that Dino would inherit and one day run the company. Franco Gozzi shrugs, turns down the corners of his mouth; he is not so sure. 'The business was evolving, everything changes… Mr Ferrari himself, he would tell me, "I am not an

industrialist, I am not a car manufacturer. I am an artisan." His life was here in Modena. He was the right person at the right time. If you look at the business now, it requires a different sort of character. I am not sure Dino was that person.'

We leave Franco and Gabriella Gozzi in the apartment they have shared since they married in 1964, an apartment that is both a family home and a repository of so much of Ferrari's past, its essence. I could listen to Franco all day, but we have a lunch appointment – at the famous Montana restaurant that nestles alongside the Fiorano test track back in Maranello – with Florentine businessman and car collector Massimo Cecchi and, of course, his beautiful little Dino.

The iconic Dino road car appeared 40 years ago as the 206 GT, a miniature exotic with an aluminium body and an all-alloy 2-litre V6 engine. Better known is the later 246, which had a more powerful, 2.4-litre, iron-block version of the V6, albeit with heavier steel bodywork to push along. Heavier and notoriously rust-prone, though there's no sign of the Italian tin-worm on Massimo's flawless 1971 example.

There's no Ferrari badge on the 246 GT – Dino was launched as a separate brand; in fact the only prancing horse is on the chassis plate tucked away inside the engine bay (below).

But you know within an instant of turning the ignition key that this car has the heart and soul of Ferrari. That isn't just a V6 behind you – it's half of a Ferrari V12 – and it revs with such energy and such presence that you soon forget the unexceptional 195bhp power-peak, instead savouring the intake roar through the three Weber carburettors and the exhaust's bark through the four chromed tailpipes slung beneath that perfect Kamm tail.

Massimo, of course, knows that this engine thrives on revs. I'm not expecting the Dino to feel quick – contemporary road testers recorded 0-60 in a little over 7sec – but when he pins the throttles wide open through second and third it sprints with affecting vigour. You

just need to keep it above about 3500 – it can occasionally stumble on part-throttle at the bottom of the rev-range, but at the top-end it feels like it'll happily pull all the way to the 7800rpm red line and keep doing it for hour after hour – just like a race engine would.

It's a real event, this little car, even from the passenger seat, looking out through the deeply dished windscreen, the sensual curves of the front wings rushing past the greenery as we climb into the hills just south of Maranello. The seats themselves are tiny, the backs barely reaching your shoulders and fixed at a semi-reclined angle. When it's my turn I find the driving position initially odd – not only am I semi recumbent, but the steering wheel is a real stretch away; it also seems to be angled towards the headlining, while my knees are slightly splayed around it and the pedals are heavily offset to the right. Oh, and the five-speed gearbox with its exposed gate has first on a dog-leg, across towards me and back. Helping stabilise my accelerating heart-rate are an encouragingly progressive clutch and quite brilliant visibility for a mid-engined car, helped by amusingly thin screen-pillars. Directly ahead is a lovely little oval-shaped instrument pod that's packed with gauges, the important ones clearly visible under the slim, leather-wrapped rim of a tiny, three-spoke steering wheel.

Everything about the Dino speaks of lightness, subtlety and delicacy, and having watched Massimo deftly palm the chromed, ball-topped gearstick around the gate, I'm surprised at the sheer physicality of driving it. The unassisted steering feels initially light once you're on the move – you almost nudge it into a corner – but once it's in there it loads up massively, so much so that in tighter turns you want to haul yourself up straighter in the seat to get more leverage. The pedals and gearshift need firm applications too, and the downshift from third to second requires you to match the revs perfectly – ideally by double-declutching – to avoid a most indelicate scrunching sound. Get it right and it's hugely satisfying. I managed it, ooh, at least twice, eliciting a cheer from the ever-encouraging Massimo alongside.

The faster you go, and the more you tune into the chassis, the more fun it gets. The Dino rides fluidly, no doubt partly thanks to the tall sidewalls of its 205/70 V-rated Michelin radials which sit on 14in(!) Cromadora alloys. They also no doubt contribute to its malleability at the limits of grip. This car feels as if it's constantly moving around a central axis, its attitude dictated largely by your right foot. It'll power-oversteer too, as Massimo ably

demonstrates later, smearing the tail wide as we exit some of the tighter corners. The controls might be heavy, but down at the road surface the little Dino is wonderfully light on its feet.

Best of all, though, the engine feels as if it's bursting with energy, just like it must have done when it was new. It sounds quite marvellously throaty when you hold the throttle flat, all the way through four, five, six thousand revs, while on the over-run there's a micro-fusillade of pops and coughs. Just as well we've got the windows down, all the better to hear it. In fact I'm so absorbed with driving the Dino that after 30 minutes I'm not even aware of the eccentricities of the driving position. That's how good it is. At one point we pass a stationary 599 GTB wearing 'Prova' plates, the factory test driver pausing to log an observation; I glance at the car, at the wonderful scenery and at Massimo, who genuinely seems to be enjoying himself despite the occasional syncro-defeating downshift, and it feels as if these roads could have been made for the Dino – or maybe it's the other way round…

That night we eat out at the Cavallino restaurant, just opposite the factory gates back in Maranello, and wash down some more first-rate pasta with some Ferrari-branded Modenese lambrusco, which tastes surprisingly good, for lambrusco. You can see why some people live and breathe the marque – round here you can even eat and drink Ferrari.

SPEAK TO ANYONE WHO KNEW DINO and a clear picture emerges, of a bright, personable, enthusiastic young man with a genuine love of cars. Carlo Benzi, who worked on the admin side at the Scuderia, can remember being driven from Modena to Maranello on several occasions by the young Ferrari. 'Dino had a lot of passion for cars, for both engines and design,' he says. 'In fact he often used to advise his father about these things.' Dino was never fit enough to race, but his father did provide a number of road cars which he drove with enthusiasm, initially small Fiats but later a 2-litre Ferrari that Dino and the young test driver Sighinolfi would take into the hills.

Doug Nye, the leading Ferrari historian, has spoken to a number of people who knew Dino. 'Everyone recalls him as having been a very pleasant and engaging young man – obviously pale, awkward in his movements and increasingly fragile – a useful ally, with his father's ear – but straightforward and open, not a politician…' As Franco Gozzi says: 'Everybody says he was a good, normal boy – not a genius maybe, but it is impossible to find someone

Cars called Dino. Going clockwise from below, 'sharknose' 156 F1, 206 GT, 196 S at Watkins Glen in 1961, 246 Tasmania down under in '68, 1973 308 GT4, 206 S at the Ring in '66, 166 F2 at Monza in '68, 156 F2 chasing a Maserati 250F in the '57 GP di Modena; 1969 206 SP and 246 S at Sebring in 1962. Opposite above: 246 F1 in the Galleria

who speaks against the boy.'

American racer and Carroll Shelby spent many hours with Dino during the summer and autumn of 1955; in Brock Yates' book, Shelby recalls Dino as being shy around strangers but open and affable with friends. He also remembers him losing weight quite noticeably in this period, while his legs became so stiff he had difficulty walking. By the end of the year he was mostly idling the days away with the mechanics and customers who packed the old Scuderia, which was by then a car delivery building. The young Ferrari spoke pretty good English, something his father never did, which meant he got on well with the Americans and Brits who were by now regularly frequenting the Scuderia. 'Dino was a good guy,' says Shelby, 'always smiling.'

But he was also a very sick young man. By early 1956, with Modena shrouded in the winter fog typical of the region, Dino's health was deteriorating rapidly. He was spending more and more time in bed, tended by his mother, visited after work by his father, and – possibly – sketching his proposals for a new V6 engine.

The end came on June 30. Although there was for many years a degree of mystery surrounding his illness, most who have since studied his case history agree that as well as suffering with muscular dystrophy, Dino also contracted nephritis, a disease of the kidneys, which his debilitated system could not fight. Eventually his kidneys gave out. His life had spanned just 24 years, five months and eleven days.

WE'RE ON THE VIALE TRENTO TRIESTE, standing at the exact spot where the Scuderia Ferrari used to be, where Enzo and Laura and Dino used to live. It's mid morning, the second day of our visit. These days there's a commercial bank on the site, and an engineering business owned by Piero Ferrari, independent of Ferrari SpA. There's also a multi-storey car park – in fact the only clue that this is the birthplace of the whole Ferrari legend is a nondescript sign for the car park: 'Garage Ferrari'. Look across the wide, busy road, however, and plenty of the old street remains. We're met by Giancarlo, another

Below from left: site of Scuderia today, and as it was. Enzo and Dino with 'Nando' Righetti, gentleman racer and valued customer – if he crashed his new Ferrari he bought another! Above: early Dino V6 engine in 246 F1. Above right: climbing the steps to the Ferrari crypt

retired Ferrari employee, who points to what used to be a car repair shop, a cafe, a Lancia dealership, another garage, apartments, shops… Trento Trieste was (and still is) a noisily bustling thoroughfare.

A few days after Dino's death, the funeral cortege formed up just here and made its way first to the local Sant'Agnese church, for a service attended by around 1000 mourners, and then out of town to the San Cataldo cemetery where his body would be placed in the family crypt. And it's Dino's final journey that we retrace now, with press officer Roberto Casolari as our guide.

On the way we pause at a rather grand apartment block a couple of streets away in Garibaldi square – this was Enzo's home in his later life – and further on we pass the site of the disused Modena racetrack, now the Park Enzo Ferrari. After a drive of 15 minutes or so, just as the outskirts of town give way to scrubby countryside and allotments, we arrive at the San Cataldo Cemetery. It's vast – ever since the middle of the 19th century, this has been the last resting place of the great and good of Modena. The perimeter wall seems to run for almost a mile, but eventually we find an entrance, park in a dusty courtyard and make our way to the administration office.

Problem. We can look at the outside of the Ferrari family crypt, but we can't go inside, and we can't take any photos, at all. Roberto puts a call through to his bosses back at Maranello. Nothing doing. So we wander around the

impressive Romanesque central square and look at the outside of the crypt – and then just as we're about to leave, something very wonderful happens. A call comes through from the office of Piero Ferrari himself: we've been granted access; his driver is on his way with the key to the crypt. Twenty minutes later he's here.

With a combination of mounting excitement and due reverence we crunch down the gravel path, climb the steps, and watch as the key is turned in the lock and the big, heavy iron gates are swung open. And then we step inside.

It's cool, quiet, serene, rather like a small chapel. The walls are granite and marble, carved with latin inscriptions, and there's a high, translucent, domed ceiling; around us are the tombs of Enzo Ferrari, his father, his mother, his brother… all bearing little enamelled portraits of the deceased. And over to our right, alongside that of his mother Laura, Dino's tomb, with a small portrait of that now-familiar smiling face. Ing. Alfredo 'Dino' Ferrari, 1932-1956.

There's a bouquet of what look like dark red roses placed on the floor; and on the shelf above Enzo Ferrari's tomb, a small, slightly dusty model of an F40. No-one says a word for several moments, the silence eventually broken by Shep's camera. *Schlick*. It's been quite a morning.

LESS THAN A YEAR AFTER DINO'S death, the first V6-engined Ferrari appeared. It

was a Grand Prix car, the 156, built to the then-new F2 regs, and cast on the cam covers of the 1.5-litre V6 was the legend 'Dino'. It debuted in the Gran Premio di Napoli on April 28 1957 – 50 years ago almost to the very day of our visit – and finished third. So began a line of Dino engines and cars, some of which can be found at our next destination – the excellent Galleria Ferrari in Maranello.

It has been an unforgettable two days, but the most vivid memories will be of the hill roads and that fantastic 246 GT, a car that – if you're lucky enough to drive a really good one, as I did – fully deserves its reputation. It's a totally engaging baby supercar with a sweet balance, a cracking little engine and a big, big character.

Ferrari, of course, has emphatically denied that there will be a new Dino, and there's no deviation from that line during our visit. But as an enthusiast, of course, you can't help dreaming… So imagine a small, beautiful, lightweight, mid-engined car, with a charismatic 3-litre quad-cam V6 or V8. Imagine it in aluminium with a Dino badge and a price tag of around £60K.

The story of Dino the man is inevitably a sad one. But when I think of him now, it'll be on those test routes, ripping along in a Ferrari sports car in brilliant late-spring sunshine, smiling broadly.

As Franco Gozzi says, Dino wasn't a genius. But he was a proper enthusiast, a talented designer and a promising engineer. He was also a much-loved son. He was a good guy.

CLAIM 3 ISSUES OF

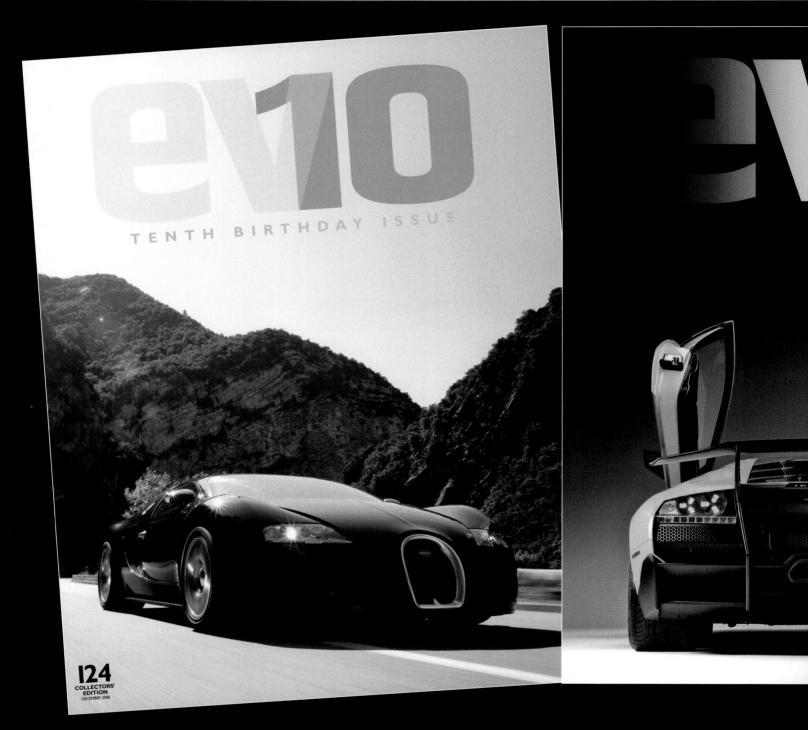

If **evo** is for you, your subscription will continue at the low rate of just **£21.30** every 6 issues by Direct Debit, saving you 19% on the shop price. If you decide not to continue receiving your monthly issue delivered direct to your door, simply cancel within your trial period and you'll pay no more than the £1 already debited.

SuperBug!

In 2006 we drove the
1000bhp Veyron across
France for the ultimate
supercar showdown

Select 'handling mode' via a button next to the gearshift and the rear aerofoil rises to provide more downforce in corners

It's

7.30am on Monday, July 10, 2006, and although the sun has been burning behind a thick blanket of humid haze for over an hour, this moment feels like a new dawn. A tight-fitting French Racing Blue cover is slowly peeled from the thick-set curves of the fastest and most expensive car in the world. What's revealed isn't especially outrageous, nor of outlandish proportions, but it has a magnetism, a gravity about it. Not surprising, perhaps, for the Bugatti Veyron has enough power to slow down the Earth's rotation…

The clear-up operation from the Le Mans Classic is in full swing and the gargle and bark of a Ferrari 330LMB and Aston DBR1 leaving the pits and driving down to the waiting transporter bounce off the high grandstands that we're sheltered behind. The scintillating din barely registers. The Veyron is sucking the colour and noise out of everything around it and, despite its sombre green and black suit, to my eyes it's in glorious Technicolor. I've seen Veyrons on show-stands and in photos, but today an epic journey is stretching ahead of the Bugatti and me. Suddenly the fat, squat and slightly cumbersome shape looks like the most beautiful car in the world.

Our mission is simple: drive the Veyron from Le Mans in the heart of France back to the factory in Molsheim, near Strasbourg, right on the German border. In round numbers that's 420 miles and, in a normal car, five or six hours of autoroute and N-road driving. This is *evo* though, and nothing is ever that simple. For a start we want to sample the Veyron on roads that aren't just arrow-straight, and secondly we want to work out just how good the Bugatti really is. After much delicate negotiation, the men from Molsheim have agreed to us meeting a few choice friends along the way…

They've been chosen on the basis that each represents a unique flavour in the broad supercar palette. First on the menu is the Pagani Zonda,

'A tight-fitting French Racing Blue cover is peeled from thick-set curves'

a bespoke masterpiece with lavish attention to detail and a deep-rooted aversion to unnecessary weight. If the Veyron feels as precious and as nimble as the Fabergé-like Zonda, it'll be a special car indeed.

The Ferrari Enzo is perhaps the main course. It's the fastest, most shocking and most aggressive of the new breed of supercars. It pulsates with malevolence, oozes charisma and has *that* badge on its nosecone. Bursting with aggression and F1-inspired tech, for many the Enzo is simply the ultimate 21st century supercar.

Our last contender does without studied outrageousness, shuns elaborate design and instead focuses purely on dynamic brilliance. The Porsche Carrera GT has a teutonic single-mindedness that is breathtaking. It's a demanding car to drive, for sure, but it offers rich rewards for those prepared to work for their thrills. Built to the most exacting standards, it'll be a formidable test of the Veyron's agility, feedback and quality.

By the time the sun falls tonight we'll know if the Veyron really does represent a bold new supercar era, if it's so accomplished that it effectively makes everything else an irrelevance. Or maybe the Enzo, Zonda and Carrera GT will expose it as an expensive dragster. Who knows? Not me, but as I fall down into the Veyron's tight-

> ### 'Maybe it will be exposed as an expensive dragster'

fitting sport seat I really don't care…

I'm denied the opportunity of firing the 8-litre quad-turbocharged W16 into life, the engineers having already started the job of warming the fluids of the 1000bhp leviathan. It's an odd noise, not tuneful at all; flat, harsh, like two traditional V8s running in unison on a fast idle. From the outside it's almost painful, not in volume (although it is surprisingly loud) but because it seems to get into your very core and oscillate your internal organs. Inside, it's much quieter, the roughest edges of the W16's voice polished away to a nondescript hum.

You sit low in the optional sports seats, uncomfortably so at first because the Veyron seems very wide and the bonnet falls away from view. The glass-house starts at shoulder height (a bit like an Audi TT's), so you feel a little claustrophobic despite the ample room all around. The A-pillar seems to invade your space too, obstructing great chunks of the view to the left. Intimidating is the word, I think.

Ahead of you is a huge rev-counter reading to '8' but with the incremental markings in red from 6500rpm, a smaller speedo to its right and a 'power gauge' to its left. It swings from '0' to '1001', depending on how heavy your right foot is. Quite when you have time to read it I'm not sure. The thick-rimmed three-spoke steering wheel looks and feels fantastic and, along with the machined aluminium centre console and sumptuous leather on every other surface, it gives the Veyron a uniquely luxurious feel.

To my right, the leather-clad, oblong-shaped gearshifter sits high on the transmission tunnel. From 'P' you simply flick it right to go into auto mode, push right again for Sport mode, or bypass all of that with a pull back, which selects

first gear and leaves you in charge of shifts – via steering-wheel-mounted paddles or by clicking the shifter back and forth. In my first tentative moments with the Veyron I want all the control I can get and pull back for first.

The W16 strains against the massive ceramic brakes and as I gently ease off the left pedal the Veyron's massive metric 365/710 tyres start to roll. The way it glides effortlessly away makes it feel just like a torque-converter auto. Phew. The steering is smooth and linear and quite light – in fact it feels very much like the rack of the latest Audi or VW in consistency and weighting. The way the broad front rubber responds to your actions is very different from any VAG product, however. Small inputs have a big effect; the Veyron feels pointy, hyper-alert, yet with no hint of nervousness. I hadn't expected that. To be honest, I expected it to feel imperious but slightly inert. The Veyron feels much better than that before we're even out of the legendary 'Circuit des 24 Heures Du Mans' gates.

It's rush hour in Le Mans town, and as smoky Renaults and wrung-out Peugeots vie for position the Veyron is temporarily the slowest car in France. It's always disconcerting driving a supercar through unfamiliar streets, but in the Veyron it feels like an even bigger responsibility, an imaginary price-tag hanging from the rear-view mirror as I trickle through roundabouts and try to blend as inconspicuously as possible with the everyday traffic. Of course it doesn't work, people pulling U-turns to follow or simply stopping in their tracks to get a longer look at the Veyron. Everybody seems to know that this is 'the 250mph Bugatti'.

Despite the mayhem all around, my tension quickly dissolves. The Veyron is ridiculously

Above: level of detailing is everything you'd hope for in your million-euro-plus-taxes supercar, as is output of quad-turbo W16 (right). Rear wheels are a massive 21.25in in diameter

easy to drive. Yes, you have to get used to that big A-pillar, but once you've learned to lean forward a little on left-handers (or alternatively wind your neck back to look through the side window) it all feels effortless. The ride is stiff even in its default setting, but such is the torque and so smooth are the gearchanges that this sort of low-speed manoeuvring really is a pleasure.

The Bugatti is happy then, but I'm impatient. I've waited a long time to try the Veyron and just ten minutes into my time with the car I need to feel the killer 1000bhp punch. This speaks volumes for the Veyron's sense of cohesion. As you start to squeeze more confidently on the throttle, every control, every element of the chassis feels perfectly in tune with the sledgehammer engine and, although even half-throttle produces almost uncomfortable gobs of torque, the Veyron feels utterly secure. It almost demands that you let it stretch its legs, if only for a few seconds…

Now, I know I should build up to it and finally unleash the W16 on an empty autoroute. Somewhere I can savour its savagery, feel it rip

Bugatti is surprisingly compact when you see it amongst traffic, but somehow imposing at the same time. Natural cruising pace seems to be around 130mph... First challenger to arrive is Zonda

through three gears, but I can't stop my right foot's irresistible meeting with the Veyron's plush carpet. As we peel off from another tight roundabout it's time. The Mulsanne straight opens out before me – where better to experience the fastest road car ever created? Despite a few lumbering trucks on the horizon, I know the Veyron is ready to rip the blinkers from my eyes and show me what real performance feels like.

Second gear, maybe 30mph on the speedo and the faint click of the throttle hitting its stop. The engine note hardens, overlaid with multiple turbos drawing breath, and then... everything goes quiet. Simultaneously the huge trees lining the road melt into a rich, green, fluid blur. In that instant your neck tries and fails to fight the Gs, your head is pinned against the seat and your lips involuntarily form a succinct four-letter word. Somehow you sense the power reaching its peak and flick the right hand paddle back. Has it changed gear? Well, it must have because the intense, ferocious acceleration is getting stronger...

The Veyron at full noise is a strange sensation. At once sickeningly violent and perfectly controlled. No wheelspin, no spine-tingling cry from the engine, just a dull rushing sound and immense, face-deforming accelerative force. Your brain shuts down non-vital functions when the Veyron is channelling all 1000bhp through its huge tyres. You don't hear the engine or road noise, don't really feel anything through the steering wheel or seat. You simply stare at the horizon and try to assimilate the information that's smashing into your retina. Distances are squashed and your brain knows that above all you need to see what's ahead in perfect detail. Because pretty soon you'll be crashing into it...

I glance at the speedo and it's reading a number about 80kph faster than can be possible. Five seconds of full throttle in the Veyron is enough to get you into some very big numbers, and very big trouble. Fortunately the ceramic brakes are even more violent, the Bugatti shedding speed at a prodigious rate. This really is another level of performance. I have a feeling our trio of ultimate supercars currently spearing through France are about to be eaten alive...

Le Mans is soon receding quickly in our mirrors. We're on the A11, heading towards Troyes, where we'll meet both Ferrari and Porsche. On a lightly trafficked autoroute the Veyron rumbles on relentlessly, speed imperceptibly creeping skywards. It seems to find its natural gait between 120 and 140mph, which in the context of France's current deeply anti-speeding climate is very dangerous indeed. But I suppose if you're going to get banned, it might as well be in a Veyron...

The Bugatti is swallowing great chunks of central France and I'm relaxing with it when a set of tiny bright xenon lights slowly closing on the Veyron grab my attention. The temperature is soaring to over 30-degrees now, and it takes at least ten miles before the lights burst out of the heat-haze and the sharp, insect-like structure of a Pagani Zonda forms suddenly in the Bugatti's wing mirrors. Game on...

Harry's in the Zonda and knows the pleasantries can wait; he's as keen as I to see how 2000kg and 1000bhp shapes-up against 600bhp and 1250kg. The Zonda looks lithe and athletic as it pulls alongside, like a lean sprinter to the Veyron's bulky weightlifter. We both select third and sit side-by-side at about 60mph, 15 litres and 28 cylinders primed and ready. Harry gives the signal and we smash accelerators into bulkheads simultaneously.

The Zonda's bellowing V12 is audible above the W16 even as the turbos start gulping, but after maybe half a second of holding station the Pagani seems to have run into treacle. The Veyron is piling on speed in a relentless lunge, each gear melding seamlessly with the next. The Zonda is nowhere, a small spec bobbing around in the Veyron's wake, sucked back into the heat haze by the time the Bugatti is on the far side of 150mph. The Zonda is a massively fast car, but the Veyron is something else entirely. Imagine a Nissan 350Z lining up alongside a 911 Turbo; imagine how quickly the Turbo would waste the 350Z. That's what the Veyron does to a 600bhp Zonda.

Pulling over for fuel at the next service station, Harry looks as stunned as I am. 'What gear were you in?' he asks. 'Does it really matter?' I reply. 'Erm, I suppose not really,' is all he can manage in a state of mild shock. I call Barker, who's in the Enzo. He can't hear his phone above the din, so I leave him a short but telling message. Today is shaping up to be a very good day indeed…

'The note hardens, overlaid with multiple turbos drawing breath…'

The other half of our supertest – Enzo and Carrera GT – en route for the rendezvous with the Bugatti and Pagani. These two are *very* closely matched

The message that Bovingdon left on my mobile was mostly logistical. 'We've picked up the Veyron and we're heading east… blah blah… should be at Troyes by about 1pm… blah blah'. Then, after a significant pause, the verdict I'd been waiting for: 'It's *f***ing* fast.' Polite young man that he is, Bovingdon doesn't often resort to such crudities, so the emphatic delivery, and the chuckle that followed, were designed to impress on me that the cars we were convoying down were significantly slower.

When you've just taken a break from caning a 650bhp Ferrari Enzo to pick up your voice-mail and you hear that, it takes some believing.

The tall, wide carriages of our early-morning Eurotunnel shuttle had disgorged the low, wide Enzo and Carrera GT into northern France with plenty of time to make the rendezvous, so progress had been discreet. Well, mostly. On a couple of occasions while mooching along in the Carrera, Arash Farboud and myself would suddenly leap out of our seats as Paul Bailey ripped by in the Enzo, the sound of its lightly silenced V12 buzzing through the Porsche and our bodies like an electric current.

Porsche is subtlest of our quartet, which makes its performance all the more stunning. Interior is plainest too, though birch-topped gearstick (below right) is a nice touch

Now, if you're wondering if this is the same Paul Bailey who writes about his Carrera GT in these pages, you might be disappointed to hear that indeed it is. He added the Enzo to his collection only a few days ago but has already found time to fit an almost straight-through Tubi Style exhaust. He attended a big Ferrari meet the day after he collected it and a fellow Enzo owner sidled up and said he didn't know they'd made an electric version. That was the end of the standard system and, for Arash and me, the start of a number of stealthily delivered V12 muggings. Sod.

And if you're wondering if this Carrera belongs to Arash Farboud of Farboud GTS fame then, again, it's yes. As you can imagine, we've got plenty to talk about, which makes us sitting ducks for Bailey. We've chatted about how the GTS project he licensed to Chris Marsh is going (it's not far off launch), how his new, quite different car, the Arash AF10, is developing (modelling begins soon) and, jokingly, whether he has a middle name to use for a third car (he has).

We've also discussed what the Carrera GT brings to the supercar party. As far as Arash is concerned, it's quality, a feature that is evident in the neatness of the cockpit design and the superb finish. It's there too in the solid straight-line stability, the excellent top-of-the-pedal brake feel and the precise gearshift. Spearing down the A26 towards Reims, the GT feels all Porsche.

It doesn't feel in the least bit lacking in grunt, either. Take hold of the birch-topped gearlever mounted high on the gradient of the slim centre console, snick it into third, nail the throttle and the Carrera bolts up the road, its 604bhp V10 yowling like a civilised F1 engine. It feels so planted and confidence-inspiring that you want to keep on grabbing gears and wringing it out to 8000rpm until it will go no faster.

'The Carrera GT bolts up the road, V10 yowling like a civilised F1 engine'

Later we'll find out what it asks of its driver on a demanding road but I've already rediscovered the challenge of the clutch. Numbered 1208, this is one of the very last GTs and is thus equipped with Porsche's best effort at making the small, twin-plate ceramic clutch user-friendly. Yet getting the GT off the mark cleanly still demands a fair amount of sensitivity (or whoops of revs, if you prefer) because the engagement is so abrupt that it's easy to stall the seemingly inertia-free V10. In the end I elected to feed the clutch in at tickover, get the GT rolling and squeeze on the throttle once it was home. Once you're going, the clutch action isn't an issue, and the surprisingly intrusive low-speed drivetrain chatter gets left behind as the gritty V10 climbs the rev range.

In isolation, the smooth, low-slung Porsche is a real head-turner but here it's totally upstaged by the Ferrari, and the visual contrast is just as sharp on the inside. After the Carrera's neat but somewhat unadventurous cockpit – its three-spoke steering wheel and overlapping dials are very similar to a Cayman's – the Enzo feels

like a sports prototype. Its smaller, flat-topped wheel is dotted with buttons, its cabin is glossy with carbonfibre and the fit of various facia panels is deliberately spacious. Later, our Bugatti chaperone will gasp at the gaps around the instrument binnacle that reveal the ducting to the air vents and the knuckle joint of the steering column. I'll remind him that the Enzo weighs less than 1400kg.

Turn the key, push the red start button and with an attention-grabbing whoop the Ferrari's mighty 6-litre engine barks into life. Even at idle the V12 has a slightly vicious edge to it thanks to the significantly lightened and simplified exhaust. Pull back on the right-hand carbon paddle to select first, squeeze the throttle, hear the V12 load up and modulate as the auto clutch feeds in, and you're away. Easy.

Slightly lighter steering, a similarly pliant ride and confident straight-line stability give the Ferrari the same comfortable, assured gait as the Porsche as we close in on Troyes. However, while there shouldn't be that much difference

between their performance – 650bhp and 1365kg for the Enzo plays 604bhp and 1380kg for the Carrera GT – it doesn't take long to sense that the Ferrari is even quicker. Its V12 is smoother and more responsive low down, so the Enzo snaps forward lustily when the Carrera's engine is still coming to the boil, and it matches the German car's thrilling top-end rush too. Arash, sitting alongside, concedes that the Ferrari has the edge: 'That's what an extra pair of cylinders does for you,' he suggests. And, yes, we did try to catch Paul napping in the Carrera but he was expecting us and enjoyed every last decibel. I will have revenge of sorts, though…

THIRTY MINUTES AFTER WE'VE parked our half of the group test in the truck park at the service area, the Veyron and Zonda S arrive. In the blistering heat, the £2.5m quartet looks like a mirage. For half an hour we mill around just gawping at them while all around us there's the soft *sher-click* of cameras and camera phones.

A middle-aged man in the crowd says

'The Zonda's 7.3-litre V12 has much of the Ferrari V12's character'

something to me and I grasp that he's asking what any schoolboy would: how fast? My schoolboy French just about runs to that, so I point to the cars in turn. 'Pagani, trois-cent-vingt, Porsche trois-cent-trente, Ferrari trois-cent-cinquante, et Bugatti… quatre-cent'. Put like that, the enormity of what the Veyron engineers have achieved gains some perspective. My new French friend sucks his teeth. Quite.

The Veyron is the car that does the big numbers: 1000bhp, 400kph (250mph) and near-as-dammit £1million. The big question, the one that the Enzo, Carrera and Zonda are here to help answer, is this: do the numbers define the Bugatti or is the Bugatti a great supercar that just happens to do the numbers?

It's not like any supercar you've seen before. It

doesn't shout its potential like the glitzy Pagani or the ruthlessly angular Ferrari. Squat, wide and soft-edged, the Veyron looks heavy and potent. It's not even particularly big: the figures show that it casts a shadow similar to that of a Ferrari F430. Indeed, the Veyron is shorter than all of its rivals here and narrower than the Enzo and Zonda. It certainly packs a lot in though, at a hefty 1950kg no less than 700kg more than the Zonda.

Aesthetically it's not to everyone's taste but, like Harry, I'm a fan. Back in 2000 I pinned a picture of the Bugatti concept to my office wall; I liked the fact that it looked different, smooth yet menacing. A lot has happened to it in those six years. Back then it was the Veyron 18/4, powered by a normally aspirated W18 engine with 'only' 555bhp, and it sported a minimalist lightweight

interior. The extraordinary decision of VAG boss Ferdinand Piech to almost double its horsepower and go for 250mph set in train a protracted, incident-strewn and often too-public gestation. The lowest point came in 2003, the year it was due to be presented to the media, when Piech's successor, Bernd Pischetsrieder, drove it and rejected it, declaring it too demanding, too much like a race car for the target audience.

Three years later, under the guidance of Dr Thomas Bscher, it has been redeveloped and, finally, signed off. But can a 1000bhp, 250mph, 2-ton supercar really be handled with any ease? I have my doubts but I'll find out soon enough. Not right now though. Hard though it is, I'm going to resist and get some miles in Harry's Pagani, just to reference all the slow cars!

Although a Zonda F would have been perfect, Harry's S has been upgraded with the racing-spec ECU and exhaust and gets close to the F's 600bhp. As in the Enzo and Carrera, you drop down into a cockpit that makes it very clear that carbonfibre is a major constituent in the car's construction, and tiny Pagani does it as beautifully as anyone, perhaps better. There's a more bespoke, homespun feel to the rest of the rather fussy facia and trim, and under a baking sun the Zonda's glass-topped cabin doesn't seem so clever but the air-conditioning just copes.

The 7.3-litre Mercedes V12 behind has

much of the Ferrari V12's character without its filling-jangling edge and gives the Zonda an effortless muscularity at low revs. It's helped by a remarkably low kerb weight of 1250kg, of course, yet despite the lack of inertia the Zonda has a hefty feel thanks to its meatily weighted steering. Shame that the gearshift of the six-speed CIMA manual 'box can be a bit sticky.

Harry's leading in the Bugatti and I'm itching to see it stoked-up but the traffic won't allow it. Somehow the Veyron looks poised to blast away and after a few miles staring at its full rump I realise it's because it has a face: the tail-lights are eyes, the generously wide rear wings look like puffed-out cheeks and the central exhaust pipe looks like a mouth puckered ready to blow anything behind into the weeds. Only a couple of times do I get a hint of its acceleration, and the first time I'm fumbling for a lower gear as the Veyron scuttles into the distance. Next time I've got the Zonda primed, right gear, right revs, and when the car holding us up pulls over, I floor it. The response is instant and mighty, the noise fabulous and for, oh, maybe one whole second there's nothing in it, and then the Veyron draws away. In terms of outright urge the Zonda feels close to the Enzo, and its best has proved inadequate. Now I know what Bovingdon meant.

At the next services we swap cars and I've got the key to the Bugatti. After the others, its interior is more luxurious than sporting, with full carpeting and vast expanses of leather and Alcantara. It's mostly simple but with lavish

Enzo's interior (top) feels like a race car after the Bugatti; Pagani is different again, with more of an eccentric, hand-crafted feel

Bugatti interior reeks of quality; novelties include power gauge (below right), which reads up to 1001PS (987bhp), though Bugatti insiders say 1050bhp has been seen on the dyno. Whichever, it's got the measure of even the mighty Zonda

'Not since I rode in a 2000bhp dragster have I felt acceleration like this'

details, like the machine-turned centre console and the apparently hand-finished, cast aluminium steering wheel. I sit myself behind it and Julius Kruta, our Bugatti representative, talks me through the controls. His most pointed piece of advice has nothing to do with the speed of the Veyron: 'Please, when you've adjusted the seat, make sure the lever is locked down.' Ah, yes; imagine flooring the throttle and finding yourself backing rapidly away from the wheel and pedals because the seat hadn't locked onto the runners…

After the exuberance of the other engines, the Bugatti's 8-litre W16 is a bit dull. It doesn't burst into life; rather it churns gradually up to tickover speed like some great industrial machine and settles there with an indistinct multi-cylinder drawl. It's more impressive from the outside, or with the windows rolled down, rumbling like a pair of hefty V8s running in close harmony. 'It sounds more like a powerboat than any other car I know,' says Metcalfe.

What's impressive right away though is the feeling that there's no slack, no wooliness anywhere in the Veyron; the steering feels direct, connected; brake response is immediate yet progressive and the ride is taut yet absorbent. This is as it should be, of course, because any free play here will be exaggerated and become a liability at big speeds, but somehow I was expecting a softer car, probably because of its styling, the fully trimmed interior and the auto-style gearlever.

For a short while I'm happy trundling along behind Julius and Harry in the Zonda, feeling my way in. However, once you've grinned at the absurdity of the power dial, or 'boast gauge' as someone described it, and used the paddles to cycle up and down a few gears to suss out the

shift quality (excellent), the urge to simply nail the throttle becomes irresistible.

A long, clear straight appears, the Zonda stays in the inside lane and I jink the Veyron into the outer lane. Behind me is Bailey in his Enzo and, from the sound of its V12 downshifting a couple of gears, I reckon he knows exactly what's about to happen. The Bugatti's throttle pedal hits the carpet. Nothing happens for a split second – there are heavy clonks as the gearbox rummages around for the right gear – and then my world changes forever. Not since I rode in a 2000bhp dragster have I felt acceleration as mind-warping as this, and the way the Veyron sustains the intensity of the initial lunge as the speed ramps up and successively longer-striding gears go home is truly staggering. It feels like we've gone from about 100kph to 300kph in the time it takes to say 'lock me up and throw away the key'.

Coasting down, I'm aware of a buzzing sound. After a second or two I realise that it's the Enzo catching up. I pull across and Bailey comes alongside. We make eye contact and with my fingers I gesture three, two, one and drop my hand. The Enzo howls off and after a second I

floor the Veyron. The sound of the Ferrari being wrung out gets louder as the Bugatti eats into the gap, and then I'm there, staring at the Enzo's broad-hipped back end, being bombarded by the blare of its tailpipes. Just as I ease off so as not to run into it, Bailey looks in his mirror, sees it filling rapidly with Bugatti, and dives for the inside lane.

At the next stop he says it was 'like being on a trackday when you're really on the ragged edge round some long corner and you look in the mirror and see something wanting to get by. I was gutted.' Yup, the Bugatti is decisively, indisputably the quickest car in a straight line, and that's without the advantage of a standing start. In launch control mode, the four-wheel-drive Veyron rips off the line to hit 100kph (60mph) in just 2.5sec. We've timed the Enzo at 3.4sec; the McLaren F1 managed 3.2sec.

I have only a couple of complaints so far, the first being that for all of its monumental power the engine has almost zero aural character, the sound of vast quantities of air being sucked in and compressed by the four turbos drowning out any rumble. The second is that the big, centrally-

'You can use more of the performance than you ever thought possible'

placed rev-counter should be the speedometer; the gearbox is so efficient at managing upshifts that you don't have to watch for the red line and the engine digs deep whatever the revs, but you can find yourself travelling at ridiculous speeds in a few moments.

Asked to predict the quickest car after the Veyron, we all agree that it will be the Enzo by a whisker from the Zonda by a whisker from the Carrera. It doesn't work out quite like that when, intrigued, we conduct a series of wholly unscientific run-offs.

Round one, and Harry's in his Zonda while I'm in the Carrera. On the first run I get the drop and can't be caught. We re-run but this time Harry gets an unfair advantage, which leaves it feeling like the best of three. The last run is peachy, the Carrera buzzing along at 5000rpm when we go. As I expected from the earlier runs, the

Porsche edges out the Zonda, much to Monsieur Metcalfe's chagrin. 'I'm amazed,' he says later. 'The Zonda was right in the sweet-spot for the last run and still the Carrera edged away. It just doesn't feel like that.'

Hanging at the same revs for its head-to-head with the Enzo, I reckon the Carrera has a chance but the Ferrari leaps ahead by a couple of car lengths almost immediately. The fantastic yowl of the Carrera's V10 is almost drowned out by the cry of the Enzo and when its V12 dies suddenly (turns out Bovingdon clipped the rev-limiter), I expect to draw level. But a fraction later I have to upshift the Porsche and the gap is restored, from which point the Ferrari slowly but surely stretches away.

The reason the Carrera performs better than any of us expected is quite simple: its V10 does its best work at the top of its rev-range, and that's

where it stays in an all-out rush up the gearbox. Will it prove less impressive on give-and-take roads? We'll soon find out.

I'M BAGGING THE VEYRON again because in a few miles we'll be on twistier roads up in the hills, and if the wheels are going to fall off the Bugatti, so to speak, this is where it will happen. Snapper Gregory leads our fabulous convoy away from the autoroute in our long-term Octavia vRS and he's not hanging around. Overtaking slower traffic requires only a tickle of throttle in the Veyron and it's good to be able to hear the engine's heavyweight rumble during these brisk overtakes which, according to the power gauge, require only about 400PS (394bhp). Super-fast ones reveal that the engine's most devastating urge is delivered with 800-900PS on the dial.

The Bugatti copes well with the lumps

3201 W 67

Above: Enzo chases Zonda (the Bugatti's already out of sight).
Above left: everywhere we stopped, a crowd seemed to gather.
Top: Bugatti's huge central exhaust isn't actually big enough to
release all the waste gases – there are also two smaller pipes,
barely visible in this pic, on either side

and bumps of these minor roads, too, feeling relaxed and controlled, the ESP traction control activating only once when I request full power over some bumps. Ferreting around later, we discover there is a button beneath the facia to turn ESP off but, really, would you? Even on part throttle, the urge the Veyron summons is so fierce and escalates so quickly that I reckon even Michael Schumacher would think twice about provoking two-tons of very grippy car on tight roads.

Clear of all the villages and into the hills, the sinuous road is perfectly surfaced and I activate 'handling' mode, which lowers the car front and rear and deploys the active rear spoiler for more downforce. Metering-out the power is a bit of a challenge but, amazingly, the Veyron proves agile, precise and composed. There's a bit of turbo lag noticeable but against expectation the Bugatti feels light on its toes, tacking into turns eagerly and allowing you to use much more of the performance to blast out of the corners than

you'd ever believe possible. I'm amazed and deeply impressed.

When we reach the plateau, the surface deteriorates and there are more crests, compressions and cambers to cope with. Although the mass of the Veyron is betrayed by small, sharp crests and the odd mid-corner lump, this doesn't stop it covering the ground at a terrific rate, even the shortest of straights allowing it to flex its turbos and put a few lengths between itself and the Carrera behind.

The grip and traction, and the willingness of the Bugatti to change direction, show that it isn't just a straight-line supercar. 'They could have just made it go incredibly quickly and no-one would really have minded, but they haven't,' says Harry, who discovered as much on the original launch in Sicily (086).

Not surprisingly, the Carrera seems a bit limp straight after. Few cars wouldn't. It feels more *alive* though because you're more directly connected with the car beneath you and more

responsible for its progress with the manual gearshift and peakier delivery. After a couple of miles along these roads you're absorbed in the process of going quickly, which can be a challenge because the Carrera is a car that feels like it will never understeer and also a car that you wouldn't want to oversteer. Entry speed is critical, the nose slicing for the apex with roll-free aggression and the heavier rear swinging in behind, which is fine if you can pick up the throttle but can feel slightly precarious if the corner tightens. The diff has a limited-slip function on the overrun but the only electronic aid is traction control; there's no stability control to help out.

It's an amazingly precise tool with exceptional brakes and it finds enormous traction but dynamically I feel it's a little highly strung.

'Right away, the Zonda feels more supple than the other cars'

Harry agrees: 'It's a brilliant driver's car, all the major controls feel great on the move, inspiring a feeling of oneness with the machine, so I'm surprised it proves such a handful at the limit. It's not what you expect.' On the other hand, Jethro is smitten. 'It's true that you don't get that feeling that the rear is part of the turn-in process, which means it's a little harder to gauge where the grip lies, but it makes each corner a clinical process. If that sounds boring maybe it's the wrong word. What I mean is there's no wasted movement; the time between you acting and the car reacting seems to dissolve until there's no lag, you're simply flowing as one with the car and the road.'

Harry sees parallels between the Carrera and the Enzo, which he's just stepped out of: 'The idea of drifting the Enzo through corners, balancing the chassis to available grip as the forces build, is the last thing on your mind. It's more about watching the steering-wheel-

mounted change-up lights flicker into life as the rev-limit approaches then tugging the paddle for another gear, revelling again in the brilliant power delivery, then slamming on the brakes, which are sensational, and popping in a couple of downshifts as you dive into the apex.'

Sounds like just the thing for upstaging the Veyron so I slot myself into the Ferrari while Bov installs himself in the Bugatti. In some respects the Enzo *is* like the Carrera – super-sharp front end, high roll stiffness and appreciable structural integrity – but its punchier engine should make it more effective here. However, half a mile in, it's clear that the Ferrari and I have got our work cut out, and not just because the Veyron is shockingly fast when the road uncoils. It's also incredibly quick into the turns and fires out of them like it's on slicks. Attempting to stay in touch, the Enzo's steering is light on feedback and the car is out of its comfort zone, anti-lock triggering over the

bumps into the turns, ASR killing the power mid-corner for what feels like an age, just when you want a slug of V12 torque to keep the Veyron's rump in view. Yes, I could switch ASR out but to be honest the Enzo feels as edgy as the Carrera at the limit and even a few, neat degrees of tailslide would see the Veyron still romping away. I can't believe it.

You'd guess that the Bugatti would be quick on any road that has a few decent straights, but the last six or seven miles has been corners almost all the way. My flabber is thoroughly gasted.

'That was pretty incredible,' says Bov. 'If you had to guess you'd probably put the Veyron's weight at 1500-1600kg. There's quick, assured turn-in, very good body control and phenomenal traction. The 'box is incredible and allows you to keep the engine on-boost, and the seamless gearshifting allows you to downchange into a corner without upsetting the car's balance.'

The last leg of the journey sees Bovingdon in the Enzo and me in the Zonda. It's out of a different mould, the Pagani, not as stiffly set-up as the Ferrari and Porsche, perhaps not quite as torsionally rigid either, but dynamically polished nonetheless and much more involving than the Veyron. Right away it feels more supple than the others, absorbing more of the surface's imperfections, yet it's still poised and alert, and once you're working the wheel, the initially heavy feel at the chunky rim seems to drop away.

The 7.3-litre V12 might not have the reach of the Enzo's V12, though this one revs to 7000rpm, but the Zonda's lack of mass coupled with long gearing means that second and third gear are all you need on these roads. This is a good thing because the 'box can be frustratingly obstructive. So while Bovingdon is firing in lots of shifts, in the Zonda I'm relying on instant throttle response and astonishing tractability to stay in touch, and I do, just. Turn-in is crisp and, more than in any other car here, you can feel the grip at the front end and work the throttle to bring the rear into play. The conservatively set traction control soon gets switched off, allowing you to push the rear tyres up to their limit and, if you're feeling frisky, beyond. It's marvellous entertainment and just a pity that the unfashionable steel brakes on

Chateau St Jean at Molsheim, next door to the original Bugatti factory and now home to the assembly shop for the Veyron, marks the end of our epic journey

Harry's car are a bit rumbly – it came straight to this test after a trackday at Spa.

As we're trundling along the last stretch of dual carriageway before we reach Molsheim, the Veyron comes belting past. It's Paul Bailey, again, but this time there's no shattering bow-wave of sound, just a heavy drone and even more speed.

JOURNEY'S END IS Chateau St Jean, where Ettore Bugatti lodged his valued customers, friends and drivers. It's a short walk from the site of the original Bugatti factory, and the brand new assembly workshop for the Veyron is built in its grounds. There's a Veyron prototype parked just inside one of the huge, renovated barns, surrounded by low settees and the heady aroma of leather. Walk to the back of this showroom and through another door you'll find a type 35, the Bugatti that for many people defines the marque; beautifully engineered, stylish, lightweight and

spectacularly successful in competition. Would Ettore consider the Veyron a Bugatti for the 21st century or, muses Bovingdon, 'the fastest truck in the world'?

There's no question that the Veyron is an astounding achievement. To build a 1000bhp, 250mph road car is remarkable enough, but to make that car comfortable, easy to drive and crushingly capable on the sort of twisting roads that would test a hot hatch is little short of miraculous. At the outset of this test, none of us could have imagined that the Veyron would leave the Enzo trailing in its wake on such a road. It sounds absurd even now.

So, do the numbers define the Bugatti or is the Bugatti a great supercar that just happens to do the numbers?

Harry first: 'The whole Veyron concept has been built around making 1000bhp usable. In that it's a tremendous success, it has moved the world

of supercars onto a new level in terms of speed and comfort, but as for emotionally, it hasn't moved the game on one jot.'

Is it the Veyron's lack of a decent, inspiring soundtrack that lets it down? Tongue slightly in cheek, Bovingdon suggests not. 'Nail the throttle and you don't miss a stirring soundtrack, in fact you don't hear anything. It's as if your brain is shutting off non-vital functions to concentrate on the sheer rate of things coming towards you.

'Seriously, the steering is quick and accurate but there's very little information flowing back through the rim, nor the incredible, transparent sense of road surface and grip levels through the seat that the Zonda and Carrera are blessed with. It doesn't feel as alive, as dependant on your inputs, but if you want the fastest car in the world, then the Veyron is unequivocally the ultimate supercar. It blows the Enzo, Carrera GT and Zonda into the weeds. That sounds

'The Veyron really does seem to defy physics in the corners'

ridiculous but it's no exaggeration. It's a fantastic achievement and I admire it greatly. But over all those miles I never really found any affection for it.'

'It is very odd, isn't it,' says Metcalfe, 'making a 1000bhp supercar feel unemotional is one hell of an achievement…'

I probably like the Veyron more than either of them, not because it's the fastest production car ever but because I still can't believe, first, that it works and, second, that it works so astonishingly well. Against all expectation it's not simply a car for going absurdly fast in a straight line; it really does seem to defy physics in the corners, feeling much lighter than it actually is, changing direction with alacrity and precision and getting its power down more effectively than cars with several hundred horsepower less. That's the towering achievement as far as I'm concerned.

Is it really a great supercar, though? If you want to be invigorated by the sound of a complex, highly tuned engine digging deep or reaching for the red line, and engaged by a chassis that delivers lucid feedback and challenges and rewards with equal measure, then no. The level of refinement the Veyron offers in the weighting, action and smoothness of its major controls, the perfect pitch of its ride and the tangible sense of quality of its construction make it desirable, but these are qualities you'd expect in any £1m car, not supercar-specific attributes. The bottom line is that the Veyron is already assured its place in the history books, but it isn't going to alter the course of supercar evolution.

Allowed the keys to just one of the four, Bovingdon has no hesitation. 'There have only been a couple of cars that have made me think about giving up this job in order to get one that would allow me to afford them, and the Carrera GT is very definitely one of them. I love everything about it, from the way it looks to its stunning construction via its insatiably rev-hungry V10 engine.'

Harry thinks he owns the best car already. 'It's been a real privilege to drive all of these cars back-to-back. They're all wonderful, enthralling and mind-blowingly fast, but they're all very distinct characters, too. There are no losers in the strictest sense, but I enjoyed the Zonda the most; it gave me the biggest thrill, and that's saying something in this company.'

What of our Carrera and Enzo owners, Arash Farboud and Paul Bailey – do they have a burning desire to own a Veyron? Too right they do. Arash has already been a guest at Chateau St Jean and is now emptying piggy banks and digging down the back of the sofa to get the deposit together, while Paul expects he'll be able to afford one next year. I reckon what did it for him was having to pull over for the Veyron while he was ringing the Enzo's neck. That's got to hurt.

Staggered though I am by the Bugatti, I find myself, like Harry, drawn to the Zonda. Not for its design but for its dynamics. I prefer its more 'organic' feel to the ruthless, incisive edge of the Carrera GT, the full-on but slightly numb feel of the Enzo, and the remarkable but ultimately uninvolving competence of the all-wheel-drive Veyron. Bizarre as it sounds in such a test, I especially like the fact that the Pagani feels special at modest speeds.

Enjoy video footage of evo road tests at www.evo.co.uk

	VEYRON	ENZO	ZONDA	CARRERA GT
■ Engine	W16	V12	V12	V10
■ Location	Mid, longitudinal	Mid, longitudinal	Mid, longitudinal	Mid, longitudinal
■ Displacement	7993cc	5998cc	7291cc	5773cc
■ Cylinder block	Aluminium alloy, dry sumped	Aluminium alloy, dry sumped	Aluminium alloy	Aluminium alloy
■ Cylinder head	Aluminium alloy, dohc, four valves per cylinder	Aluminium alloy, dohc, four valves per cylinder	Aluminium alloy, dohc, four valves per cylinder	Al alloy, dohc, four valves per cylinder, variable valve timing
■ Fuel and ignition	Electronic engine management and fuel injection, quad-turbo	Bosch ME7 management, sequential multi-point injection	Electronic engine management, sequential multi-point injection	Bosch ME7.1.1 management, sequential multi-point injection
■ Max power	1000bhp @ 6000rpm	650bhp @ 7800rpm	555bhp @ 5900rpm	604bhp @ 8000rpm
■ Max torque	922lb ft @ 2200-5500rpm	485lb ft @ 4000rpm	553lb ft @ 4050rpm	435lb ft @ 5700rpm
■ Transmission	Seven-speed DSG twin-clutch gearbox, four-wheel drive with fixed split: 30/70 front/rear	Six-speed manual, sequential paddle-shift, rear-wheel drive limited slip differential	Six-speed manual, rear-wheel drive, limited slip differential	Six-speed manual, rear-wheel drive, limited slip differential
■ Front suspension	Double wishbones, coil springs, electronically controlled dampers	Wishbones, pushrod links, coil springs, horizontal gas dampers	Double wishbones, coil springs gas dampers and anti-roll bar	Wishbones, pushrod links, coils, horizontal gas dampers
■ Rear suspension	Double wishbones, coil springs, electronically controlled dampers	Wishbones, pushrod links, coil springs, horizontal gas dampers	Double wishbones, coil springs gas dampers and anti-roll bar	Wishbones, pushrod links, coils, horizontal gas dampers
■ Brakes	Carbon-ceramic discs, 400mm front, 380mm rear, ABS, ESP	Carbon-ceramic discs, 380mm front, 380mm rear, ABS, TC	Vented discs all round, 355mm front, 335mm rear, ABS, TC	Carbon-ceramic discs, 380mm front and rear, ABS, ASC
■ Weight (kerb)	1950kg	1365kg	1250kg	1380kg
■ Power-to-weight	521bhp/ton	484bhp/ton	451bhp/ton	445bhp/ton
■ 0-62mph	2.5sec	3.7sec	3.7sec	3.7sec
■ 0-125mph	7.3sec	9.5sec	10.0sec	9.9sec
■ Max speed	253mph	217mph	200mph-plus	206mph
■ Price (2006)	c£872,000 (EUR1.1m plus taxes)	c£450,000 (2005)	c£350,000	c£323,000
evo RATING	★★★★★	★★★★★	★★★★★	★★★★★

Veyron is quite simply the fastest car we've ever driven, both in a straight line and along twisting roads, but it still couldn't supplant the Zonda or the Carrera GT in our testers' affections

close to the edge

America's Pikes Peak is the toughest hill climb of them all. In 2007, Richard Meaden took it on

Pictures **Andy Morgan/Jay Benyouloir/Rupert Berrington**

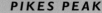

Oldest. Longest. Highest. Scariest. There's no doubt Pikes Peak is one of the wonders of the motorsport world. I've been aware of this illustrious mountain for as long as I can remember and, since the advent of YouTube, have spent more time watching *Climb Dance* – the short film of Ari Vatanen's record-breaking 1988 climb in a Peugeot 405 T16 – than is strictly healthy. However, my quest to *compete* in the world's greatest hill climb began a few years back, when I was lucky enough to experience 'America's Mountain' on a press trip organised by Porsche Cars North America to promote the Cayenne Turbo (evo 072).

It was an amazing event, and the first time anyone had been given permission to drive the road at speed outside the hill climb itself. To guide us, and to prevent any of us plunging into the abyss, Porsche had enlisted the help of some of the greatest Pikes Peak competitors to sit alongside the small group of international journalists present. By sheer good fortune my guardian happened to be Paul Dallenbach.

A multiple winner of the event, and a former outright record holder, Dallenbach proved a great tutor, and although we only drove the full course in anger once, it was enough to convince me I had to come back. Blame it on oxygen starvation, but in the

giddy euphoria of reaching the 14,110ft summit, I clambered out and pronounced, somewhat breathlessly, that the next time I drove the Pikes Peak Highway it would be as a competitor in the hill climb...

Strapped finances and, it has to be said, a lack of courage prevented me from sorting anything for a couple of years. This year, however, everything fell into place: a well-timed email to Paul, an uncharacteristic flush of bravery and PlayStation 3/Gran Turismo HD sponsorship securing me a place as Paul's teammate in the 2007 'Race To The Clouds'.

Over the following months initial excitement faded to a nagging background

level of nausea at the thought that perhaps I'd bitten off a bit more than I'd be capable of chewing. We were, after all, talking about a highly specialised event of legendary status and brutal reputation. At 12.42 miles in length and packing in some 156 turns, the course of the Pikes Peak International Hill Climb (PPIHC) is an awesome mixed-surface challenge for man and machine, climbing from the start line at 9390ft (2862m) to the oxygen-starved summit finish at 14,110ft (4300m).

And then there was my car, which would be entered in the Open Wheel class – the oldest and purist Pikes Peak group. Many great American racing heroes have raced and won in open-wheel cars since the event's inception in 1916, most notably the Unser clan, yet no one can remember an Englishman racing on this most American of mountains in this most American of divisions. No pressure or national honour at stake then…

As you'd expect, while the spirit of these cars remains the same, the design and performance has changed out of all recognition. Right up until the 1970s they were simply Sprint or Indy cars adapted to the demands of a dirt road, but the open-wheelers of today have morphed into purpose-built rear-engined monsters, powered by vast V8 engines and wearing aerodynamic devices of cartoonish proportions. Absurd and awesome in equal measure, they are machines quite unlike any other.

If you visited Goodwood's Festival of Speed back in June, you may be familiar with my Pikes Peak steed, the PVA-06, since Paul Dallenbach drove it to great effect up Lord March's sodden driveway. I was also there, mainly to say hello to Paul and to meet crew chief Kevin Kidwell and his sons Corey and Jason, but also to have a seat fitting. If I'd pushed I could have driven the car too, but, with no disrespect to Lord March, I wanted my first taste of this 800kg, 750bhp, methanol-burning beast to be in its natural environment, not a leafy driveway in Sussex.

A FEW SHORT WEEKS later I find myself at a motocross track just north of Denver and a couple of hours north of Pikes Peak. Paul and the car's owner, the immensely trusting Leonard Arnold, thought it would be a good idea for me to discover just what 950bhp per ton feels like on a loose surface. (Arnold later confesses that the exercise was also to see whether a rookie Brit was up to the job. Or, as he put it, 'We wanted to see if you'd be slow or crap yourself.' Well, at least he's honest.)

How does it feel? Spectacular. Explosive. Addictive. Yet despite appearances to the contrary, the car never feels intimidating. Sure, it's easy to come to that conclusion when driving on an open expanse of arid Colorado plain rather than a narrow and vertiginous mountain road, but the way the car flows, the progressiveness to its slides, the easy, clutchless shifts afforded

by its five-speed sequential transmission and the way its extraordinary 6.6-litre V8 pulls crazily in every gear all make it every hooligan driver's fantasy made real. After ten minutes Arnold is happy I'm not going to soil myself or, worse, drive slowly, and the car is packed back onto its trailer and hauled to Colorado Springs for 'tech' – Pikes Peak speak for scrutineering.

The breadth of machinery raced at Pikes Peak is remarkable. An abundance of classes and a liberal, inclusive attitude mean everything from a matt black 125bhp Toyota Corolla to a 1200bhp Freightliner 'big rig' have homes within the various divisions. In between are bellowing Stock Cars, wallowing Protrucks and 'Monster' Tajima's awesome Unlimited-class Suzuki XL7 Hill Climb Special. The assembled throng is quite a sight.

With the car through 'tech' and me signed-on, we make our way back to the town of Manitou Springs and the Comfort Inn, our base for the next week. Along with several other PPIHC competitors, Kevin Kidwell uses the hotel car park as a makeshift paddock: the red and blue open-wheelers looking ludicrous amongst the Acuras and SUVs. Nestled in the shadow of Pikes Peak, it makes the perfect base for race week, as the schedule is punishing in the extreme. Thanks to the Pikes Peak Highway's popularity with tourists, it remains open right up until race day itself, and with the toll booths opening to the public at 9am every day but race day, the

Hill climb course consists of a mixture of tarmac (left) and gravel. Below left: Pikes Peak humour (we hope). Below: Meaden seems to be enjoying his first acquaintance with the PVA-06 'open wheeler'

'THE WAY IT PULLS CRAZILY IN EVERY GEAR MAKES IT EVERY HOOLIGAN DRIVER'S DREAM'

three practice sessions have to be held early. Very early. And so it is that I set my alarm for 3am Tuesday morning in readiness for my first full-on taste of an open-wheeler on the mountain it was built to conquer.

A VETERAN DRIVER and multiple Pikes Peak winner once said, 'You can't begin to think you really know this road until you've driven up it about 150 times.' This makes pretty demoralising reading when the sum total of your high-speed experience of the road in question amounts to one sweaty-palmed ascent.

With so many corners to learn, the organisers wisely divide the course into three sections: the Lower Half, which is split evenly between tarmac – or pavement as our American cousins call it – and gravel, and takes you from the start line to the halfway point at Glen Cove; the Mid Section, which is all pavement and runs to the 16 Mile Paddock; and finally the Upper Section, which is exclusively gravel and stretches from Devil's Playground to the summit.

The Mid Section is where our first morning of practice will take place, so I've at least got the luxury of starting on a familiar sealed surface, but I'm haunted by the fact that corner speeds will be increased and that terrifying sheer drops line much of the road in the section.

wishbone, grab front and rear of the roll cage, then place your right knee on the side bar. Then scoot your left leg up, tuck both feet up and drop into the reclined seat. The wheel feels close, but with no power assistance it needs to be. All three pedals are in the conventional places, but the brake pedal is double size and sits either side of the steering column to enable left- or right-foot braking. As my last serious attempt at the former resulted in me driving through a hedge, I vow to keep it

steady and stick with what I know.

Now for my favourite stage of pre-flight: starting the engine. Fingering the toggles for ignition, fans, fuel pump and oil pressure protection system makes a satisfying *flick-flick-flick-flick* before finally I push the black rubber starter button and wait for the thunder. Slowly at first, then with conviction, the big Chevrolet motor hammers into life, hollering through unsilenced pipes before settling into a pulsing, laid-back dragster idle. I love the smell of methanol in the morning.

From the moment I told the lads in the evo office that I was entering Pikes Peak, a certain Mr Bovingdon dared me to recreate the classic *Climb Dance* moment when Vatanen drives one-handed, shielding his eyes from the dazzling sun. I'd all but

pumping oversteer and lung-bursting effort. As I park at the top of the run I'm gulping at the thin mountain air like a fish out of water, completely shot to pieces by a few minutes of intense, heart-pounding effort. So this is the reality of racing at 12,000 feet when you live barely 100 feet above sea level.

I've decided not to look at any times, as I reckon it could be demoralising at best and dangerous at worst. Besides, I prefer to follow Paul's advice and creep up on a

'ONE MISTAKE COULD EASILY SEE YOU TANK-SLAP INTO OBLIVION'

time. Apart from feeling like I'm going to have some kind of respiratory failure, I'm encouraged by how much fun the PVA-06 feels on the pavement. The steering is much heavier than it was on gravel, and the gravel-spec rear tyres suffer significant sidewall deflection in the turns, but the handling characteristics remain progressive and exploitable, and all that power and torque simply annihilates the gradients.

With another few runs under my belt I'm beginning to feel as though I'm attacking the course, braking deeper into the corners and getting back on the throttle earlier and earlier. It's an absorbing process, one made all the more critical by the certain knowledge that one mistake could quite easily see you tank-slap into a rock face – or oblivion. I've never driven anywhere that comes close to giving you this sense of complete responsibility for your own destiny, or one that demands you place such complete and utter faith in your own ability. It's true to say that nobody's forcing you to push so hard – you could easily drive slow and stay safe – but who wants to go slow?

Bizarrely, when you drive up here as a tourist at 25mph, you spend your whole time peering over the edge and giving yourself the total willies. Yet when you're strapped into an open-wheeler

After a short-and-sweet driver's briefing at 5.15am, I walk nervously back to the car. With arm restraints velcroed and taped to my forearms (these are clipped into the five-point harness to prevent arms flailing in the event of an accident), the seriousness of what I'm about to embark upon hits me soundly in the stomach. I think about using the nearby 'Porta-John', but as some comedian has positioned it on the edge of the precipice I decide against it.

Getting into the car is a ritual in itself: place your left foot on the left-front

forgotten Bov's challenge, indeed I'd made sure I bought a tinted visor specifically to avoid having to prize one of my snowy-knuckled mitts from the wheel, but no sooner have I been flagged away from the start line for my first timed run than I'm hooning around one of the biggest, baddest, bowel-slackening fourth-gear curves with one hand shielding my eyes simply in an effort to stay on the road. This isn't showboating, it's survival.

After that the rest of the run goes in a flurry of chest-squeezing acceleration, arm

attempting to drive as fast as you dare, such is your focus on the road ahead that the drops don't even register. It might as well be a different road.

After six runs we have to call it a day, and as I climb out and grab a bottle of water, Leonard approaches. 'You wanna look at the time sheet?' he asks, without waiting for an answer. 'You did an awesome job, man. You're third fastest!' I can't quite believe what I'm hearing, but a quick glance down the sheet confirms the news. Paul is quickest with a 2:07.63, Spencer Steele is

Opposite: Meaden with the team, including three-times Pikes Peak winner Paul Dallenbach (blue race-suit). Below: powering up the hill. Bottom: makeshift paddock in hotel car park

next with a 2:11.67 and there I am with a 2:14.08. Cue handshakes all round and a few sideways glances from the open-wheel regulars. Not bad for a Brit rookie!

DAY TWO OF PRACTICE is a nasty wake-up call, both literally – another 3am start – and metaphorically, for we're driving the Upper Section. Really fast and all loose, it combines long fourth- and fifth-gear sections with big drops and no barriers. While I'd be lying if I said I had no gravel surface experience, I don't in all honesty feel that a couple of rallies in a Ford Ka and a clapped-out mk2 Escort almost ten years ago really count as prime preparation for what I'm about to face.

To make things worse, the Upper Section starts with a fifth gear approach to a long, blind and fast-as-you-dare left-hander, which then drops downhill towards Bottomless Pit: a fourth-gear right-hander where all that protects you from a 6000ft drop on the outside is a shin-high stone wall. And it just gets scarier from there.

I feel like my granny could make a few seconds on me during my first run, for the PVA-06 is constantly skating around, rear wheels digging and spinning for traction, rocks and dust flying everywhere, hands constantly punching corrections through the wheel. I get to the end but, what with my fear of the fast corners and my scrappy technique through the smattering of tight, rocky hairpins, I feel lost. And slow.

Crumbs of confidence begin to form, as does the belief that I'm becoming familiar with the ambiguous-looking entry to many of the corners. Bit by bit I gradually feel like I'm carrying more speed, but as I turn in to what I think is an easy left, the numbing realisation dawns that it's actually a different corner: a tightening left with a drop to the outside. I come off all the pedals and throw some opposite lock at the problem. Everything goes quiet, the sickening swoosh of loose gravel the only sound I hear. The tail sweeps wide, momentum taking us towards the edge before finally, miraculously, the chunky Goodyear Blue Streak Pikes Peak Specials (I love that name) find some traction and I tentatively get back on the power. To the hapless photographers who throw themselves down the scree slope in order to escape I can only apologise…

Thoroughly spooked, I return gingerly to the team, all my hard-won confidence of yesterday broken into little pieces. I decide to sit out the next run to get my

Left: sights of Pikes Peak hill climb 2007; 165 riders/ drivers entered this year. Bottom row, centre: crew chief Kevin Kidwell and his sons, all of whom work on the cars in their spare time

head together, a process aided by rival open-wheel driver Spencer Steele. A truly genuine guy and a driver known for his super-committed style, he takes the time to chat, and to try and rebuild my confidence. 'I know you're finding it a bit dicey on the loose,' he says, 'but you gotta keep working the throttle when you get on the fluff [the loosest gravel] to get those rear tyres digging through to the hard base beneath. It's tough to do, but you'll feel the benefit. Keep at it man, you're doing great.'

Encouraged, but still too uptight to let the car flow, my best Upper Section time of 3:30 puts me in eighth place. Less than great, but OK considering. Then I'm devastated to hear someone tell Paul he's done a 2:10, and I retreat to our Chevy TrailBlazer hire car, distraught at the prospect of having to find almost a minute and a half from a time that already had me pushing much harder than I wanted to. I emerge ten miserable minutes later to discover Paul's best run was actually

3:10. That'll teach me to listen in on other people's conversations…

DAY THREE IS THE BIG ONE, for we're running on the Lower Half with our best time counting as our qualifying run. I've been looking forward to this, not just because it means we can have a lie-in until 3.30am, but also because I'm looking forward to the mix of fast, sinuous pavement and trickier, flowing gravel – and the fact that trees now mask the worst of the drops. They're still there, but what you can't see won't hurt you. Right?

The section also highlights the increasing compromise required to find a good set-up for the full Pikes Peak course. Where once drivers and engineers would work on a softer, gravel set-up, teams now have to decide between sacrificing pace on the pavement with a softer set-up for more speed on the loose, or going stiffer and lower for more downforce and stability on the pavement.

Paul, Leonard and Kevin are all of the opinion that you won't win with a chassis tailored to a gravel set-up, and with Paul's circuit racing experience he's able to push harder on the pavement than the guys who feel more comfortable on the loose, while still maintaining a strong pace on gravel despite the stiffer than ideal settings. This suits me too, as my limited experience

means I'm more likely to get closer to the car's limits on the pavement.

Unlike the Upper Section, I really enjoy the Lower Section from the off, and although there are a couple of early corners that consistently catch me out, I feel happy that I've got the bogey corner – Engineer's – nailed, as it's tailor-made to end a driver's race. I love the charge through Picnic Ground too, for it allows a prolonged run flat out in fourth and fifth gears. The quickest open-wheel cars will be hitting almost 125mph through here.

Somewhat unexpectedly, my love of the pavement is soon overshadowed by a growing enjoyment of the gravel. I feel more relaxed today, and my newfound loose-limbed style allows the car to work more happily. Spencer Steele's advice has also sunk in and I'm finding more drive, control and forward motion by working the throttle more actively and precisely. Paul has also told me to short shift, relying on the huge torque to push us up the

'THE TAIL SWEEPS WIDE, MOMENTUM TAKING US TOWARDS THE EDGE…'

inclines and fire us out of the corners rather than wasting time with crowd-pleasing wheelspin.

It's taking time to truly use all the road and let the car slide from edge to edge, but slowly things are beginning to click. The way the car slithers and squirms around, even in top gear, is beginning to feel natural and I'm finding the Lower Section's rhythm more consistently. This is my favourite section and my most enjoyable session so far, and I'm extremely pleased to find that I've managed a best of 5:15.84, which is good for sixth place (and just a second and a half off fifth). Meanwhile Paul is upholding the team's honour with a 4:47.39 – first in class.

RACE DAY DAWNS crystal clear. Since we last drove the course there have been two monumental Colorado thunderstorms, and much of the surface-sweeping accomplished by the cars and motorbikes during the three days of practice has been undone. Gone is the vague hint of a clean line through the gravel, replaced by a fresh surface of loose stones spread over a hard base. Paul is disappointed, as the surface doesn't suit the rear-drive open wheelers. Like other seasoned competitors he's obsessed with the condition of the course, scanning its surface and talking in hushed, reverential tones of the days when 'a blue

groove' could be seen all the way up the mountain, where all the loose stones had been swept off by the cars' soft-compound tyres, leaving a faint coating of rubber on the hard-packed surface beneath.

Today there isn't so much a blue groove as a brown mess. Nonetheless, there's a buzz about the mountain, with high expectations that Monster Tajima could be in record-breaking form. For my part I'm simply looking forward to enjoying the privilege of being able to race flat-out up this amazing road. I'm not even terribly nervous, which is unheard of for Meaden on race morning.

After years of anticipation and a week of highs and lows it's impossible to describe how I feel as the official starter waves the green flags and I accelerate across the start

line. I'd expected elation, but as I shift into second gear devastation is the best word I can think of, for the clutch is slipping badly. I can't believe it. The guys changed all the clutch plates and the half shafts as a precaution only yesterday, and the car hasn't missed a beat all week. This can't be happening!

I'm hoping beyond all hope that it manages to bite, yet deep down I know in my heart that it's only going to get worse. Every time I attempt to transmit 600lb ft to the grippy pavement the clutch gives little resistance. Despite popping off the rev limiter in fifth we register a depressing 65mph through the Picnic Ground speed trap. The prognosis is hopeless and I'm totally beside myself with anger and disappointment.

Cussing until I'm hoarse is no match for the wave of angst that's crashing through my system, so I punch the steering wheel repeatedly as hard as I can. It hurts – really hurts in fact – but not as much as conceding

A despondent Meaden sits with his stricken PVA-06 where its clutch finally expired – halfway up the course – and watches 'Monster' Tajima on his way to a new record

that, after a 4500-mile flight, a succession of 3am starts, countless moments of raw fear and sheer exhilaration and the tireless efforts of Kevin and the crew, I'm not going to reach the summit.

There's a glimmer of hope when we reach the dirt, for the reduced grip levels spare the frazzled clutch at least some of torque onslaught. I even manage some tight lines through sections I'd previously found tricky, but the enjoyment is short-lived, and by the time I reach the halfway point at Glen Cove (coincidentally the point where photographer Andy Morgan and Emma, my wife, are watching) the clutch is finally crying enough. I pass the crowd like some sort of demented lunatic, doing my best to shatter my right hand on the steering wheel while the crippled car limps on, sputtering around one last uphill hairpin before I grudgingly pull in and kill the motor.

As I sit motionless in the car the silence is deafening. I try to cry but can't, and as the crushing sense of disbelief sinks in I throw off my harness, remove my crash helmet and climb out. A few brave souls wander down to commiserate, one proffering a welcome bottle of water. I put on a brave face and even sign a few autographs, but I really just want to be left on my own. They

get the message and leave.

Meanwhile the race continues. First David Donner, then Paul Dallenbach power past, their heads briefly cocking to the right as they spot my bright red car before turning once more to focus on the flat-out right-hand kink ahead of them. I'd do anything to be in their shoes, charging on towards the summit, but instead I'm left here, an empty shell, my insides hollowed-out by the corrosive misery of such a cruel mechanical failure. I may be standing two-and-a-quarter miles above sea level but I can safely say I've never felt so low.

The last man to tackle the mountain is Monster Tajima. He's been driving like a man possessed all week, and as he punches past my lay-by his outside wheels kiss the dirt as he squeezes the maximum from the road and his Suzuki special, flying through Cove Creek and on, out of sight, towards Ragged Edge. Just 10min 1sec after crossing the start line, he crests the summit to set a new course record.

Even in my morose state I can't fail to feel a fizz of adrenalin as a marshal's radio crackles with the news that Rod Millen's 13-year-old record has finally been eclipsed. When the same radio brings belated word that, despite mechanical woes

of his own, Paul has won the Open Wheel class with a time of 10min 55sec, I actually crack a smile.

The exciting news, not to mention the head-straightening solitude, has done me good. So does the eventual sight of Andy and Emma, who have both made the wheezy ascent from Glen Cove to find me. Failing to finish may hurt like hell, but it does little to diminish what has been the most incredible week of my life. Both the car and the road have comfortably exceeded even my pumped-up expectations, while the satisfaction from having successfully faced genuine lie-awake-at-night fears and felt the thrill of beginning to master such a fabulous and formidable car on two wildly contrasting surfaces has brought me an unmatched sense of achievement. Despite the dreadful disappointment I conclude that, come what may, I'll be back next year, more determined than ever to reach that elusive summit.

Many thanks to Leonard Arnold, Paul Dallenbach, Kevin, Corey, Jason and Kellie Kidwell, Mike Leary, Susie and Jay Bonvouloir, Patrick Seurynck, Phil Layton and all at the PPIHC.

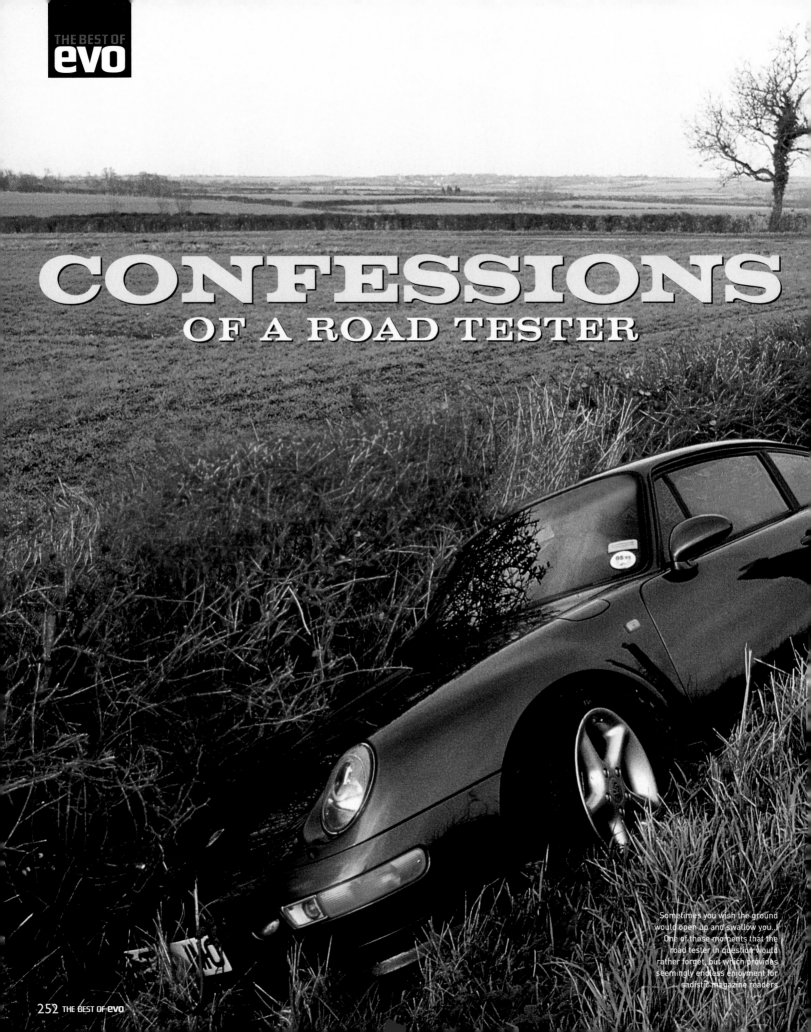

CONFESSIONS
OF A ROAD TESTER

Sometimes you wish the ground would open up and swallow you... One of those moments that the road tester in question would rather forget, but which provides seemingly endless enjoyment for sadistic magazine readers

Magazine road tests haven't always been high-tech. Things haven't always gone smoothly. And just occasionally everything's gone horribly wrong. Peter Dron remembers some of the incidents that never made it to print, and other road test veterans confess their testing sins

My first visit to MIRA (the Motor Industry Research Association's test track, near Nuneaton) was dramatic. It was November 1976 and, with *Motor*'s road test editor and two other testers, I spent a cold, slightly damp morning, timing four cars around the banking, checking speedometer accuracy, measuring turning circles, hill-starting, attaching and removing test equipment, and so on.

None of this was out of the ordinary, especially the weather. The routine would soon become dull, with considerable irritation and a few moments of terror, but on a tester's first day it all seemed new and exciting. (The few moments of terror occurred either on the banked 'high-speed' circuit, once you entered the curves at over 125mph, or when you got out of shape on the 'Number 2' circuit, used mostly for brake-fade tests: the bends were helpfully marked out by oildrums filled with sand. These days they have girly plastic posts.)

At midday, the road test editor said, 'Right, let's go and have some lunch.' For some reason, the splendidly-named Oddfellow's Arms, overlooking MIRA, was out of favour, and we headed off in convoy, in two cars, to a more distant hostelry, on roads made treacherously slippery by melting snow and cow muck. The road test editor was leading, in a Toyota Corolla Liftback; I was following, in a Honda Civic. He was a skilled driver, but perhaps a bit too keen to prove it that day to the 'new boy'. Despite maximum attack on

the slithery lanes, he had no chance of getting away from the Civic in the unimaginably crude Toyota. Eventually, he was so sideways in one right-hander that I said, 'Shit, he's lost it!' My optimistic passenger said, 'No. He'll hold it.' He didn't, and fell off into the ditch on the left.

Driver, banging the steering wheel with both fists, and passenger, crying with laughter, were unharmed, and the Toyota seemed none the worse for wear, although stuck. We dropped Our Leader at a garage, and headed off for lunch. An hour later, we found Our Leader and a grease monkey, driving a Transit pickup with a slipping clutch, still vainly attempting to extract the Toyota, but merely dragging it backwards and forwards. As soon as a couple of us jumped into the ditch and assisted with a shove, the Corolla popped out like a cork. The fruitless to-ing and fro-ing had crumpled all the panels on one side, but the suspension seemed undamaged, so we went back to MIRA and did the acceleration runs. Our times beat the manufacturer's claims, perhaps because of the makeshift aerodynamic alterations, perhaps because of the road test editor's pent-up fury.

The published road test advised: 'On slippery surfaces, [the Corolla's] Japanese-manufactured Dunlops lacked grip and a combination of rear-end steer (due to poor location of the live axle) and indifferent traction could cause the tail to step out of line, calling for immediate and accurate correction?' Yes indeed.

MIRA was first used by *The Motor* and *The Autocar* (both retained the definite article in

those days – it is about time the practice was reintroduced for **the evo**) back in the 1950s. One of the most famous road-testing anecdotes of all occurred in the very early days. A tester on his second visit, while showing a colleague around, failed to distinguish between the shallow water-splash trough (for cars) and the deeper pond designed for lorries. Apparently, the Singer Gazelle convertible remained afloat for a surprisingly long time. The two occupants had time to pull their craft first to one side of the trough, and then to the other, enabling each to scramble out. Scratching their heads, they watched as the murky waters slowly enveloped the car and it sank out of sight. The trough was emptied and the car towed to the Members' Garage where, after having its sump drained and refilled, it was eventually persuaded to restart. To the man who had driven the car into the water fell the task of taking it home. To dry out, our hero turned the heater volume up to maximum, which made the interior mist up severely. This was cured by opening the windows, but then there was a series of popping noises, as the kapok stuffing in the hood lining expanded and burst the seams, floating away like gossamer on the breeze.

My own worst experiences at MIRA involved the Transflo fuel meter, which measured steady-speed consumption. Nobody shed a tear when the introduction of fuel injection with high-pressure fuel lines rendered it redundant. The device was fitted between fuel pump and carburettor, counting each cc of fuel entering the engine. Attaching it could be a fiddly, knuckle-chafing job. On one occasion in the late '70s a notoriously laid-back *Motor* staffer (now an **evo** contributor, renowned for his vivid writing style) even managed to plumb it into the cooling system.

One day I was removing the Transflo from a car 6ft up on a hoist in the Members' Garage. As I yanked the tube free, a small amount of fuel escaped. Simultaneously one of the attachment springs flailed about, making a sufficiently solid electrical connection to produce a big fat spark.

'Fire!' I shouted. But my colleague was dreamily elsewhere, and only began to lower the hoist when I introduced adjectives and turned up the volume. By the time the car was at ground level, the flash fire had extinguished itself, but it was a scary moment.

'The Singer Gazelle convertible remained afloat for a surprisingly long time'

It was not only installation and removal that made the Transflo an object of detestation: obtaining the consumption graph that appeared in *Motor*'s road tests required a three-mile lap of the full 'high-speed' circuit at 30mph, and at 10mph increments up to 100mph or whatever speed below that the car could comfortably maintain. This was unbelievably tedious, and on one occasion disastrously so. It was 1980, and I had collected a Renault Fuego at the launch in Nice one Sunday morning and driven over a snowy Route Napoleon back to England, then got up early on the Monday to do the tests at MIRA.

With all the other tasks in the bag, we had only the steady-speed consumption tests left. It was mid-afternoon when I discovered that falling asleep at the wheel did not happen only to 'other people'. It happened to me at 80mph and I am not

Top: 328 spins onto the infield at Castle Combe; half an hour later it was into the barrier on the same corner. The occasion was Autocar's Best Handling Cars day. It didn't win. Centre: the fifth wheel. Left and above: testing BMW suspension travel

sure if the scream of my fellow tester woke me; it may have been initial contact with the barriers on the entrance to one of the triangular circuit's three banked curves. The barriers consisted of steel hawsers and vertical wooden posts at intervals of about 10ft. Still attempting to steer, even though the means to do so had been ripped out and were lying on the track way behind me, I came to a halt with the car perched perilously atop the banking, having demolished 36 of those stout posts, which I discovered set a new circuit record. This stood for a year or so until two Rolls-Royce testers were travelling in convoy at around 130mph, and the leading car shed part of its exhaust system, which interfered with the steering of the second.

Later, we moved our testing to Millbrook in Bedfordshire, which was closer to where we all lived, and had a better range of test tracks, especially the high-speed 'bowl', which becomes interesting, and sometimes eerily terrifying, from 150mph. The local pubs are better, too.

JOHN BARKER

It was a big surprise to suddenly be looking in the rear view mirror to see where I was going, at 100mph. Moments before it had been an ordinary exercise, extracting figures from the late-'80s Nissan Maxima on the Millbrook proving ground's mile straight, in the rain. I'd just clocked the ton heading towards the north end of the straight, which opens up into a vast, car park-like apron of asphalt that rises gently towards a steep grass bank.

I turned slight left onto it, braked, and felt the anti-lock grab coarsely at the outside rear wheel. Uh-oh. The Maxima flipped neatly around on the glassy surface, so I was now spearing towards the bank at huge speed, backwards. I was terrified to find that the brakes did bugger all – does ABS work in reverse? – and braced myself for the impact.

'The Maxima flipped neatly around on the glassy surface, so I was now spearing towards the bank at huge speed, backwards'

I sensed the asphalt rising, then there was a massive jolt as the Nissan hit the steeper angle of the grass bank... and just kept going, ploughing up backwards, up and up, running out of energy only after it had climbed about 40ft.

All was quiet. The V6 idled, the wipers swished, but surely the car was bent double. Bugger, bugger, bu... But the ride wasn't quite over – what goes up must come down. My foot was still hard on the brake as the Maxima gathered speed on the wet grass before burying its nose in the French drain at the base of the slope.

Damage? By some miracle, virtually nothing; just a one-inch crease on a rear pillar. Amazing. It took part in the *Autocar & Motor* group test later that week. The Millbrook recovery crew had a laugh, though. The Maxima's exhaust had acted like a soil sampler on the way up and chugged out eight-inch tubes of dark clay on the way down. Showing me one of them, one of the lads said 'we found this on the driver's seat'. Ha, bloody ha.

IAN FRASER

They've long since faded away, those puzzling white lines at 90 degrees to the verge on a long, straight section of the A11. They were the mute witnesses to road-testing expeditions 30 or 40 years ago. In the early hours of the morning, the weekly rags and some of the monthlies would use those distance markers for performance measurement.

Top speed runs, speedometer calibrations, standing quarter miles and the ubiquitous 'nought to....' times were all done with a driver, a hawk-eyed observer, a bank of stopwatches, a clipboard and pencils. No-one ever got into space by such methods, but it was cheap, reliable and surprisingly accurate when averaged over runs in opposite directions.

It was a dodgy way to earn a living, though. Then as now, few people had any perception of how fast other cars were approaching them. Furthermore, wandering deer, stray livestock and itinerant tractors caused premature ageing. Since there was nowhere else to go, we persisted in this folly, even as machinery got faster and faster. When I started figuring cars, an Austin Healey 100/4 was highly regarded because it would saunter up to 60mph in about 11seconds, but a gullwing Mercedes 300SL was viewed with some suspicion because the fortunate few who tested it came back with 0-100mph times of around 16seconds.

By far the greatest pestilence was mechanical failure – clutches frequently gave up the ghost during acceleration runs, while a Holden Monaro 350GTS snapped its propeller-shaft. On another epic occasion, severe and sudden axle-tramp beset the Ford Falcon I was figuring and the differential broke up and went through the casing. In the dark, middle of nowhere, very inconvenient.

The move from road to disused airfield meant rigorous brake testing could be undertaken with impunity. Mostly the hydraulic fluid boiled after a few quick stops but on one occasion a Chrysler Valiant's shoe pivots broke and jammed the drums tight on. Another long walk to the phone, this time under a hot sun. Less exercise these days, so cars have something to answer for after all.

MARK HALES

I remember the narrow escapes. Like in the mid-'80s when colleague David Vivian decided to impress me with his closing speed at the wheel of a brand new Ferrari 328, one of the first in the country. We had been under strict instructions not to harm this car in any way – not that it was something we ever tried to do, but the road test editor was clearly nervous about the test department's 'unholy alliance' going to Millbrook with a car that was already changing hands for double the list price. Vivid got it out of shape on the brakes and overtook me on the grass, spinning neatly between rows of concrete bollards. After which, like the inside of his wallet, nothing was found to be disturbed. I was rarely that lucky and my worst experience by far was with the only TWR-modified new-shape Jaguar XJ in existence.

A racer's reputation always led snappers to request more sideways than the last time, something which I have since learnt to resist. I obliged, but the edge of the road was dusty and the left rear wheel slid a few inches further and just caught the sharp, square edge of a shallow Cotswold kerbstone which tore out the tyre's sidewall. The car slewed wildly across the verge, then, like a billiard ball rattling into a pocket, it slipped neatly into a concrete gully where it wedged tyres against one wall, roof against the other, all of it completely invisible from the road. As the horrified onlookers sped closer to check on my state, I stood on the driver's door, levered the passenger one towards the vertical and climbed out to make my excuses. It was one of those Buster Keaton moments which I dearly wish I could have enjoyed.

Tom Walkinshaw was on the phone the following day, and I took the call, fully expecting the bollocking I so richly deserved. A soft spoken Scots brogue asked simply, 'I just wanted to make sure you're alright. We can always build another car...' Sometimes, a man doesn't live up to his reputation...

JEFF DANIELS

Moments I'd rather forget. Plenty of those in the late '60s and early '70s. The De Tomaso Pantera whose RHD-conversion brake linkage fell apart, leaving only the handbrake (max 0.07g) for stopping from 70mph in the limited remains of the braking straight; the Monteverdi 375L whose throttles stuck wide open at 130mph near the end of the MIRA horizontal straight (ignition off, sideways with no power round the turning loop); the various devices, from MG Midget 1500 to Aston Martin V8, whose transmissions – drive shafts, usually – failed under the impact of the standing start or the 1-in-3 hill start. The joys of attaching the fifth wheel. The horrors of extreme understeerers on the MIRA banked turns – Vauxhall Ventora, Mazda RX3, almost anything American; the wire fence inching closer, the knowledge that more lock would unstick the front end, while lifting off would unstick the back (when I confessed these fears to Innes Ireland, then sports editor of *Autocar*,

From the top: Barker explores the handling limits of the late-'80s Nissan Maxima, before exploring its off-road abilities by driving it up a steep, grassy bank. Backwards. At 100mph. Ruf 911 suffered high-speed blowout at the Nürburgring. Barker again, this time affixing 1990s-style test gear to a Ferrari 456GT. Figuring a Ferrari isn't a sin in itself. Unless Ferrari themselves don't know about it at the time... (and won't speak to you for two years afterwards)

Top: Motor's photographer has instructed youthful Barker (right) to drive 21 Turbo onto seafront at Mablethorpe, promising it will 'make a great picture' (patently untrue) and 'definitely won't get stuck' (ditto). Centre: pristine GT1 before Mr Meaden restyled the front spoiler (he still can't bring himself to recall that particular Performance Car test). Bottom: Meaden again; another PC highlight

he growled 'Laddie! Let yourself start thinking like that, and you're finished as a quick driver!'). Brake-testing cars that faded out of sight long before the tenth stop. And above all, I suppose, the maximum speeds illegally achieved in the dawn twilight on carefully reconnoitred stretches of public road. Honestly, today's road testers might hardly know the meaning of sweat – except that they have to live with acceleration, braking, and above all cornering forces we could only dream about back then...

DAVID VIVIAN

Maybe this tale would have sat better in last month's 'Power issue'. Maybe I'm just a sad, pathetic performance junkie. But I suppose the most truthful confession I can make is that I always seemed to be at Millbrook whenever anything even remotely

'extreme' was going on.
Like the time, back at Motor in the '80s, we invited British rallycross ace John Welsh to subject his 560bhp Zakspeed-engined, four-wheel-drive X-Trac Ford Escort to the full, Piesler-wired, standing start routine. Or perhaps it was the other way round. For it soon became apparent that our test gear had never been subjected to anything quite like this.

I vividly remember joining John in the remarkably un-macho looking Escort (it didn't even have flared arches for Christ's sake) for the warm-up runs. It was important the engine (just 2 litres and four cylinders) was properly limbered-up before it was subjected to maximum turbo boost. As we rounded the bottom of Millbrook's mile straight for the return run, John started to tickle this up by means of a large thumbwheel that looked like a water tank's stop cock just beneath the dash. He'd look at a gauge, carefully nudge the wheel clockwise, select second and floor it. The first time he did this I nearly swallowed my tongue. The second time, after what looked like a full quarter-turn of the stop cock, I couldn't blink. And the third time, when John gave me a wink and the circled thumb and index finger 'OK' gesture, my sinuses unblocked for the first time in ten years.

The right moment, I felt, to step outside. For the timed runs I installed young Mr Simister and then watched, from a safe distance, as the Escort hit 30mph in 0.8sec, 60mph in 2.6sec and 100mph in 6.6sec. He emerged looking particularly pink – always a sign that Simmo had had a good time.

COLIN GOODWIN

Moments? I've had a few. Have you ever done that old favourite of thinking that the car in front had moved off and driven into the back of it? I have. I was sure the colleague in the 360 Modena had pulled out across the junction but unfortunately the huge bang as the nose of my 996 Carrera removed the tail of his 360 indicated that he had not.

Ages back we were doing the figures on an Alfa SZ and were using cumbersome fifth wheel timing kit. I was working the gear and a colleague was pedalling the SZ. We did a couple of 0-60 runs and then lined up for THE ONE. Unfortunately, in his excitement my pal left the SZ in reverse. He revved the V6 to about six grand and dropped the clutch. I nearly

went through the screen (er, no belts) and the fifth wheel left its impression on the side of the Alfa. We laughed like drains of course.

The Millbrook test facility has a two mile-long banked circular test track which is separated into about six lanes. At 100mph in the topmost lane you can take your hands off the steering wheel. One day I and a fellow tester thought it would be fun to set our Bentley Continental T's cruise control to 100mph and see if we could do a lap with both of us sitting in the back. After a couple of test laps the driver climbed into the back. Just as

> 'We thought it would be fun to set the Bentley's cruise control to 100mph and see if we could do a lap with both of us sitting in the back'

the passenger was climbing into the back the cruise control clicked off and the car careered off down the banking. The cabin was a hive of activity as we fought to stop £250,000 going for a burton.

There have been many moments over the years, enough for a book. Dickie Meaden will tell you about the time that he was passengering me in a Ford Probe and I spotted a bend ahead that looked remarkably similar to the old Masta kink at Spa. 'Do you think it's flat?' I asked. It wasn't unfortunately and Meaden hasn't driven with me since.

JOHN SIMISTER

Nowadays we have dirt-free, glitch-free and trauma-free speed-measuring systems that use GPS and many megabytes. It was not always so. In the far-off days of mid-1980s Motor magazine we used the famous fifth wheel, like a bicycle wheel, originally clamped to the rear bumper and sending pulses to a data logger. But not many cars had suitable bumpers by then, so we used suction clamps instead.

These were not reliable. You had to find a sufficiently large and flat surface for the suckers, which in the case of a particular Mazda 626 was low on a rear door just ahead of the wheel. All was well until the suckers let go, and the highly expensive, precision-built ensemble was now being dragged along by its retaining strap. And the slower I went, the further towards the rear wheel it went.

What could I do? I tried snaking from side to side to fling it away from the car. I even tried a handbrake turn

so the Mazda would come to rest before the fifth wheel was flattened. None of this worked. So I just decided to stop, and wait for the crunch. I watched it all in the door mirror as several hundred pounds' worth of fifth wheel got run over. I was not alone in my equipment destruction, though. Our then technical editor, now a senior Ford PR man, lost it completely when another fifth wheel flew off. Wordlessly he hurled it over the barrier at the end of Millbrook's mile straight, where no doubt it remains.

Later we used a hub unit which clamped on to wheel nuts. But what do you do with a wire wheel? Tie the unit on with garden wire bought in a panic from the garden centre up the road, of course. Which is fine until it gets a wobble on and breaks free, flailing along a Morgan Plus Four's front wing.

I once broke a Plus Eight's rear wheel in a spin on the rough cobbles at the Chobham test track, too. The wheel tucked under the axle so the ride height was still normal, so it took a while to discover why forward motion was no longer available. It's a wonder Charles Morgan will still talk to me.

BRETT FRASER

Some things are best done in the dark. For other stuff, daylight is by far the better option; it certainly is when you're trying to max a Jaguar XJ-S 6-litre for CAR magazine around the two-mile circular banked bowl at the Millbrook proving ground.

As you may have read elsewhere, at 100mph on the bowl you can take your hands off the wheel. At 150mph or more, however, you've got to hang onto the wheel like your life depends on it. Which it does. Because at that speed the centrifugal forces want to chuck the car into – or maybe even through – the Armco.

Not that I've told virgin road tester Colin Goodwin any of this. I don't want him to see how scared I am and I need him to operate the stopwatch.

It's damn spooky in the top lane of the bowl in the dark. The Jag's headlights aren't designed for running flat-out so I have to rely on faith that there's nothing blocking the track. Other than the blurred Armco to my right, I have no points of reference and the curvature of the track turns it into an endless and ring-puckeringly tight corner.

My head pounds through the concentration and I break into the cold sweats of the truly petrified. I really don't want to be here but for the sake of accurate figures I go three complete revolutions of the bowl. Then, and with huge relief, I back off the throttle for the slowing-down lap.

That's when Goodwin asks if he should start the stopwatch now. I never have liked him...

WHEN ROAD TESTS
GO BAD

Richard Meaden recalls the most terrifying ride of his life, passengering in a Ferrari F50

There's only one thing more traumatic than crashing a car during a road test, and that's being in a car when someone else crashes it. When that someone else happens to be a proud and unhealthily confident Ferrari F50 owner, driving around a brutally unforgiving test track, you've got yourself a 24-carat road test nightmare.

The fateful day in question is the culmination of a special Ferrari feature put together for **Performance Car** magazine. Having spent weeks pestering a network of friends and acquaintances to track down an F50 owner, the sight of the blood-red supercar glistening like a jewel in the car park convinces me that the day will be a memorable one. It is, but for all the wrong reasons.

We want to shoot the F50 driving alongside an equally stunning yellow F40 around the outer circuit of Chobham's Long Cross Proving

Ground. Having completed one exploratory lap, the owner invites me to sit alongside him. Well, you would, wouldn't you? One slow lap of the track later, photographer Dom Fraser gives the thumbs up: a signal F50 man takes as an invitation to nail his Ferrari's accelerator to the floor. Alarm bells began to ring when I note his driving style. Steering with both hands sitting at 12-o'clock on the straight as he tips the fully committed F50 into one of Chobham's super-quick turns by pulling both hands to 9-o'clock, then letting go with his right hand to change up a gear, while we're mid-corner at perhaps 100mph (always a nice touch, that).

Thanking God for Dario Benuzzi and the adhesive qualities of Goodyear's GS Fiorano tyres, we emerge onto the longest straight, but the worst is yet to come. We're in fifth gear now, bright tacho needle pointing vertically, big V12 gulping lungfuls of air and hauling hard. My legs fidget as the voltage of

Meaden captured the whole thing on video. F50 owner's eccentric steering style (top) sounded alarm bells. Barker was on hand to sweep up the bits (notice a recurring theme here?)

raw fear sparks through my synapses, while ahead looms Chobham's daunting, steeply banked left-hand corner. Unbelievably our man's still got the loud pedal pinned. What really freaks me out is when his previously narrowed eyes widen in terror as the realisation dawns that he should have been braking hard at least 100 metres ago. He stabs at the middle pedal and throws both sweaty palms to 9-o'clock while I curl into a ball and close my eyes. We're history.

Tyres howl, the big, angry V12 slews past my right shoulder as we begin a sickening spin down toward the apex of the corner. Out of the corner of my

eye, a large cube of concrete perhaps a metre square flashes up at the door sill. A deafening bang and a savage impact slams us into a sickening airborne spin as fabulously expensive car hits immovable object at perhaps 80mph. Then silence. Leaves and dust fall into the cockpit. I think I utter an incredulous oath under my breath before opening the door, only for it to fall off in my hand. Later, as his £300,000 wreck is hauled away, our man apologises, shakes my hand and utters a line that still makes me shiver to this day. 'My friend, if I can't kill you, nothing can kill you. You are immortal...' ∎